PROFESSIONAL ETHICS

PROFESSIONAL ETHICS

Michael D. Bayles

Westminster Institute for Ethics and Human Values

Wadsworth Publishing Company
Belmont, California
A Division of Wadsworth, Inc.

Philosophy Editor: *Kenneth King*
Production Editor: *Donna Oberholtzer*
Designer: *Adriane Bosworth*
Cover Designer: *Jane Rockwell*

Printed in the United States of America
1 2 3 4 5 6 7 8 9 10 — 85 84 83 82 81

Library of Congress Cataloging in Publication Data

Bayles, Michael D.
  Professional ethics.

  Bibliography: p.
  Includes index.
  1. Professional ethics. I. Title.
BJ1725.B29   174   81-3345
ISBN 0-534-00998-0   AACR2

To Marge, for making everything worthwhile

Contents

Preface

The ethics of professional conduct is being questioned as never before in history. Lawyers, physicians, engineers, accountants, and other professionals are being criticized for disregarding the rights of clients and the public interest. Perhaps society is reconsidering the role of professions and professionals. In any event, many difficult ethical challenges are being faced by both professionals and the public. Given the important roles professionals are playing in society during these last decades of the twentieth century, everyone is concerned with professional ethics.

When I first taught professional ethics to undergraduates in 1978, no general materials were available. In particular professions, especially law and medicine, some good materials on ethical issues did exist, but no book provided an overview of ethical issues in several professions. The first aim of this book is to fill that void. While emphasizing law and medicine, its principles apply to all professionals who are in a consulting role. Many of the principles also apply to professionals in nonconsulting roles. Examples from a number of professions are provided, and readers should try to apply the principles to still others.

A second major aim of this book is to examine professions from the viewpoint of the average citizen in a liberal society. Much literature on professional ethics adopts the viewpoint of practicing professionals. This book instead adopts the perspective of clients and other members of society. The overriding consideration is to determine the ethical norms citizens in a liberal society have good reason to accept. A liberal society and its citizens are devoted to the values of governance by law, freedom, protection from injury, equality of opportunity, privacy, and welfare. This approach to the issues, then, renders the discussion relevant to those who are not planning to become members of professions as well as to those who are.

A wide conception of ethical issues is adopted. It includes issues of fees, advertising, and social organization to provide services, as illustrated by national health insurance, as well as professional discipline. Although some people deny that these are strictly ethical topics, they involve significant value choices confronting professionals and society. Elements of political, social, and legal philosophy are thus pertinent.

The first two chapters are primarily introductory and provide a background for those that follow. The first chapter discusses the scope of professional ethics, what can be expected from its study, and possible causes for the present concern with professional ethics. It then defines professions, distinguishes consulting from scholarly professions, and notes significant characteristics of professions in the United States during the last part of the twentieth century. Chapter 2 addresses the relations between professional norms and ordinary ethical norms applicable to everyone, the justification of professional ethical norms, and the distinctions between various types of norms.

Chapters 3 through 6 analyze the substantive obligations of professions and professionals. Although these chapters can be read in any order, it is preferable to read them in the order presented, especially Chapters 4 and 5. Chapter 3 primarily concerns access to professional services. The first section discusses economic norms, such as those relating to unauthorized practice, fees, and advertising, which have often hindered access to services. The next section focuses on social organization, as illustrated by group services, national insurance, and national service, to provide medical and legal services. The chapter concludes with a discussion of the ethics of accepting clients who have unethical purposes. Chapter 4 considers the ethical obligations that arise from accepting a client. The first section considers the ethical nature of the professional–client relationship, and the second section professionals' obligations to clients that result from viewing the relationship as fiduciary. Chapter 5 discusses the obligations of professionals to people who are not their clients and how these obligations are to be balanced against conflicting obligations to clients. Chapter 6 analyzes obligations professionals have to their profession, even though ultimately for the benefit of society, such as research, reform, and maintaining respect for the profession.

The last chapter discusses methods of ensuring that professionals conform to ethical norms. It reviews criteria for admission to professions and the success of self-regulation. After criticizing arguments for professional autonomy, the chapter considers issues of lay participation in the professions, improvement of disciplinary mechanisms, and professional education in ethics.

This book is intended for use in a wide variety of courses. I have tried to present enough information about professions and to avoid technical philosophical vocabulary so that it can be used in lower division undergraduate courses. At the same time, I have tried to provide sufficient depth and detail so it can be used in upper division courses and in courses on the ethics of particular consulting professions, especially law and medicine. For the latter use, teacher and students in classroom discussion should be able to supplement the examples with others from their particular profession.

Throughout the book, I have offered my own opinions about the obligations of professionals. Readers are encouraged to question and challenge my assumptions and arguments. One problem with traditional education in professional ethics has been that accepted norms, especially those enshrined in professional codes of ethics, have not been questioned. Only by challenging assumptions and reflecting on them can one come to understand the reasons for ethical norms and conduct.

This book developed out of lectures to upper division undergraduates who were planning to enter professions, especially law and medicine. In response to classroom discussions, it went through several revisions—some topics were deleted, others were added, and those that were retained were clarified. A previous version was also used at Western Michigan University in Professor Michael Pritchard's course on professional ethics. He kindly sent me useful comments based on this experience.

So many other people have contributed to this book that it would be jointly authored were they willing to take responsibility for the result, but in some instances I have perversely ignored their suggestions. Kenneth Kipnis, Wade Robison, and the publisher's anonymous reviewers provided useful and often detailed comments on earlier versions. Michael Rumball, as my research assistant, worked hard to ferret out study problems and relevant research materials. My wife, Marge, tested the readability of the text and was a source of several examples and steady encouragement. Neither last nor least, versions of the manuscript were competently and efficiently typed by Ann C. Marx, Pat Harris, Fran McFall, Lois Weston, Angela Robitaille, and others.

"Professional Autonomy" in Chapter 7 is reprinted in slightly revised form from "Against Professional Autonomy," *National Forum: The Phi Kappa Phi Journal* 58, no. 3, Summer 1978, pp. 23–26, with permission.

The University of Kentucky Research Foundation provided funds to aid in the preparation of an early typescript. The University of Western Ontario Foundation, Inc., provided funds for research assistance. The Westminster Institute for Ethics and Human Values, London, Canada, supported work on the book and provided for typing the final manuscript.

1 Problems of Professions

In their daily practice, professionals confront a wide variety of difficult ethical and value problems. Consider the following cases and the types of problems they present.

Clients may ask for help that requires conduct professionals consider ethically wrong. For example, a physician practicing in a remote Alaskan community is approached about an abortion by a seventeen-year-old woman who is three months pregnant. The physician is ethically opposed to abortion except to save a woman's life. This woman's health is not good, but she is likely to survive the pregnancy. She is unmarried and lives at home with her family. Her employment prospects are poor, and her father cannot easily support another child. After much discussion, she finally admits that her father is responsible for the pregnancy. If the physician does not perform the abortion, the young woman will probably not be able to afford the expense of traveling to another community to have one. Does the physician have an obligation to perform the abortion despite personal moral opposition?

Professionals also confront problems about the appropriate scope of their services. An architectural firm is temporarily short of clients and will have to let several employees go if it does not obtain more work. The local government is looking for a consulting engineering firm to design a sanitary sewer extension project. Although the architectural firm has not previously designed sewer systems, and such work is not usually considered appropriate for such firms, it believes it can do the job. Should it approach the government to try to secure a contract to design the sewer extension?

There are also problems about the types of fees professionals charge and arrangements for collecting them. A vice president in charge of production at a large corporation wants to build a new plant. To present his idea to the board of directors, he needs a rough design. He asks a friend who is a consulting engineer to make one. If the board approves the plant, the vice president assures his friend that he will get the design contract as well as payment for the rough design. Should the board not

1

approve the new plant, then unfortunately the engineer will not be paid. Can the engineer ethically agree to make the rough design? Would it be fair to other engineers to obtain business by such a contingent fee agreement? Is it ethical for the vice president to make such an agreement?

Conflicts of interest raise still other questions. A member of an accounting firm serves without pay on the board of directors of a local nonprofit organization. If the director is not involved, may his firm ethically audit the books of the organization?

Other kinds of problems involve conflicts of interest between clients. For example, a large law firm has two clients being handled by separate legal teams. Their cases are in different courts within the state. The case for client A requires arguing for a particular point of law, but the case for client B involves arguing against the same point of law. Can the firm ethically represent both clients?

Obligations to inform clients also create problems. A dentist has a patient who constantly smokes a pipe. Clenching the pipe between his teeth has caused some teeth to shift, slightly affecting the alignment of his bite. The smoke badly stains his teeth and has caused some minor precancerous sores of the type that rarely become malignant. The patient is concerned about the sores. To try to get the patient to stop smoking, can the dentist ethically tell him that the sores are "precancerous lesions" without further qualifications?

Professionals also have problems about their obligations to others. A family physician sees one spouse and diagnoses a venereal disease. The patient requests that the other spouse not be told of the disease because it might destroy the marriage, which the patient still wishes to preserve. Should the physician advise the other spouse to be tested for venereal disease?

Another example is a criminal defense attorney whose client tells her he has concocted an alibi and wishes to take the stand to present it. What should the lawyer do? Should she place her client on the stand to perjure himself? Should she withdraw from the case? If so, will the client then simply not tell the next lawyer that his alibi is false? Should she simply put the client on the stand, let him tell his story without direction, and then not argue that evidence? If so, will not the jury conclude that the client is lying?

Other problems revolve around the ethics of research. For example, a university computer science professor is contacted by a government security agency. The agency would like her to develop a system for accessing computers when the codes are not known. Can the computer scientist ethically undertake this task?

Problems about informing on the ethics of colleagues also arise. A nontenured university faculty member learns that the department chairman frequently visits female graduate assistants at home and suggests that they sleep with him. Does the faculty member have an obligation to report the chairman's actions to the dean or another university authority? Another example is a junior member of an accounting firm who learns that one of the senior partners spends two to three weeks each year at a lodge owned by a corporate audit client. Does the junior accountant have an obligation to report this activity to the appropriate disciplinary committee?

THE PROBLEMS

These cases, some of them among the most debated in professional ethics, illustrate the types of ethical problems professionals face and also provide some idea of the scope of professional ethics as a field of study. Some people restrict professional ethics to ethical dilemmas faced by particular professionals, so that matters of fees, advertising, the specification of the separate spheres of practice of professions, and social schemes to make professional services widely available are not, in their view, properly a part of professional ethics. The preceding cases indicate the broader scope of professional ethics adopted here.

Broadly construed, professional ethics encompasses all issues involving ethics and values in the roles of the professions and the conduct of professionals in society. Three broad areas of concern can be distinguished. First, the goal of making professional services equally available to all raises questions about the legitimacy of advertising, the cost of services, and the appropriateness of restricting certain services to particular professions. The question of the desirability of insurance or legal services corporations are also part of this concern. The second area of concern is the relationship between clients and professionals, in which problems such as taking advantage of client dependence, withholding information, and disregarding confidentiality of information can arise. The third area of concern is the effects on others of professional conduct in behalf of clients. These others may be either a specific individual, as in the example of a physician telling a patient's spouse of the risk of a venereal disease, or society more generally, as in a lawyer's client committing perjury (which is a crime against society's interest in the legal process). Thus, professional ethics is not simply an application of narrow ethical theory. It involves aspects of political, social, and legal philosophy as well.

The study of professional ethics will not automatically make one an ethical professional or enable one to always know what is right or wrong. Although intellectual study cannot develop a motivation to ethical conduct, most people most of the time want to do what is ethically correct. Sometimes, however, they fail to see the ethical questions surrounding a course of action. The study of professional ethics will hopefully sensitize one to the ethical dimensions of professional practice and help one think clearly about ethical problems. In addition, conflicting considerations often make many ethical choices difficult. The study of professional ethics can enable one to develop some general principles to use in difficult or unusual cases. Finally, consideration of the social or political aspect of professional ethics will enable one to better understand the role and importance of professions in contemporary society.

Historical Perspective

Why has professional ethics become such a popular and important topic in recent years? The reasons for its popularity may not be the same as those for its importance, but they are closely related. The popularity of professional ethics largely stems from dramatic, widely publicized cases. Watergate stands out as the most spectacular of recent examples of unethical professional conduct, largely by lawyers. Watergate also brought with it exposures of corporate fraud and bribery that accountants and investment advising firms failed to detect or covered up. Physicians have been exposed and criticized for unnecessarily prescribing brand name drugs in exchange for benefits from the pharmaceutical industry and accused of defrauding the government in Medicare and Medicaid programs by billing for services that were not performed.

Historically, the professions have controlled admission to their ranks, regulated the conduct of their members, and defined their role in society. The lay public regarded professionals with respect and entrusted their lives and fortunes to their judgments. Although antipathy and suspicion have occasionally been directed towards individual professions, such as the attacks on lawyers in Charles Dickens's novels, by and large people concurred in professionals' self-judgment that all the decisions in and about their respective fields should be exclusively theirs. Now, however, criticism has become widespread and is directed at almost all professions.

Contemporary discontent with professional conduct may be deeper than professionals believe and may be based on more than the occasional ethical aberrations of a tiny minority of professionals, as the professions themselves are apt to see it. An eminent sociologist has written that "the professional complex, though obviously still incomplete in its development, has already become the most important single component in the structure of modern societies."[1] In the twentieth century, the number of professions and their members has grown dramatically. Although their origins date back several centuries, accounting, psychiatry, and many branches of engineering are largely twentieth-century professions. In 1900 there were 1,234,000 professional and technical workers in the United States, constituting $4\frac{1}{4}$ percent of the working population. By 1970, the number of such workers had vaulted to 11,561,000, constituting $14\frac{1}{2}$ percent of the working population.[2] And the increase is even greater than these rough figures indicate. The figures for 1970 do not include college teachers and groups such as musicians, artists, and entertainers, which are included in the data for 1900.

As society has become more complex and dependent upon technology, the professions have become increasingly central to its functioning. For years, violations of professional ethical codes were frequent and unpunished, yet did not spark the kind of criticism that is currently widespread.[3] At the least, the recent criticism reflects the development of consumerism. Concern about withholding information from clients, unnecessary surgery, advertising, fees, and the unavailability of professional services all reflect a new emphasis upon consumer rights.

Modern society has become centralized on the basis of complex technology and an increasingly complex legal system. As a result, many more decisions significantly affecting our lives are made by professionals. Control has shifted from the average individual or a political representative to professionals. Given the traditional self-regulation of the professions, democratic control, individual freedom, and other values of liberal society (discussed further in the next section) may be threatened.[4] The rise of modern industry during the late nineteenth and early twentieth centuries was accompanied by a political and social struggle to preserve and promote the well-being of the larger society. State and federal legislatures developed laws—such as workmen's compensation—to restrict or meliorate the detrimental effects of large corporations upon employees and the public. This effort culminated in the New Deal legislation of the 1930s. With the rise of the professions, a somewhat similar struggle may be occurring to redefine the professions' role in society so as to preserve and promote freedom, welfare, and other values.

From this perspective, the study of professional ethics must be more than the application of traditional principles of professional ethics to new problems. It must be an analysis of the proper roles of professions in a liberal society. One cannot simply accept the prescription by professionals of their own roles. As one lawyer notes, "The public contempt for lawyers stems rather from their adherence to an unethical code of ethics, paradoxical though that may seem."[5] Although the responsibilities and situations of individual professionals vary, common elements stem from their role as professionals. Only against an understanding of the values of liberal society and the general role of professions can the peculiarities of ethical issues confronting the different professions be properly analyzed and perhaps resolved.

Values of a Liberal Society

If the professions are to serve society, their roles must be examined from the viewpoint of average members of society. Therefore, this book analyzes professional ethics from the perspective of the average citizen, who is a consumer of professional services and is affected by professionals working for others. The average citizen needs good reasons to accept the ethical norms that regulate professional practices. These norms must be justifiable to a reasonable person living in the society in which the norms operate. A reasonable person is one who is not mentally ill, who has sufficient intelligence to understand the norms and their implications for most concrete situations, and who obtains facts, listens to arguments, and supports his or her views by reasons. It is assumed here that such people are self-interested with limited benevolence; that is, they do not care for all others as much as for themselves.

If one assumes that a reasonable person desires life, bodily and mental integrity, and at least the wealth of personal property, then one can present arguments showing that a reasonable person has good reasons for accepting certain values of a liberal society. The chief values relevant to professional ethics are governance by law, freedom, protection from injury, equality of opportunity, privacy, and welfare. Space does not permit a full discussion of these values and the arguments for them.[6] However, rather broad agreement on these values exists in a liberal society, despite differences over the methods or bases of their justification and the details of their weighting. Consequently, this presentation is confined to a brief statement of these liberal values and some reasons why a reasonable person would accept them.

Governance by law. Public authority should be exercised in accordance with rules to which citizens can conform and that are adequately communicated to them. This ideal extends beyond strictly governmental authority and applies also to such areas as hospital administration, public audits, and many other activities involving professionals. Without governance by law, a reasonable person would be unable to act so as to avoid possible penalties. Nor could one rely on the conduct of others.

Freedom. People should be free from limits imposed by others to act as they desire to the extent that such freedom is compatible with other values. In general, people should be free from the control of government or others in making important decisions about their own lives. Of course, freedom must be limited to preserve or promote other justifiable values. A reasonable person would value freedom because it enhances the satisfaction of desires (the individual knows best what will do so) and because one simply wants to control and direct one's own life even if one may not decide as wisely as others might.

Protection from injury. People should be protected from injury—loss of life, bodily or psychological integrity, or wealth—by force or fraud. This value concerns the essentials of life in society. Without protection from injury caused by others, social life is not possible.

Equality of opportunity. People should have the same chances to reap the benefits of society. Discrimination on the basis of sex, race, religion, or ethnic origin, for example, deprives people of an equal opportunity. So far as human beings control social conditions, only ability and effort should be relevant to social success. Self-interested people want as great an opportunity as possible for themselves and cannot accept a society in which these opportunities are restricted unnecessarily. Consequently, they do not have good reason to accept a value that would give them fewer opportunities than others. Although they can accept a value providing themselves more than others, the others would not have good reason to accept such a value, so it is difficult to have such a social ideal. Moreover, reasonable people have benevolent reasons for allowing others an equal chance at social benefits, even though they may not be as concerned for others' success as for their own.

Privacy. People should have privacy, that is, control over the information others have about them. Privacy takes several forms—solitude, intimacy, and private or personal affairs. A reasonable person has good reason to accept privacy as a social value because lack of privacy may adversely affect one's wealth and prestige (business deals can be lost if others know of plans in advance), because privacy contributes to valuable intimate personal relationships, and because of the psychological benefits of occasional solitude to reflect and collect one's thoughts.

Welfare. People should have welfare, or the goods needed to fulfill those self-regarding wants necessary to a minimal standard of living. A minimal standard of living refers to the conditions for normally good health, personal necessities, and security in them. Reasonable people want more than a minimal standard of living for themselves, and it is prudent to be assured that one will never have less than such a standard. As with equality of opportunity, others will also want assurance of a minimal standard of living, and reasonable people have sufficient benevolence to desire this for others, even if they desire a much higher standard for themselves.

The role of professions in liberal society must ultimately be tested against these values. To the extent professions preserve or promote them, they are properly constituted. Professionals may affect many other values of clients or others in addition to these general social values and be held to additional ethical standards in their dealings with clients and others.

THE PROFESSIONS

No generally accepted definition of the term *profession* exists, yet a working concept is needed for our study of professional ethics. Because the purpose of this study is to consider common ethical problems raised by and within professions, a good definition will delineate characteristics of occupations with similar ethical problems. (These characteristics may prove to be related to some of those problems in important ways.) One need not characterize professions by a set of necessary and sufficient features possessed by all professions and only by professions.[7] The variety of professions is simply too great for that approach. Rather, some features can be taken as necessary for an occupation to be a profession, and others as simply common to many professions and as raising similar ethical concerns.

Three necessary features have been singled out by almost all authors who have characterized professions. First, a rather extensive training is required to practice a profession. Lawyers now generally attend law school for three years, and in the past they underwent years of clerkship with an established lawyer. Many, if not most, professionals have advanced academic degrees, and one author has plausibly contended that at least a college baccalaureate is necessary to be a professional.[8]

Second, the training involves a significant intellectual component.[9] The training of bricklayers, barbers, and craftspeople primarily involves physical skills. Accountants, engineers, lawyers, and physicians are trained in intellectual tasks and skills. Although physical skill may be involved in, for example, surgery or dentistry, the intellectual aspect is still predominant. The intellectual component is characteristic of those professionals who primarily advise others about matters the average person does not know about or understand. Thus, providing advice rather than things is a characteristic feature of the professions.

Third, the trained ability provides an important service in society. Physicians, lawyers, teachers, accountants, engineers, and architects provide services important to the organized functioning of society—which chess experts do not. The rapid increase in the numbers of professions and professionals in the twentieth century is due to this feature. To function, technologically complex modern societies require a greater application of specialized knowledge than did the simpler societies of the past. The production and distribution of energy requires activity by many engineers. The operation of financial markets requires accountants, lawyers, and business and investment consultants. In short, professions provide important services that require extensive intellectual training.

Other features are common to most professions, although they are not necessary for professional status. Usually a process of certification or licensing exists. Lawyers are admitted to the bar and physicians receive a license to practice medicine. However, licensing is not sufficient to constitute an occupation a profession. One must be licensed to drive a car, but a driver's license does not make one a professional driver. Many professionals need not be officially licensed. College teachers are not licensed or certified, although they must usually possess an advanced university degree. Similarly, many accountants are not certified public accountants, and computer scientists are not licensed or certified.

Another feature common to professions is an organization of members.[10] All major professions have organizations that claim to represent them. These organizations are not always open to all members of a profession, and competing organizations sometimes exist. Some bar associations, at least in the past, did not admit all lawyers. The organizations work to advance the goals of the profession— health, justice, efficient and safe buildings, and so on—and to promote the economic well-being of their members. Indeed, one author has stated that "the ethical problem of the profession, then, is . . . to fulfill as completely as possible the primary service for which it stands while securing the legitimate economic interest of its members."[11] If this claim is even approximately correct, one must expect professional organizations to be deeply involved in securing the economic interests of their members. Nevertheless, such organizations do generally differ from trade unions, which are almost exclusively devoted to members' economic interests. One does not expect to find carpenters' or automobile workers' unions striking for well-designed and constructed buildings or automobiles, yet public school teachers do strike for smaller classes and other benefits for students, and physicians and nurses for improved conditions for patients.

A third common feature of the professional is autonomy in his or her work. Given the present concern with reconciling professions and liberal values, how far such autonomy should extend is an open question. The minimum lies perhaps in the tasks of the work itself.[12] For example, surgeons are free to use their own judgment about the details of operating procedure and lawyers to use their judgment about how to draft a contract, provided they remain within the bounds of acceptable professional practice. If professionals did not exercise their judgment in these aspects, people would have little reason to hire them. However, many professionals now work in large bureaucratic organizations in which their autonomy is limited by superiors who direct their activity and overrule their judgments. Nurses are often thought to have an equivocal status as professionals simply because their superiors can overrule their judgments about specific aspects of their work. In these cases, however, an element of autonomy remains since the professionals are expected to exercise a considerable degree of discretionary judgment within the work context. Thus, an element of autonomy is a common and partially defining feature of a profession, though it might not be a necessary feature and the extent of such autonomy is debatable.

One may bias an investigation of professional ethics by using normative features (those saying how matters *should* be) to define or characterize professions. One common bias is to characterize professionals as primarily devoted to providing service and only secondarily to making money.[13] Such claims may be legitimate contentions about what should govern professions and motivate professionals, but they do not define the professions. If lawyers are, in the words of one of the earliest American writers on legal ethics, George Sharswood, "a hord of pettifogging, barratrous, custom-seeking, money-making" persons, they nonetheless constitute a profession.[14] An extreme example of the use of normative features to define professions is the following "consideration" presented by Maynard Pirsig: "The responsibility for effectuating the rendition of these services to all that need them and in such a manner that the public interest will best be served is left to the profession itself."[15] In this one condition, Pirsig manages to assume three different normative principles. First, services should be provided to all who need them. Second, the services should be provided so as best to promote the public interest. Third, the profession itself should be the sole judge of the method for achieving the first two principles. Even if these normative principles are correct, they should not be erected into the defining features of a profession.

Distinctions among kinds of professions are usually related to the kinds of activities pursued by most but not all members of the professions. An important distinction in professional ethics is between *consulting* and *scholarly* professions.[16] The consulting professions, such as law, medicine, and architecture, have traditionally practiced on a fee-for-service basis with a personal, individual relationship between client and professional. A consulting professional (or a professional in a consulting role) acts primarily in behalf of an individual client. A scholarly professional, such as a college teacher or scientific researcher, usually has either many clients at the same time (students) or no personal client (jobs assigned by superiors in a corporation). A scholarly professional usually works for a salary rather than as an entrepreneur who depends on attracting individual clients. Of course, this distinction is blurred in many cases. For example, a junior lawyer in a large law firm is more like a scientific researcher, and nurses have individual clients even though they usually work for a large organization (hospital). Among the consulting professionals are physicians, lawyers, accountants, consulting engineers, architects, dentists, psychiatrists, and psychological counselors. Other persons with tasks similar to some of the consulting professions include nurses, pharmacists, stock brokers, the clergy, insurance brokers, social workers, and realtors. Among the scholarly professions are nonconsulting engineers, teachers, scientists, journalists, and technicians.

These differences between the roles of consulting and scholarly professionals are crucial in defining the kinds of ethical problems each confronts. The economic considerations of the consulting professional—fees, advertising, and so on—are not important problems for the professional employed by a large organization on a salary. Although consulting architects and accountants have many ethical problems in the professional–client relationship, research scientists or engineers in large organizations do not normally deal with clients. University teachers do have clients, but they typically confront them in a group and have fewer problems of confidentiality, and so forth.

This discussion focuses on the consulting professions. Special emphasis is placed upon the legal and medical professions because they are among the oldest and largest professions and have often been models for newer professions. Moreover, they have the most developed codes of professional ethics, and there is considerable documented material about problems that arise. Finally, most people will deal with a physician or lawyer sometime during their life, whereas fewer people will deal with an architect or consulting engineer.

Three salient features of the role of the consulting professions in the United States during the last half of the twentieth century lie at the heart of the problem of their positions in a liberal society. First, they all provide an important service. Consulting engineers and architects design the structures and facilities essential to modern life—buildings, houses, power stations, transportation systems, and so on. Most of us depend on the medical and dental professions to protect our health and well-being, even our lives. The legal profession provides services essential for justice and equality before the law. Accountants, as auditors, testify to the financial integrity of institutions and keep track of the wealth in society. The services of professionals are important for individuals to realize the values they seek in their personal lives—health, wealth, justice, comfort, and safety.

Second, not only do the professions serve basic values, they also have a monopoly over the provision of services. In many professions, one must be legally certified to practice. Laws often make it a criminal offense to practice a profession without a license. Attempting to do without professionals or to be one's own professional can realistically have only minimal success. If one decides to be one's own physician, one cannot obtain access to the most useful medicines and technology; most drugs can only be obtained legally with a prescription from a licensed physician and from another professional, a pharmacist. Although one may legally represent oneself, the legal profession has waged continuous war against allowing people access to information that would enable them to handle their own legal problems, such as divorce and probate of wills.

The monopolistic aspect of professional practices has frequently brought professions into conflict with each other and with other occupational groups over the provision of services. Architects and engineers have long debated their respective spheres of practice, as have lawyers and accountants. The legal profession has also been anxious to define the respective spheres of practice of realtors and insurance and title companies. The medical profession now confronts questions concerning the services provided by nurse practitioners and physician's assistants. A little noticed battle has concerned the practice of midwives, especially lay midwives, at home births. In many states, delivering a child is considered the practice of medicine and only licensed physicians may offer to do so.[17] In a recent California case, three lay midwives were prosecuted for the unlicensed practice of medicine, and the Supreme Court of California upheld the constitutionality of the law with respect to childbirth.[18] A woman's right of privacy, it held, does not extend to the choice of the manner and circumstances in which her baby is born.

The legal monopoly of professional services has an important implication for professional ethics. Professionals do not have a right to practice; it is a privilege conferred by the state. One must carefully distinguish between a right and a privilege in this context. A right is a sound claim that one be permitted (or assisted) to act in some manner without interference. A privilege is a permission to perform certain acts provided specified conditions are fulfilled. With a privilege, the burden is upon the person obtaining it to demonstrate that he or she has the necessary qualifications. For example, one must pass tests for the privilege of driving a car. In the case of a right, the burden is upon anyone who fails to respect it, for example, by prohibiting the publication of one's opinions. Individual professionals have only a privilege to practice; in addition, the profession as a whole is a privileged activity created by the state to further social values.

A third feature of the consulting professional's role is that although some professions have secured legally protected monopolies, none of them has been subject to much public control. Monopolies such as public utilities that provide essential services have usually been subject to strict public control as to the conditions and types of services provided. In contrast, the professions have claimed and been accorded a large degree of self-regulation. They have claimed that because of the intellectual training and judgment required for their practice, nonprofessionals are unable to properly evaluate their conduct. Thus, in addition to control over membership and the disciplining of members, the professions also control the conditions of practice (including until recently the setting of fees and the regulation of advertising).

The combined effects of these three features—serving basic social values, monopoly, and self-regulation—are central to the issue of the role of professions in a modern, liberal society. Monopoly and self-regulation, if exercised improperly, may be detrimental to society and the quality of human life. As the number of professions and professionals increases and their decisions become more essential for the operation of a technologically complex modern society, the conduct and ethical principles of the professions as well as the enforcement of standards become a matter of increasing importance to everyone. If the principles of professional conduct are designed to favor professionals more than their clients and others, then liberal values are threatened. Monopolies are created for the benefit of society, and if they do not serve society well, then they are not justified.

Some problems with professional principles may arise from a failure of professions to revise accepted ethical principles to adequately reflect the changing conditions of society and the professional roles. Two sociologists suggest that the professions are beginning to adopt characteristics of modern industry, specifically a more bureaucratic structure of practice.[19] They specify six differences between traditional professional practice and the modified form they see evolving.

1. Practice as an isolated individual is changing to team practice.
2. The use of knowledge from a single discipline is being replaced by use of knowledge from diverse disciplines.
3. Compensation is changing from fee-for-service to salary.

4. The limits on altruism involved in solo professionals' entrepreneurial private practices (the concern with attracting clients and making a living) are decreasing.

5. The opportunity for colleague evaluation is increasing.

6. The privacy of the professional–client relationship is decreasing.

Examination of these six changes indicates that the last three depend on the first three. Colleague evaluation and privacy in the professional–client relationship depend largely on whether a professional practices as an individual or as part of a team. The entrepreneurial limit on altruism depends on the fee-for-service system. With a fixed salary, a professional can literally afford to be altruistic.

The factors of team approach, use of knowledge from diverse fields, and compensation by salary, partially result from the increasing knowledge required for professional practice. The growth of engineering knowledge and the complexity of many structures now being built require the efforts of many different types of engineers. Electrical, structural, and other engineers must be involved in the design and construction of skyscrapers, large bridges, and so on. The growth of medical knowledge has forced specialization since physicians cannot keep fully informed about all aspects of medicine. No one specialist can provide total patient care, so the team approach involving various physicians and nurses is now often used for hospitalized patients. Although compensation by salary is not as widespread in the medical as in the accounting and legal professions, as group practice develops, more physicians will become salaried. Similar developments have occurred in the legal professions. Although the profession is just beginning to officially recognize specialization, it has existed in practice for a number of years. The development of large corporate law firms during the late nineteenth and early twentieth centuries encouraged specialization and salaried employment. In addition, the enormous proliferation of laws, especially with the advent of governmental regulatory activity in the 1930s, has made it difficult for any one lawyer to keep abreast of the entire legal field. Despite these developments, however, about half of all lawyers and physicians are still engaged in individual or small partnership practices.

Finally, practitioners within professions are not homogeneous. The differences in income, status, and type of practice between a partner in a Wall Street law firm and a small-town solo practitioner are tremendous. The large law firm usually has retainers from corporate clients, whereas the solo practitioner handles one matter for one client. Large accounting firms also can be virtually certain of continuing to work for corporate clients, while small accountants have little such security. The disparity is so great in the legal and accounting professions that different ethical or enforcement procedures have been suggested for large and small firms.[20] The conditions they face, it has been claimed, require such different applications of the same general ethical principles as to make a single system inappropriate. The medical profession is not as stratified as the legal and accounting professions, but a great difference still exists between a well-known specialist in a large urban center and a general practitioner in a rural community. The status of specialties has been evident in the career choices of medical students during the past decades. Medical research and surgery have been the most prestigious, and general or family practice the least. Although family practice is becoming more respected and the choice of more students (as a specialty!), this difference has not disappeared.

SUMMARY

Professional ethics seeks to determine what the role of professions and the conduct of professionals should be. As a discipline, it includes aspects of social, political, and legal philosophy as well as individual ethics. The study of professional ethics will not automatically make one more ethical, but it should develop sensitivity to ethical problems and clearer thinking, provide some general guiding principles, and help one better understand the role and importance of professions in contemporary society. Professional ethics has gained popularity due to recent dramatic cases of unethical conduct or difficult issues, but deeper reasons may underlie this new popularity. The contemporary concern with professional ethics reflects consumerism and the need for society to reconsider the role and conduct of professionals. This study adopts the point of view of the average citizen interested in preserving the values of liberal society—governance by law, freedom, protection from injury, equality of opportunity, privacy, and welfare.

The professions are characterized by three necessary features—extensive training, a significant intellectual component to practice, and the provision of an important service—as well as three commonly found features—certification, the organization of members, and autonomy in work. An important distinction can be made between consulting and scholarly professions. This book focuses on consulting professionals who act in behalf of clients (individuals or corporations) on a fee-for-service basis. Three salient features characterize the role of consulting professions—provision of services related to basic values, a monopoly or near monopoly of services, and self-regulation. These features lie at the heart of the relation between the professions and the values of liberal society. The structure of professional practice may be changing from that of a single practitioner paid on a fee-for-service basis to one of team practice using knowledge from diverse disciplines and paid by salary. Finally, members of professions are not homogeneous but range from those working in large organizations to solo practitioners.

NOTES*

1. Parsons, "Professions," p. 545.

2. From U.S. Bureau of the Census, *Historical Statistics of the United States, Colonial Times to 1970,* Bicentennial ed., part 1 (Washington, D.C.: GPO, 1975), p. 140.

3. See Chapter 7, "Self-Regulation."

*See the bibliography at the back of the book for complete references.

4. Branson, "Secularization of American Medicine," p. 17–28. Notes the conflict between traditional medical practices and the values of freedom and equality.

5. Lieberman, *Crisis at the Bar*, pp. 15–16.

6. For a general development of these political values and principles, see Bayles, *Principles of Legislation*.

7. Wilbert E. Moore recognizes this point and offers a scale of professionalism; see *The Professions*, pp. 4–5. The definitional technique used here could be modified to a scale system by assigning points to the possession of those characteristics that are not necessary but are often found in professions. Both the scale system and that used here agree that an occupation may be a profession yet lack some features found in most professions.

8. Ibid., p. 11.

9. Professionals "profess to know better than others the nature of certain matters, and to know better than their clients what ails them or their affairs. This is the essence of the professional idea and the professional claim" (Everett C. Hughes, "Professions," in *Professions in America*, ed. Lynn, p. 2).

10. See Moore, *The Professions*, pp. 9–10; Pound, "What Is a Profession?" p. 204.

11. R. M. MacIver, "The Social Significance of Professional Ethics," in *Cases and Materials on Professional Responsibility*, ed. Pirsig, p. 48.

12. See Freidson, *Profession of Medicine*, pp. xvii, 42, 70, 82.

13. Wade, "Public Responsibilities of the Learned Professions," in *Cases and Materials on Professional Responsibility*, ed. Pirsig, p. 38; MacIver, "Social Significance" (note 11), p. 48. Moore's use of this feature as one item on a scale is less objectionable because the service orientation is not a necessary feature; see *The Professions*, pp. 13–15.

14. Sharswood, *Essay on Professional Ethics*, pp. 147–148.

15. Pirsig, *Cases and Materials on Professional Responsibility*, p. 43.

16. Freidson, *Profession of Medicine*, pp. 70, 75, 188.

17. George J. Annas, "Childbirth and the Law: How to Work within Old Laws, Avoid Malpractice, and Influence New Legislation in Maternity Care," in *21st Century Obstetrics Now!*, ed. David Stewart and Lee Stewart, 2 vols. (Chapel Hill, N.C.: NAPSAC, Inc., 1977), vol. 2, p. 558.

18. *Bowland v. Municipal Ct. for Santa Cruz City*, 18 Cal. 3d 479, 556 P. 2d 1081, 134 Cal. Rptr. 630 (1976).

19. Gloria V. Engel and Richard H. Hall, "The Growing Industrialization of the Professions," in *Professions and Their Prospects*, ed. Freidson, p. 85.

20. Philip Shuchman, "Ethics and Legal Ethics: The Propriety of the Canons as a Group Moral Code," in *1977 National Conference on Teaching Professional Responsibility*, ed. Goldberg, p. 271; see also Abraham J. Briloff, *"Quis Custodeit Ipsos Custodes?* Accountants and the Public Good," *National Forum* 58 (Summer 1978): 29.

STUDY QUESTIONS AND PROBLEMS

1. Which of the following questions concern professional ethics? Why or why not?

   a. Should a corporation pay a government lawyer an honorarium for a lecture?

   b. Should carpenters be paid the same hourly wage as bricklayers?

   c. Should a physician smoke marijuana?

d.   Should an accountant report suspected illegal activity by a firm she is auditing to the Securities and Exchange Commission?

e.   Should an engineer report to the police that his neighbor is driving a car with one headlight and both taillights out?

2.   Study the newspaper for a week and collect all the articles that concern professions. What ethical issues are raised? Are the stories favorable or unfavorable?

3.   Why have the professions grown so rapidly during the twentieth century? Name five professions that are new in the twentieth century.

4.   What are the values of a liberal society? Are some of them more important than others? If so, which ones? Why?

5.   Which of the following categories of occupations are professions? Why are they or are they not professions?

a.   physicians

b.   horticulturalists

c.   law clerks

d.   journalists

e.   radiologic technicians

f.   military officers

g.   TV repair people

h.   major league baseball players

i.   editors of book publishing firms

6.   What ethical difference does it make, if any, whether an occupation is a profession? Why?

7.   What differences between consulting and scholarly professionals may be relevant to questions of professional ethics?

8.   Do licensed barbers constitute a monopoly? How do they differ, if at all, from lawyers?

9.   Choose a profession and list as many differences as possible between the way it is practiced now and the way it was practiced sixty years ago. Are these differences also found in other professions?

2 The Structure of Professional Ethics

Professional ethics may be viewed as a system of norms. The term *norm* has several meanings. It is commonly used in social science to refer to criteria of behavior accepted within a group or to the statistical average of a characteristic. These are descriptive uses of *norm*. The concern here, however, is with what the behavior of professionals *should* be rather than with what it is, and with the criteria that *should* be used to evaluate professional conduct and professions rather than with those that are used. Consequently, *norm* has an evaluative or normative use. It is the most general term for justifiable criteria for evaluating professions, professionals, and their conduct.

Professional ethics does not concern all the norms that apply to professionals, only those that pertain to them in their professional conduct and activities. Thus, although a justifiable norm may specify that parents have a responsibility for the well-being of their children, this is not a norm of professional ethics. One may call those norms that apply to everyone *ordinary norms*. Examples of ordinary norms are the requirements to keep promises and not to murder.

Three crucial questions about the norms of professional ethics are: (1) How are they justified? (2) How are they related to ordinary norms? and (3) What kinds of norms are there? This chapter examines these three questions.

FOUNDATIONS

Relationships

There are four possible relationships between professional and ordinary ethical norms; professional norms are (1) identical with, (2) specifications of, (3) functionally related to, or (4) independent of ordinary norms. These distinctions are illustrated by the following logical form of a norm. Person X, with characteristics C, in situations S, may or should do A in manner M. A norm specifies who should or may do what, when, and how.

If professional norms are identical to ordinary norms, none of the variables differ. And if no special norms exist for professional ethics, then it does not exist as a separate field.

If professional norms are specifications of ordinary norms, then S will vary according to the type of situation a professional encounters. Professional norms are simply ordinary norms made more concrete. For example, "one should not lie to a judge" simply specifies one type of situation in which one should not lie; it applies with equal force to lawyers and nonlawyers. The fact that a person is a professional gives no additional weight to the norm that one should not lie to judges. Frequently, descriptions of situations will implicitly refer to a professional role. For example, a statement that one should not operate on a patient without his or her consent implicitly refers to (or at least strongly suggests) the role of a surgeon or physician.

If the description of the situation implicitly refers to features defining professional roles or explicitly identifies a person as a professional, then the norm is functionally related to ordinary norms. It is functional because the function or role of professionals is taken into account in justifying and applying the norm. Functional norms will usually specify both characteristics (C) of the persons to whom they apply, as well as situations (S) often encountered by professionals.

Finally, if professional norms are completely independent of ordinary ones, all the variables filled out in functional norms (C, S) may differ from those of ordinary norms. More importantly, the norms are not justified by, nor applications of, ordinary ones or the values supporting them. Instead, they constitute a distinct ethical system alongside of, and perhaps taking precedence over, the ordinary ethical system. This view may perhaps be illustrated by the similar position of some religious norms. Religious norms concerning baptism, confession, and diet, for example, are not justified by reference to ordinary norms and do not apply to people who are not members of a particular religious sect.

Ethical Relativism

Before considering which of these relationships between professional and ordinary norms is valid, it is important to clarify the concept of ethical relativism. The central feature of ethical relativism is that norms always refer to a particular reference group.[1] Two apparently contradictory statements can both be true; for example, "Bribing officials to award engineering contracts is permissible *in Korea*," and "Bribing officials to award engineering contracts is not permissible *in the United States*." According to the ethical relativist, different norms may be correct in different societies or for different groups. The ethical relativist does not merely maintain that people have different beliefs (sociological or descriptive relativism) but that these different beliefs may all be correct. The arguments against this ethical theory are well known and will not be rehearsed here. Ethical relativism is not accepted for this book.

There is a difference between ethical relativism and the view that the same norm is applicable in all societies but may require different conduct due to different conditions or perhaps social roles. For example, physicians may be subject to a norm requiring them above all to "Do no harm." This norm would usually require that physicians try to resuscitate patients who suffer cardiac arrest. Usually, dying is a harm. However, some people contend that some patients would in fact suffer harm were they resuscitated, such as patients suffering excruciating pain from cancer who are almost certain to die in a few days. Their life would be so miserable that it would be worse than death. Whether or not this claim is correct, the point is that these people do not reject the principle "Do no harm." Rather, they contend that actions which usually avoid harm may in some situations actually cause it. Thus, to hold that the same norms or values justify different actions by people in different social roles or situations is not ethical relativism.

The view that professional norms are independent of ordinary norms is a version of ethical relativism.[2] If professional norms are not justified by ordinary norms or the values supporting them, then professional norms must apply only to a particular group. What is ethically correct for professionals is independent of what is correct for others. It is difficult to understand how professional norms independent of ordinary norms could be justified. One might think that they could be justified by a perhaps tacit social contract among professionals, but this view has two problems. First, it presupposes a nonrelativist norm, namely, that contracts should be adhered to. Second, it would not justify norms concerning conduct towards clients and other persons who are not members of the profession and thus not parties to the contract.

Besides the difficulties with justifying an independent professional ethic, it is also inadequate for conduct towards others in society.[3] Religious norms, such as Jewish dietary laws and priests' vows of chastity, do not apply to others. However, whenever religious duties affect people who do not belong to the sect, ordinary ethical norms may limit them. Because professional activity almost always affects nonprofessionals, some broader-based ethic would limit any independent ethic.

Justifications

Professional norms pertain to persons occupying roles defined by social norms. The norms defining roles need not be ethical ones; they simply state the actions that people with certain characteristics may or must do. The qualifying characteristics and some basic activities define professional roles. To determine the defining characteristics and activities of various professionals, one looks to the statutes and other licensing regulations. They specify the qualifications for being an accountant or nurse, for example, and the kinds of activities these professionals are entitled to engage in (that others are usually prohibited from performing). Admission to the bar and permission to perform certain actions, such as to represent other persons in court, define the role of a lawyer. Other norms are not definitive of a professional role but do indicate the appropriate activity of a professional. For example, norms prohibiting solicitation (personally seeking business) by physicians or lawyers do not define their roles but specify their function in society. The norms defining other roles are often not written down anywhere; they are generally accepted social norms, such as those for the parental roles.

Some writers suggest that professional norms can be justified by the ideal or value of a profession.[4] For example, the ideal of the medical profession is health and healing. Its fundamental norm, many physicians contend, is "First, do no harm." In order to heal and avoid doing harm, confidentiality of professional–client relationships is essential. Other norms can be similarly derived from the basic ideal or value a profession serves.

This approach is defective, however, for it virtually insulates the professions from other liberal values. Each profession predominantly serves only one or two of the values of a liberal society—lawyers, legal justice; physicians, health; architects and engineers, beautiful and safe structures. Other values of liberal society must also be considered. Just as religious norms—such as requiring school prayers or using poisonous snakes—are limited by ordinary norms when they affect persons outside the sect, so too professional ethics must be limited by a profession's impact on society. Just as founding professional ethics solely on the primary value or ideal served by a profession fails to adequately consider the other values of liberal society, it also cannot adequately reconcile professional ethics with ordinary ethics, which includes all the values of liberal society.

Norms for professional roles are to be justified by their promoting and preserving the values of liberal society. The justification involves more than the primary value a profession promotes, although it plays an important part. One must look at the effect of professional activity upon different groups. Professional activities affect three distinct groups—the professionals, their clients, and the general public.[5] Professional activity should promote the wealth of the profession-als and the interests of clients related to the professional function (such as legal justice or health) and should not be detrimental to (should preserve) the liberal values of clients and others in society. Different values will be affected depending on the context. For example, confidentiality promotes the value of privacy of clients, and making services available promotes equality of opportunity.

Norms are justified by balancing the effects of conduct conforming to them on the different groups and their values. Sometimes a norm will promote one value for at least one of these groups and preserve all values for others. Sometimes that is not possible, and difficult choices must be made between favorable and unfavorable effects upon different values of different affected groups. The interests and values of clients sometimes coincide with, and sometimes conflict with, those of the broader community. A criminal lawyer's client has an interest in avoiding punishment that is contrary to society's interest in the prevention of crime and protection from injury. Similarly, a patient with a communicable disease has an interest in being free in the community, which is contrary to society's welfare. Professionals often mediate between individuals and society.[6] Sometimes the values of the general public do not all point in the same direction; for example, a housing project may promote the welfare of some persons but harm that of others who are forced to move. In such cases, professional norms must provide a proper balance between the effects on the values of professionals, clients, and the public. This balance is determined by considering what a reasonable person holding liberal values would desire for himself or herself in the respective roles.

If professional norms are justified by their promoting and preserving the values of society, then the nature of those values is crucial. In a Nazi society, the norms for physicians might include identifying and performing involuntary euthanasia on those who, by Nazi standards, are unfit. One must here distinguish two levels of justification. At one level, professional norms are justified by the values of society. A professional ethic completely incompatible with accepted social values will not endure; any viable professional ethic must be largely congruent with the accepted values of a society. However, as the Nazi example shows, the accepted social values may be unjustifiable. At a higher level, a complete justification of professional ethics involves the justification of societal values. The values of freedom, privacy, equality of opportunity, governance by law, prevention of injury, and welfare identified in Chapter 1 are here taken to be justifiable. Major differences from these values alter the professional norms that are justifiable. Although there are differences in interpreting these values, they are widely enough accepted in the United States and other Western countries to render viable a professional ethic based on them.

The social role of professions can be relevant to the evaluation of professional norms by liberal values. For example, the activities in which particular professions are exclusively entitled to engage can be critiqued by their promoting and preserving social values, especially the freedom of clients. The proper social role of a profession can affect the weight given to various norms. As an analogy, consider norms for nurturing children. An ordinary norm is that children should be nurtured. Most societies assign this job to biological parents as the best way to promote the values of all affected. People in a parental role are not expected to weigh the interests and needs of their children equally with all others; in some contexts, they are entitled to benefit their own children at the expense of others. The balancing of conflicting norms is different for parents than for others, just as the balancing and weighing of confidentiality can be different for professionals than for ordinary citizens.[7] Lawyers have a stronger commitment to preserve the confidences of clients about past crimes than ordinary citizens do; otherwise, lawyers could not adequately defend their clients. As parental roles to care for children create an obligation for parents that other people do not have, so occupying a professional role can entail obligations for professionals that others do not have.

The claim that professional norms can differ from ordinary ones due to professional roles does not entail ethical relativism. Ultimately, the norms of a professional ethic must be justified by the same values as other norms in a liberal society. However, this claim recognizes the different tasks involved in professional roles and implies that no simple, absolute norms hold in every situation. The same norms do, though, apply in similar situations. Norms do not vary simply because the people in the situations accept different norms. Any such relativism would immediately justify the norms accepted in a Nazi society. Nor is bribing persons to obtain contracts ethically justifiable in some countries simply because that is the general practice in them.

Although many professional norms are functionally related to ordinary ones and can be justified in the way described, that is, by considering the effects of professional functions on the values of different groups, not all professional norms are functionally related to ordinary ones. Professionals are people, and ordinary norms apply also to them. For example, professionals should not assault or defraud others. A number of complaints against professionals are for violations of such ordinary norms—for example, lawyers appropriating clients' funds for their own use. These situations do not often cause ethical perplexity. How one determines ordinary norms is the subject of normative ethical theory, a subject that cannot be developed here; it requires a separate book. However, such ethical theories justify basic ethical norms that are widely shared, such as those against theft and assault. For the most part, these are the types of ordinary norms considered in this book, so the absence of a theory justifying them should not create difficulties. Such norms would be justified by any acceptable theory.

Other professional norms are specifications of ordinary ones, such as that physicians ought not have sexual intercourse with patients. An ordinary norm is that sexual intercourse requires the free consent of both parties. Since the dominant position of a professional, like that of an employer, makes free consent of a client questionable, application of the ordinary norm to the professional–client situation results in the specific prohibition. Some professional norms are, like this, specifications of ordinary norms for situations that arise frequently in professional practice.

NORMS

This section briefly explains some of the different kinds of professional norms (see Table 2.1). The differences among them are often relevant to their use.

Table 2.1 Kinds of Professional Norms

Obligations
Standards of virtue and vice
Principles of responsibility
of a profession as a whole
of individual professionals
Rules of duty
Permissions

The term *obligation* is used here to express the requirements of professional norms. Obligation is used to mean the prescription or proscription of a norm: what it is right or wrong to do (or not do) or be. Some norms do not express requirements or obligations but express *permissions*—for example, that a professional may refuse to accept a potential client if he or she considers the client's proposed course of conduct immoral. Most of the concern in professional ethics is with what professionals are obligated to do, for they are permitted to do what is not prohibited.

Standards, Principles, and Rules

Norms expressing obligations can be divided into three types: those prescribing standards, principles expressing responsibilities, and rules expressing duties.[8] Standards are used to evaluate persons as good or bad, better or worse, virtuous or vicious, and can be fulfilled to different degrees. Technically, standards alone do not constitute norms; they must be prescribed. One obvious standard is that a professional be competent. Competence is a character trait, a disposition to act in certain ways, of a professional, and professionals can be more or less competent. A norm of professional ethics prescribes that professionals have an obligation to be competent. Standards guide human conduct by presenting desirable traits (virtues) to be sought or undesirable ones (vices) to be avoided. Among the virtues that professionals should have are competence, loyalty, discretion, honesty, diligence, and candor (see Chapter 4).

Other norms, which may be called principles, prescribe responsibilities. Responsibilities do not precisely specify the required conduct but leave room for the discretion or judgment of a professional. For example, a principle is that engineers are responsible for the safety of what they design. An engineer is thus responsible for designing a safe structure, but a safe structure of a certain appearance and function can be constructed in various ways. The engineer is not required to use concrete instead of steel or vice versa. Because responsibilities allow discretion and indicate more general ethical concerns, a principle by itself does not necessarily determine what should be done in a particular situation. Instead, various principles or responsibilities may be relevant, and these have to be weighed and balanced against one another.

In contrast to responsibilities, rules prescribing duties specify particular conduct and do not leave room for judgment or discretion by a professional. For example, a rule prescribes that professionals experimenting on human subjects have a duty to obtain informed consent. A professional does not have discretion to decide whether informed consent is needed for a particular experiment or subject. Because duties are determinate, rules cannot be balanced against one another. They apply in an all-or-nothing fashion; that is, if they apply to a situation, they determine the evaluation and leave no leeway for a contrary one. Of course, rules may have exceptions, which are often stated as separate permissions, and sometimes rules may conflict. But in the end only one rule is applicable to a situation. For example, a physician treats a person for a venereal disease, and the person does not want his or her spouse told. In this case, the physician cannot both preserve confidentiality and treat the spouse. An exception must be made to either the duty to maintain confidentiality or the duty to treat.

The uses of and relations between the various types of norms are sometimes complex. Standards are often the basis for many principles of professional ethics. For example, one norm of professional ethics prescribes that professionals have the virtue of honesty. As a result, a professional has a responsibility to protect his or her client's money. Principles thus help explicate the standards that professionals must meet.

Principles can be used to justify rules. That is, a rule may be justified by showing that various principles support it, that it advances more than it hinders the considerations in proper principles. In short, one may justify a rule by showing that principles provide stronger reasons for it than for any alternatives. For example, one principle is that professionals keep confidential information obtained from clients. Another principle is that professionals should not injure their clients. Balancing these two obligations might result in a rule requiring preservation of confidences except when doing so would result in serious injury to the client.

Principles also provide guidance in situations not covered by rules. Rules can be formulated only if specific conduct is almost always right or wrong. Many cases cannot be covered by hard and fast rules. For example, a physician has the responsibility to assist the profession in making medical services equally available to all. One can make a rule that physicians should never refuse to treat their own patients or anyone in an emergency situation.[9] How many patients each physician should accept is not easily decided, however. Various principles or responsibilities may apply to this situation. For example, physicians should render service when needed and render competent service; but these responsibilities can conflict with one another if a physician accepts more patients than he or she can serve where needed and serve competently. Thus, the decision as to the number of clients a professional should accept is a matter of discretion, keeping in mind the different responsibilities.

Finally, duties require specific conduct, and violations are comparatively easy to determine. They may be specific parts of responsibilities, just as the duty not to steal clients' money is a further specification of the responsibility to protect clients' money. Much of the disciplining of professionals is for violations of duties. Although more leeway must be allowed in judging nonfulfillment of responsibilities, persistent nonfulfillment or ignoring of responsibilities may also be grounds for discipline. No valid reason exists to permit a professional to continually exercise discretion beyond reasonable bounds without discipline.

Many but not all professions have developed codes of ethics to present the relevant norms. The status of professional codes varies widely. The American Bar Association codes are usually adopted by legislatures or courts and have the force of law. Other codes of ethics, such as those of the American Medical Association or the American Society of Civil Engineers, are statements for the guidance of professional societies. Violations of the latter may result in removal from membership, but this action does not automatically involve loss of a license to practice. Most codes are of this sort.

Obligations of Professions and Professionals

Although codes claim to be fairly complete statements of professionals' ethical obligations, they chiefly comprise statements of obligations of individual professionals. This constitutes a fundamental defect since such codes fail to adequately cover obligations of a profession as a whole.[10] It is important to recognize obligations of professions as a whole and not to confuse them with the obligations of individual professionals. For example, professions are often said to have an obligation to provide services to all who need them. However, individual professionals do not have an obligation to serve all those who are in need.[11]

Obligations of a profession as a whole cannot be directly reduced to similar obligations of each member—that is, obligations of the same kind specifying the same conduct, such as an obligation to provide service equally to all. An obligation of a group (military) not to kill members of another group (innocent civilians) is reducible to obligations of each member of the first group (soldiers) not to kill members of the second (civilians). As indicated previously, however, an obligation of the medical profession to provide services equally to everyone is not so reducible to a similar obligation of each physician. It is an obligation of the profession as a whole or of all physicians together, not of each individually. Nonetheless, obligations of a profession as a whole can support some obligations of individual professionals—for example, to spend some time working for disadvantaged clients who would otherwise not receive services.[12]

SUMMARY

Professional norms can be related to ordinary ones (those applicable to everyone) in four ways; they may be: identical to, specifications of, functionally related to, or independent of ordinary norms. The conception of professional norms as independent of ordinary norms is not tenable; this view does not provide a basis for justifying professional norms or reconciling them with ordinary norms and liberal values. One must distinguish the claim of ethical relativism—that norms always refer to what is accepted in a particular society or group—from the claim that norms may require different conduct depending on the situation or the person's role. The latter view does not deny that there are some valid universal norms or values that justify the more concrete norms. Norms for professional roles are justified by their promoting and preserving the justifiable values of liberal society. One should consider how the norms affect the realization of values by professionals, clients, and the public. In justifying functional norms, the defining roles of professions in society must be justified, and then these functions must be considered in justifying other norms and giving them weight. Ordinary norms also apply to professionals, and some professional norms are specifications of ordinary ones for situations that frequently arise in professional practice.

Professional norms express either obligations or permissions. Obligations may be of any of three kinds. Standards present desirable or undesirable character traits to be sought or avoided. Principles state responsibilities that allow for discretion in the fulfillment of standards and may be balanced or weighed against one another. Rules state duties that prescribe rather specific conduct and do not allow for much discretion. Principles can explicate standards, justify rules, and provide guidance in their absence. Not all responsibilities are those of individual professionals. Some are responsibilities of a profession as a whole and cannot be reduced to obligations of individual professionals. Professional codes attempt to formulate the norms of professional ethics and are the basis for disciplinary measures of various kinds. However, they are primarily composed of norms applying to individual professionals. Thus they often omit norms for professions as a whole and fail to be comprehensive statements.

NOTES*

1. See Paul W. Taylor, *Principles of Ethics: An Introduction* (Encino, Calif.: Dickenson Publishing, 1975), pp. 18–23; John Hospers, *Human Conduct: Problems of Ethics,* shorter ed. (New York: Harcourt Brace Jovanovich, 1972), pp. 36–38.

2. See Veatch, "Medical Ethics," pp. 543–549.

3. Veatch, "Professional Medical Ethics," p. 12.

4. See, for example, Freedman, "A Meta-Ethics," pp. 14–17.

5. See *Report of the Professional Organizations Committee,* p. 8. This valuable study concerns the regulation of architects, lawyers, engineers, and accountants in Ontario.

6. "There is an intriguing tension in our legal system whereby lawyers on the one hand picture themselves as representatives of a public profession and on the other picture themselves as defending individuals against an oppressive system" (Thomas D. Morgan, "The Evolving Concept of Professional Responsibility," in *1977 National Conference on Teaching Professional Responsibility,* ed. Goldberg, p. 316).

7. Freedman, "A Meta-Ethics," pp. 2–4.

8. Bayles, *Principles of Legislation,* pp. 42–44; Ronald Dworkin, *Taking Rights Seriously* (Cambridge: Harvard University Press, 1977), pp. 22–28.

9. AMA, *Opinions and Reports,* sec. 5.50.

10. See R. M. MacIver, "The Social Significance of Professional Ethics," in *Cases and Materials on Professional Responsibility,* ed. Pirsig, p. 50.

11. ABA, *Code of Professional Responsibility,* EC 2-26; AMA, *Principles of Medical Ethics,* sec. 6.

12. ABA, Commission, *Model Rules,* sec. 6.1.

STUDY QUESTIONS AND PROBLEMS

1. Which of the following norms are professional norms and which are ordinary ethical norms? Why?

    a. It is wrong to have sexual intercourse without the consent of the other person.

    b. Lawyers should keep information from their clients confidential.

    c. Do no harm.

    d. Performing abortions is wrong.

    e. Do not design unsafe products.

---

*See the bibliography at the back of the book for complete references.

    f.   Teachers should not spank students.

    g.   One should tell the truth.

    h.   One should tell the truth to judges during court.

2. What are the four views of the relation between ordinary and professional norms?

3. In many foreign countries it has long been the practice of engineers to submit sketches and bids for engineering work. In the 1960s, many foreign projects funded by the United States Agency for International Development asked for bids. However, the codes of ethics of many U.S. professional engineering societies prohibited bidding on projects. Should engineering firms have followed the practice of the countries in which the projects were done? Or, should the U.S.A.I.D. have required those countries to follow ethical codes of the U.S. societies for projects they funded? Why?

4. How can professional norms be justified?

5. In Nazi Germany, physicians were ordered to select unfit persons for euthanasia. As Nazi values were widely accepted, should the physicians have complied? If not, what is the relation between the accepted values of a society and justifiable professional norms?

6. What are the differences among standards, responsibilities, and duties? Which are the following?

    a.   If the other party does not do so, a lawyer should advise the court of a precedent in the jurisdiction directly contrary to a legal claim he or she is advancing.

    b.   An engineer should be careful.

    c.   A journalist should present facts accurately.

    d.   A dentist must have the informed consent of her patient before performing a service.

    e.   An architect should charge a reasonable fee.

7. Distinguish obligations of an individual professional from obligations of a profession as a whole. Give two examples of each.

3 Obligations and Availability of Services

The average citizen faces three potential problems in obtaining professional help—economic, racial, and geographic maldistribution of services. This chapter focuses on the first problem—obtaining professional services at a reasonable price. The value at stake is equal availability of professional services. With some qualification, the professions do recognize a responsibility to establish equal opportunity for or equal access to their services.[1] The central problems that must be overcome are (1) that this obligation belongs to professions as a whole and cannot be directly reduced to a similar obligation on the part of individual professionals and (2) that various traditional professional norms have hindered equal access to professional services.

Two related arguments support the obligation to make professional services equally available. First, as legal privileges are granted for the benefit of society, to the extent professions have a legal monopoly upon the provision of services, they should be equally available to all citizens. The government should act for all citizens, so the benefits of a legally created monopoly should extend to all of them.

The second argument is more general. The argument from monopoly assumes that the state should act for all citizens. One reason for that assumption is the value of equality of opportunity; this value, however, directly supports the equal availability of professional services regardless of the existence of a legal monopoly. Thus, denial of equal opportunity to secure competent professional services directly infringes upon a fundamental value of liberal society.

Most consulting professionals work on a fee-for-service basis, which distributes professional services by the ability of potential clients to pay. However, the availability of some professional services is essential to providing people with equal opportunity in society generally. In particular, people without access to health care or legal representation do not have an equal opportunity to compete with others in society. Without reasonable health care, a person may be disadvantaged in obtaining an education or a job. Legal representation is also often needed to secure basic rights, such as a fair trial or a secure title to a house. The provision of health and legal services according to the ability to pay has denied

27

general equality of opportunity, because the rich have consumed a disproportionate share of them. To achieve equality, health and legal services should be *provided* to all equally, regardless of ability to pay.

The services of other professions—accounting, architecture, engineering—are less essential to general equality of opportunity. One could argue that accounting services and advice for income tax preparation are important for general equality of opportunity. Nevertheless, they are not as important as health and legal services. Consequently, the services of these other professions need only be *available* to all on equal terms. Ability to pay may be an acceptable basis for the distribution of these professional services.

Equality of opportunity and other basic values also have implications for more concrete issues in the distribution of health and legal services. First, society may not be able to provide everyone all services from which they could benefit. Equality of opportunity implies that in such an event, everyone should have equal access to those services that can be provided. Second, along with the other values, the principle of equality of opportunity helps determine which services should be available. For example, a relatively inexpensive and reliable treatment for life-threatening diseases and injuries should be made available before cosmetic services such as "face-lifts," since the latter are less important for general welfare and equality of opportunity.

These arguments support the claim that people have positive rights to certain health and legal services, but only negative rights to other professional services. Negative rights imply noninterference; that is, without good cause, neither the state nor other people may interfere with a person obtaining services from professionals willing to provide them. Positive rights are to the services themselves. They are sound claims that the services be provided.

These distinctions can be briefly illustrated by the history of the availability of abortions. For about a century, most states prohibited abortions except in limited circumstances. In 1973 the U.S. Supreme Court held that, with some restrictions, women have a right of privacy to abortions during the first and second trimesters of pregnancy.[2] This is a negative right to noninterference by the state. Under the Medicaid program, poor women have a limited positive right to medical care. That is, the government will pay for certain services. The negative constitutional right to an abortion does not automatically confer a positive right to have abortions paid for by Medicaid. Some people argue that equal protection of the laws (equality of opportunity) requires that Medicaid pay for abortions, but the Supreme Court has held that states need not pay for nontherapeutic abortions.[3] Further, a federal court held that restricting Medicaid-funded abortions to those necessary to save the woman's life unduly restricts the range of medically necessary or therapeutic abortions, and thus in effect denies equality of opportunity for health and welfare, but the Supreme Court rejected this argument also.[4]

Even when positive rights to legal and health services exist they do not directly affect the obligations of individual professionals. Such rights obligate only the government or perhaps the professions to provide the services. Thus, a patient does not have a right to have a particular physician perform an abortion for her.

Similarly, for a number of years criminal defendants have had a constitutional right to counsel, but except when assigned by a court, individual lawyers have not had a duty to represent criminal defendants. Individual professionals merely have a responsibility to assist the profession in fulfilling its obligation (see Chapter 6).

Ensuring the equal provision of professional services requires a social organization. The legal and medical professions have not only failed to promote such a delivery organization, they have often actively opposed adoption of policies to do so. (For years, the AMA opposed what it called socialized medicine, that is, national health insurance.) Moreover, traditional norms of professions concerning economic matters such as fees and advertising have hindered equal opportunity for services in all professions.

Before examining these traditional economic norms, the other two problems with the distribution of services, racial and geographic, should be mentioned. They have been more of a problem for the provision of health and legal services than for other kinds of professional services. Blacks and other racial minorities receive fewer professional services per capita than whites. This racial maldistribution results partly from economic maldistribution, since a larger percentage of the black population is poor, but its fundamental source is racial prejudice. Racial discrimination in employment has contributed to the disproportionate poverty of minorities, and thus to their inability to pay for services. Discrimination by professions has also played a role—for example, by excluding minorities from the professions. A white friend of mine, accompanying a black physician seeing black patients, found that the patients assumed he was the doctor. Lack of minority professionals does not necessarily affect the distribution of services to members of that minority, although it may. For example, women have been underrepresented in professions in the United States, but that has not affected their access to professional services as much as it has the quality of the services they receive. The quality may have been severely affected by the failure of male professionals to adequately assess the needs and interests of women, as in childbirth. Nonetheless, although few white male professionals serve predominantly black clients, many serve female clients.

The third maldistribution of professional services is geographic. The bulk of professional services is centered in the more affluent urban areas. Many rural communities lack basic health and legal services. Some counties in states like Minnesota have no lawyers. The reasons for the lack of professional services in rural areas are only partly economic. Although many rural areas are poor, sufficient economic demand for professional services often exists. One reason professionals may not wish to practice in rural communities is the absence of facilities. A poor rural county may not have a hospital, and even if it does, it will not have all the modern equipment found in large urban hospitals. Similarly, lawyers in rural communities may not have access to libraries large enough to help them keep abreast of the law. Further, as a group, professionals are often more interested than the average citizen in cultural activities, which are scarce in rural communities. Whatever the reason, it is widely recognized that rural and remote areas are often short of professional services, and some rich urban ones have more than needed.

ECONOMIC NORMS

Several traditional professional norms have hindered availability of professional services. These are largely concerned with economic matters, although they have usually been defended by ethical-sounding considerations. The general impact of such norms on access to services is as follows. The professions recognize an obligation to prevent unauthorized practice (provision of services by nonprofessionals) and thus they maintain a monopoly. Without competition from others, norms about fees and publicity prevent competition among professionals and deny potential clients information relevant to choosing a professional intelligently. Finally, norms about specialization may further increase costs. Potential clients then face unnecessarily high fees that prevent some from receiving services and prevent many of those who can afford them from being able to choose high quality services.

Unauthorized Practice

A traditional obligation of the legal and medical professions is to prevent unauthorized practice—that is, the unlicensed provision of professional services.[5] This norm has not been as strong for other professions, such as engineering, because unlicensed provision of those services is usually not illegal. Nonetheless, even those professions that have not had a legal monopoly of the provision of services have often fought to prevent their practice by unlicensed persons.

Both the legal and medical professions are currently under pressure to (1) use paraprofessionals to assist in providing services and (2) accept provision of services by others outside of the profession. Services by paraprofessionals have been more strongly advanced against the medical profession, and services by other persons against the legal profession. For example, Ivan Illich contends that much of the medical profession's resources are now devoted to treating disease and illness caused by physicians' use of high technology. He favors development of less specially trained health care workers to provide basic services to more people rather than high technological care for a few.[6] Both the Canadian Nurses Association and the Canadian Health Coalition have suggested that nurses and other health care workers should perform some of the tasks now performed by physicians, such as changing dressings and giving vaccinations.[7] Similar competitive situations for the legal profession are realtors completing real estate contracts, groups such as H. & R. Block preparing income tax returns, and title companies checking property titles.

The fundamental moral guide in the area of unauthorized practice should be the public or social good.[8] The appropriate method of analysis was developed years ago by Karl N. Llewellyn: "For the men of law are a monopoly, and monopoly is subject to regulation. The ground for monopoly is that it makes possible better service; this holds of the bar. The condition of monopoly is that it serve; this does not hold of the bar."[9] For example, lawyers' organizations fought the provision of legal services by unions for injured workers which helped more people receive services. The same point applies to other professions. In another paper, Llewellyn outlines four steps to be followed in considering the justification of prohibitions of unauthorized practice.[10] (1) Determine the proposed areas of monopolization. (2) Ask of each area why society needs to make it a monopoly. (3) Consider what is gained, if anything, for people other than the monopolists. (4) Finally, if there are complaints about unauthorized practice, consider who is complaining and why, specifically, whether it is the public or members of the profession.

The public concern in prohibiting nonprofessionals from performing certain services is to protect people from injury due to inadequate or incompetent performance.[11] This implies that a professional and only a professional possesses the requisite skills and abilities to provide the services. One legal ethics text modestly claims that the special privilege of lawyers stems from their superior competence, dependability, and breadth of view.[12] Even taken with a grain of salt, such sweeping claims are hardly plausible. Services must be examined individually, indeed, the same text suggests the following reasons for nonlawyers handling such matters as real estate transactions and tax preparations: (1) easier access to these nonlawyers, (2) equal or superior value of the nonlawyer's expertise, (3) economy and lower cost, and (4) speed in business transactions.[13] A tax accountant or realtor may better handle such matters because he or she routinely processes large numbers of them. Similarly, abortion clinics with medical technicians rather than physicians may provide better service at a lower cost. Concentrating on the provision of one type of service, they become more efficient. At least in early pregnancy, medical technicians can perform abortions as well as, or better than, physicians.[14] The superior competence of professionals cannot justify monopolization of many traditional services simply because in some cases this superior competence does not exist.

Even if professionals are more competent, one should also consider the freedom of the client to choose a lesser service at a lower cost. To justify limiting this freedom, one must show that a reasonable consumer would not knowingly choose to have the services performed by a less competent person in exchange for some other benefit such as lower cost. If an informed person is willing to risk an unclear title to property or a medical complication from an abortion or childbirth in order to save money or secure some other value, any prohibition of unauthorized practice limits his or her freedom. Many of the restricted services are much less significant, such as nurses giving vaccinations. An extremely difficult distinction to justify is the College of Nurses of Ontario not permitting registered nursing assistants to provide fractional doses of medicine.[15] People at home are capable of splitting tablets or pouring one teaspoon of medicine rather than two. It is difficult to understand why a reasonable patient may not be willing to allow a nursing assistant to do the same for him or her.

If a nonprofessional providing a service would pose a risk of injury to others, that is certainly a reason for restricting the service to licensed professionals. Thus, good reasons exist to prevent companies issuing stock with a legal opinion letter from a nonlawyer. If a reasonable client knowingly and voluntarily risks only his own well-being, however, no reason exists for prohibiting unauthorized practice.

Prohibiting nonprofessionals from rendering services is also overly restrictive of their freedom. One need only hold them to the same standard of competence as professionals. Even this requirement has been used to try to prevent competition. When an amendment to the state constitution overturned the Arizona Supreme Court's prohibition of realtors completing purchase agreements, deeds, mortgages, and so on, the Court announced that realtors would be held to the same ethical standards (including competence) as attorneys.[16] The point was to discourage them from exercising their constitutional rights by requiring them to have the same legal competence as lawyers. When a profession claims that large recognized occupations, such as realtors and title insurance companies, provide unauthorized practice, their purpose is probably to protect their own monopolistic source of income. Such claims deserve special scrutiny. Prohibition will probably only increase the cost of services and make them less available.

Another approach is for two professions, such as engineering and architecture or law and accounting, to agree which services are appropriately provided by each. One might think that such an approach would result in each profession offering what it is best skilled to provide. Unfortunately, these arrangements are often simply a division of the client pie. A client may discover that instead of having to hire only one professional, he or she will require the services of two. A couple in a relatively simple divorce can end up hiring four professionals, one lawyer and one accountant each. Were grocery stores and fast food restaurants to agree what service each would provide, everyone would perceive it as an anticompetitive agreement in restraint of trade and obviously detrimental to consumer interests. In many areas, open competition between professions is also the best way to decide which services different professionals should provide. Those who provide a service most efficiently will eventually dominate in its provision.

Only certain core services should be restricted to specific professions. The two reasons for this are that (1) no reasonable person would want an untrained person to provide the service or (2) an untrained person providing the service might burden the public. The first condition holds for only few services, but few reasonable people would want a nonprofessional to perform open heart surgery or defend them on a murder charge. Restrictions are less likely to be justified for other services. For example, a reasonable person might be willing to have a person who is not an architect design a house. Of course, as this condition says, no reasonable person would want the important services in question to be provided by nonprofessionals, so restrictions are hardly necessary.

The second condition applies to more services. For example, people who are not lawyers practicing in court might take up so much time as to seriously increase the public's costs in running the courts.[17] Untrained accountants preparing financial statements to be filed with the government could impose heavy costs on the government, which has to review the filed materials. Untrained engineers designing large structures like buildings and dams could cause serious injuries to many persons if the structures were unsafe. Similarly, bungled medical care could drain public resources when others tried to correct the resulting problems.

Greater restrictions than these two conditions allow would unduly limit the freedom of clients to choose, and of nonprofessionals to render, services.

Fees

Professional norms concerning fees have often prevented price competition among professionals. The issues of fee schedules, competitive bidding, and fee splitting arise in most professions. Contingent fees, paid only when the outcome is successful, are an issue for some professions in the United States. Examples of contingent fees are those paid only when a plaintiff recovers damages or when a community approves a construction project.

Traditionally, many local professional groups issued minimum fee schedules that were sometimes obligatory and sometimes merely recommended. The main argument for fee schedules is that they prevent poor performance for a lower cost, that is, prevent inadequate service. To attract clients, professionals might charge lower fees but render less thorough service in order to keep costs down. As with unauthorized practice, the underlying *reason* is to protect clients assumed incapable of protecting themselves by making intelligent decisions.

Fee schedules increase the costs of professional services by eliminating competition. Without competition, professionals have little motivation to introduce cost-saving techniques. Should they discover a way to reduce costs, professionals have no economic incentive to lower their fees rather than simply increase their profit.

Fee schedules also deny prospective clients freedom of choice between full service at a high price and less service at a reduced price. People who purchase low-cost automobiles do not usually expect the same quality as with more expensive ones. (Of course, sometimes they get as good a car at a lower cost, but that is the result of competition.) Consumers often make a conscious choice between quality and cost. Similar choices can be made with respect to professional services. For example, some stockbrokers now offer an economy service that does not include the stock analysis provided by other firms. A lawyer might offer a low-cost title search covering fifty years and a more expensive one covering a hundred years. A physician could offer medical examinations of differing thoroughness at different prices. Engineers might explain that they could spend less time determining structural loads and so on for a lesser fee but that the resulting construction costs might be higher due to excess allowances for safety.

The proffered reasons for fee schedules do not adequately support them. These reasons primarily support truthfulness and honesty. A professional has a duty to inform a prospective client of the limited extent of the services being provided for a lower fee and of the risks and costs involved vis-à-vis alternative services. He or she also has a duty to actually provide the proposed services. These ethical obligations, however, apply to all business transactions and do not support special price setting in the professions.

Some professional fees are a percentage of the amount involved in a professional service such as a stock transaction, probated estate, or construction project. The amount of money involved in such cases is not necessarily related to the amount of work professionals perform. In engineering, the work is more apt to be related to project costs than in other professions, but it need not be. (An engineer hired on a percentage fee will receive more if there is a cost overrun, no matter what the reason for the overrun.) With very large estates, lawyers with a percentage fee may receive compensation quite disproportionate to the work involved. To some extent, the rich subsidize the poor. Rarely do the truly indigent benefit, because the indigent do not inherit, sell, or purchase anything of significant value, and if they must probate a worthless estate, legal aid may be available. Percentage fees give rise to "windfall profits" in these areas. And these profits can be maintained only by a near monopoly of services and agreed fee schedules.

The days of minimum fee schedules are pretty well over. In *Goldfarb* v. *Virginia State Bar*, the U.S. Supreme Court held that the Sherman Anti-Trust Act prohibits minimum fee schedules for "services performed by attorneys in examining titles in connection with financing the purchase of real estate."[18] The Court explicitly left open whether the Sherman Act applies to other legal services.[19] In *Goldfarb*, a couple found that nineteen different attorneys all quoted the county bar's recommended fee or a higher one for searching the title to a house. (The fee was based on a percentage of the purchase price.) The Court held that this constituted price-fixing even though the minimum schedule was not straightforwardly mandatory. That is, an ethics opinion of the state bar had indicated that habitually charging less than the minimum fee would raise the presumption that a lawyer was guilty of professional misconduct. The extent to which the *Goldfarb* decision may be extrapolated to other professionals is unclear. Medical care is less clearly connected with interstate commerce, to which the Sherman Act applies, than is real estate. Many large engineering projects, however, do have interstate aspects.

A second, and closely related, issue concerns prohibitions of competitive bidding by professionals. The National Society of Professional Engineers' (NSPE) "Code of Ethics for Engineers" used to contain an explicit prohibition of competitive bidding for contracts.[20] The underlying fear was that clients would choose engineers on the basis of price alone, ignoring such factors as experience, training, and so on. The net result, it was thought, would be less competent work that might even cost clients more. To ensure safety, engineers' designs might call for more extensive materials and work than a more careful design would require. Other professions did not explicitly prohibit competitive bidding, but it was, nevertheless, not actually practiced. For example, if a school board needed routine and regular legal services during a year, it would not advertise for law firms to submit bids for the work; and lawyers would not bid on it if the board had done so.

The effect of prohibiting competitive bidding is to deprive prospective clients of an opportunity to secure services at as low a cost as possible. It enables professionals to maintain fees at a higher rate than might otherwise be the case. In short, it restricts competition, and the restriction is broader than necessary to prevent the feared evil of poor or shoddy work due to deceptively low bids. For these reasons, the U.S. Supreme Court has held the NSPE prohibition to be an illegal suppression of competition under the Sherman Anti-Trust Act.[21] Thus, like minimum fee schedules, restrictions on competitive bidding are now illegal.

A third general issue concerns fee splitting, the division of fees between a professional and another person. Many professions condemn or restrict fee splitting or commissions.[22] Some also restrict sharing fees or being in business with people who practice another occupation or profession.[23] On the other hand, in Canada, a referring lawyer is entitled to up to one-third of the fee of the correspondent.[24] The reason given for allowing such fee splitting in Canada is that the amount of fees is regulated. Both those for and against fee splitting argue on the basis of the client's interests but disagree as to the effects it has on them.

Two reasons support the prohibition of fee splitting except in proportion to services. First, if professionals must split their fees with referring professionals, they will have to charge more in order to cover costs and make a profit. Second, the judgment of referring professionals may not be objective and independent if they have an interest in referring the client to the professional paying the largest referral fee. As the professional's and client's interest conflict, the first professional may not refer the client to the best qualified professional.

The argument for fee splitting is that it should provide clients access to more competent professionals at lower cost.[25] Professionals who do not consider themselves competent to handle a case can either attempt it anyway in order to collect a fee, associate with another and charge a double fee, or refer the client and receive nothing. As the latter option is contrary to professionals' economic interests, they are more likely to choose one of the first two options, thus causing incompetent service or a higher fee. Were fee splitting permitted, a professional could refer a client and still receive some compensation. To ensure referrals to competent professionals, the referring professional can be made legally liable for the second one's performance or, what amounts to the same thing, responsible for all the services rendered.[26]

This argument is not sufficient. The second professional's fee would be increased to include the payment to the referring professional, so cost saving would be limited. Moreover, charging in excess of services rendered cannot be justified; it is simple theft.

Consulting with and referring a client, however, is a service that does deserve some compensation. If a client pays directly for the referral, the judgment of the referring professional then is not affected by personal gain. Further, increased malpractice suits are likely to ensure that professionals do not attempt to provide services they are incompetent to render. Of course, professionals can associate with others to do part of the work on a case. Physicians call in specialists for particular aspects of patient care; lawyers sometimes consult with others for specific purposes, such as to determine tax implications; and engineering designs often involve various professionals working on different aspects of the design—structural, electrical, and so on. Allowing professionals to charge a modest fee for a referral is most likely to help clients receive competent service and allow professionals appropriate compensation for their efforts.

Fee splitting prohibitions do not prevent referral abuses. One of the major scandals in the Medicaid and Medicare programs is "ping-ponging." In this practice, each physician charges only for the services he or she renders, but the patient is referred from one physician to another for different, but usually unneeded, specialized services. Physicians know that if they refer patients to other physicians, those physicians will refer patients back to them. The AMA *Principles* do not address directly the problem of ping-ponging. The only statement about consulting is that a physician should do so when indicated.[27] Professionals clearly ought not suggest that clients obtain unneeded services, whether to be rendered by themselves or by someone else. Doing so violates an obligation of candor to the client.[28]

"Kickbacks" are rather widespread in the professions. Three major areas may be mentioned. First, title insurance companies frequently return part of a fee to a referring attorney. Second, physicians often receive kickbacks from laboratories to which they send specimens for analysis. Third, engineers sometimes receive compensation from supply companies for ordering or recommending their products. Clients then pay more than the services are worth. If a professional charges a proper amount, then a kickback is extra compensation. This difficulty could be remedied by requiring professionals to note the reimbursement in their bills and deduct that amount. Professionals would then have no incentive to recommend products or services from which they receive the largest kickback rather than those best for the client, because they would receive the same total compensation in either case.

The difficult issue of contingent fees arises chiefly with respect to lawyers in personal injury cases. The American Bar Association (ABA) prohibits contingent fees only for representing a defendant in criminal cases, but most professions prohibit all contingent fees outright.[29] The British legal system does not allow contingent fees; instead, the losing party pays all legal fees. One objection to contingent legal fees is that they deprive a victorious party of full compensation for an injury. Damages are awarded for medical expenses, loss in income, pain and suffering, and so on. If a client suffers a $100,000 loss, the lawyer is likely to receive 33 percent or more, leaving less than $67,000. In the British system, the client receives the full $100,000 plus the lawyer's fee.

Over a century ago, George Sharswood disapproved of the general practice of contingent legal fees because of three undesirable consequences.[30] First, contingent fees change the attorney–client relationship. The attorney has a stake in winning by any means and may become blind to the merits of the case. Second, such fees encourage litigation. A client who loses is out only court costs, a rather small amount. A client who wins may receive a substantial award. Thus, a client may risk a case he would not if he were required to pay attorney fees regardless of the outcome. Third, contingent fees have a bad effect on professional character.

Other considerations contradict each of Sharswood's points. First, although the attorney–client relationship is changed, the change need not be for the worse. Because attorneys will be paid only if they win, they are apt to pursue the case more zealously. This reason, however, is sufficient to prohibit contingent fees for accountants. As auditors, accountants are not to work zealously to show a corporate profit but to provide a fair statement of the corporation's financial condition. Second, one must consider what type of litigation is encouraged. Contingent fees are unlikely to encourage frivolous litigation. As attorneys are paid only if they win, they are not apt to undertake hopeless cases.[31] Third, Sharswood's claim that contingent fees have a bad effect on an attorney's character adds nothing. If contingent fees are morally permissible, then accepting such cases will not harm an attorney's character. Presumably the bad effect is that such fees encourage lawyers to try to win by any means. However, ethical lawyers will not accept a case unless they believe they have a reasonable chance of winning by fair means. This third consideration, then, either begs the question or is the same as the first.

The main argument in favor of contingent legal fees is that they increase equality of opportunity by enabling indigent persons to defend their rights. Poor persons are often unable to pay a lawyer unless they recover. Without a contingent fee, they cannot afford to sue even if they have good grounds. Contingent fees are unlikely to encourage persons to litigate for rights not previously recognized by the courts, because such cases are unlikely to be won and attorneys are reluctant to accept them on a contingent basis.

This argument has little plausibility for consulting engineers and architects, for they are not likely to work for indigent clients. For them, the contingent fee is most likely to be a means of preventing other professionals from having the opportunity to be considered for a project. For example, an engineering firm carried out free studies under one government administration on the understanding that it would receive the full contract should a bond issue pass.[32] The issue failed and a subsequent administration, after a new bond issue passed, awarded the contract to other firms. The first firm then complained that these firms were supplanting it. Obviously, the first firm provided the contingent work primarily to get an edge on the contract. Such a practice gives an advantage to large firms that can afford to provide work without compensation until later.

One must compare the contingent fee system with alternatives. One alternative for contingent legal fees is for the losing party to pay both attorneys' fees. If plaintiffs must pay both attorneys' fees should they lose, poor persons will be unlikely to sue for their rights. Should they be unsuccessful, they will owe legal fees they cannot pay. Justice does not necessarily require a losing party to pay all legal fees.[33] In cases that go to trial, something can usually be said for each side; that is, neither party is clearly right. If losing parties must pay both legal fees, they must shoulder the whole financial burden of litigation even though their position was reasonably defensible.

Finally, the argument that contingent fees enable indigent persons to bring justifiable cases assumes that legal services are not otherwise available. If legal representation were generally available to them, the argument would collapse. Legal aid programs usually refuse cases in which representation can be obtained on a contingent fee basis. Were legal aid provided for such cases, a victorious plaintiff would receive the full compensation to which he or she is entitled.

A secondary issue concerning contingent legal fees is the amount. The fee is usually a percentage of the amount recovered, ranging from 25 percent to as much as 50 percent. In a large award or one settled easily, lawyers receive much more than they would if they billed on a standard hourly rate. A percentage-based contingent fee is justifiable in a way it is not for other legal services not provided on a contingent basis, such as title searches. Because lawyers are not compensated in contingent fee cases they lose, clients who win such cases subsidize those who lose; contingent fees are a way of pooling the resources of those who have plausible cases. They increase equality of opportunity. In real estate and probate cases, lawyers rarely receive less than the value of their services and do not have previous losses to recover.

This last argument also supports professionals giving expert testimony in personal injury cases on a contingent fee basis. The practice would also enable them to recoup losses incurred in cases lost. The AMA prohibits such a basis for fees, and the ABA prohibits hiring expert witnesses on a contingent fee basis.[34] The fear is that experts will be biased; yet, as one commentator notes, experts on retainers or generally employed by large corporations are just as apt to be biased.[35] Even the general AMA prohibition of contingent fees is questionable. The fear is that physicians are apt to make excessive claims to lure patients to unreliable treatments, but physicians are unlikely to make a reasonable profit from generally unreliable treatments provided on a contingent fee basis. The duty of truthfulness provides a reason for prohibiting excessive claims.

The AMA has permitted an analogous pooling of client resources. The 1957 *Principles* stated that a physician's fees "should be commensurate with the services rendered and *the patient's ability to pay.*"[36] In effect, the rich should subsidize medical care for the poor. The chief economic difference in theory between this method and that of a state-run medical plan financed by progressive tax rates is simply that it is decentralized. Rich patients of a particular physician subsidize her poor ones. Unfortunately, if most of a physician's patients are poor, she does not have a basis for subsidizing them. Such a system, then, does not work in areas in which most people are poor. Moreover, this policy does not allow clients any influence or voice in the system, such as they have through legislatures for state-run health insurance programs. In particular, no standards exist for size of contributions in proportion to wealth or income.

Publicity

Traditionally, most professions have severely restricted publicity—advertising and solicitation.[37] As will be discussed shortly, the restrictions on advertising were greatly liberalized during the 1970s. The restrictions on personal solicitation have not been liberalized nearly as much. The restrictions have probably been most detrimental to urban citizens seeking lawyers and perhaps physicians. The potential clients of accountants, engineers, and architects often have considerable knowledge of professional activities and a means for identifying competent professionals and reasonable costs.[38] Individuals and small businesses in large urban centers experience the most difficulty learning about lawyers.[39] Because advertising is the standard method by which people find out about available services and products, restrictions on it have tended to prevent average citizens from having equal access to professions.

The traditional reasons for limiting advertising and solicitation rest upon a conception of professionals as devoted to public service rather than to mere money making. Advertising, it is claimed, would change that image and undermine public confidence in the professions. Three policies underlie the traditional condemnation of publicity for lawyers: (1) to prevent stirring up litigation, (2) to permit wise selection of counsel, and (3) to protect the public image of the bar.[40]

The concern with stirring up litigation basically refers to an increased burden on the legal system. A similar concern might apply to advertising by physicians; it might increase demands on the health care system. Increased burdens on the legal and health care systems must be balanced by a concern for the health and legal status of potential clients. Only frivolous demands on the system should be discouraged. Without publicity, people who might significantly benefit from professional services may not receive them. Unless people recognize the appropriateness of professional services and know they are available, they will not seek or receive them. Undoubtedly, fewer people fail to recognize health than legal needs, but people are still reluctant to see physicians and dentists for routine preventive care.

How preventing publicity promotes a wise selection of professionals seems an esoteric piece of knowledge available only to professionals. The traditional premise is that a professional builds a practice by gaining a reputation in the community. Although this assumption still generally applies to the limited group using accounting and engineering services, it does not apply to professionals providing services to individuals in an urban environment—physicians, lawyers, and architects. The net effect of the prohibition on advertising has been to provide better access for the upper class than for the middle and lower classes. The policy has thus fostered inequality of opportunity.

Advertising is also claimed to lead to boastfulness and self-laudatory statements. Since the public lacks a basis for evaluating the quality of professionals, it may be misled in selecting professionals. However, even if correct, this contention does not support a total ban on advertising, but rather supports only restrictions to prevent misleading and untruthful claims.

Finally, most charitably interpreted, protecting the public image of the professions means preventing people acquiring unrealistic expectations. One can imagine professionals advertising miraculous cures for cancer, how to sue businesses and obtain million dollar judgments, or how to receive large income tax refunds. This legitimate concern, however, does not support a total ban, but only limitations on the content of advertising. People who mistakenly believe that nothing can be done for cancer or nothing can be done to obtain repairs of defective merchandise can also become disillusioned with the health care and legal systems.

The basic argument against bans on publicity, especially advertising, is that it infringes freedom of communication or speech. Freedom of communication rests not simply on the value to the speaker in expressing himself, but also on that to the potential audience (the public) in receiving information.[41] The wise selection and use of professionals depends upon full and accurate information about their availability, cost, and quality. Implicit in this justification is the limitation that the public has no interest in deceitful and misleading communications. Total restrictions on publicity are incompatible with the liberal values of freedom of communication and equal opportunity to secure health care, legal justice, and other values promoted by professional services.

Some restrictions on publicity are not only compatible with liberal values but promote them. This general issue is best divided into the content of advertising— fees and quality of service—and its time, place, and manner. Solicitation, although it involves communication, should be treated separately.

In cases involving pharmacists and lawyers, the U.S. Supreme Court has held that professional advertising of fees, at least for standard services, is protected by the First Amendment's guarantee of free speech.[42] It recognized that lawyer advertising would not be able to account for small differences in the work involved in cases. As bar associations had set minimum fees until they were struck down as violations of the Sherman Act, individual lawyers could set and advertise fees for standard services. Charges for more complex and variable services probably could not be advertised, and the Court doubted that an attorney would attempt to do so. Finally, the Court recognized that the traditional ban on advertising had limited people's knowledge of and thus access to legal services.[43] The Court left open the possibility of restrictions on advertising that is deceptive and that concerns the quality of services, and also on its time, place, and manner.

Although in upholding lawyers' constitutional rights to advertise fees the U.S. Supreme Court cited favorably AMA norms on advertising, the Federal Trade Commission has struck down these norms as restraining trade.[44] The norms on solicitation, the FTC claims, restricted competition and access to relevant information. It did, however, accept the legitimacy of an ethical norm directed at false or deceptive advertising and unfair solicitation. In light of these decisions, it is unlikely that general prohibitions against fee or price advertising by any professional are legally permissible in the United States.

Advertising the quality of professional services is probably the most difficult issue. The argument against doing so is that potential clients are incapable of evaluating the competence of professionals. Certain types of information, such as degrees, awards, or specialization and preferred areas of practice, are not conclusive of a professional's competence. Yet they are relevant, and truthful statements of this information can only aid clients in making a wise selection of professionals.

Much more difficult is the use of favorable outcomes of professional services. For example, may lists of former clients be used? To protect the privacy of clients, their consent would be necessary. Even if the relationship is a matter of public record, the client should have control over the use of his or her name. When the outcome is unfavorable, it is unlikely that professionals would use clients' names or that clients would consent to the use of their names. A simple list of clients, however, might provide useful information and not be deceptive. More likely to be deceptive would be pictures of engineering projects in which the firm had only a small role. Similarly, statements of the percentage of cases won or of cures brought about for given diseases could be quite misleading. For example, to build a reputation, some physicians beginning in transplant surgery operate only on patients with the best chances of success. Even without success rates, though, comparisons with other professionals might be objectionable. Probably the chief objection to such comparative advertising is that it would demean the profession; prospective clients would consider choosing professionals in the same way they consider choosing different detergents. Yet, some professionals are more competent than others, just as some detergents clean better than others. Consequently, on the basis of liberal values, there is little reason to prevent advertising service quality except to prohibit false, deceptive, and misleading advertisements.[45]

Nor are there better reasons for restricting the time, place, and manner of advertising professional services than there are for advertising other types of services. The concern here is the possible misleading character of advertising. The form of advertising—television, newspapers, and so on—is not itself relevant. Advertising by broadcast media or handbills is not inherently more misleading than advertising by other forms, such as telephone directories. A concern might be that so little information could be presented in a thirty-second commercial or on a billboard that it would be misleading. However, a simple statement of a professional's degrees, office location, type of practice, and the fact that he or she charges reasonable fees is not inherently misleading.

Considerations of time, place, and manner are more relevant to solicitation than advertising. The traditional concern among lawyers has been with "ambulance chasing"—lawyers contacting persons immediately after accidents and suggesting that they be retained to sue, often on a contingent fee basis. This form of solicitation has not been a problem for the other professions. And at least one commentator applauds such solicitation as helping people recognize their needs for professional service and gain access to it.[46] The ethical concern with this type of solicitation is that people may be approached when in vulnerable circumstances and may hire a lawyer without adequate reflection or consideration of alternatives. In short, undue influence and overreaching can occur, depriving people of a free and informed choice of professional services.

A classic example of the validity of this concern is exhibited in a U.S. Supreme Court case. The Court upheld the constitutional validity of restrictions on types of soliciting that pose a threat of fraud, undue influence, intimidation, and other forms of vexatious conduct.[47] After hearing of an automobile accident, Ohio attorney Albert Ohralik contacted the parents of an eighteen-year-old woman driver injured in it. He then approached her in the hospital offering to represent her. After again visiting the parents, he visited her in the hospital a second time and she signed a contingent fee agreement. He also went to the home of the driver's eighteen-year-old woman passenger, who was also injured. With a hidden tape recorder, he secured her verbal consent to represent her. He explained that the young women would not have to pay him anything and would receive two-thirds of the insurance settlement. When both young women fired him, he sued them for breach of contract and received part of the proceeds from the insurance settlement to the driver. Eventually Ohralik was suspended indefinitely from the practice of law.

Although solicitation of this sort takes unfair advantage of prospective clients, personal solicitation can help serve some of the functions of advertising. Some clients are not aware of their legal rights, and solicitation can inform them. In particular, disadvantaged persons may not know of their constitutional and other legal rights. If these rights are not secured, people lack equality of opportunity, and governance of law may not be realized. In light of similar considerations, the U.S. Supreme Court has held that solicitation by mail on behalf of nonprofit organizations using litigation as a means of political expression and association is constitutionally protected.[48] However, this argument is not likely to hold for other professions. Other professions are not usually engaged in political expression, and the mere fact that speech is involved in solicitation does not provide strong First Amendment protection.

Most other concerns with solicitation chiefly involve professionals taking clients from other professionals. Prohibiting such solicitation primarily limits competition among professionals and generally lacks justification. Most professions prohibit a professional approaching a client of another professional.[49] Three legitimate concerns do exist here. First, a professional might attempt to attract clients by criticizing other professionals. Such tactics could drastically reduce the trust essential to the professional–client relationship and undermine the value of the services. Second, professionals might suggest that people need professional services when they do not. Third, solicitation should be fair and not based on exaggerations of the professional's ability or on other false or incomplete claims. Something less than a total ban on solicitation suffices to prevent these three abuses. Greater restrictions on solicitation both limit professionals' freedom and decrease the availability of services to potential clients.

Specialization

The net effect of specialization upon access to, and the cost of, professional services is unclear. Physicians have long had certified specialties, but lawyers and engineers are only beginning to formally adopt them. Some of the general disadvantages of specialization are as follows. First, too many people enter some specialties and not enough people enter others. For years, most physicians specialized in surgery, with few in other fields. Second, with specialization, fewer people tend to enter general practice. Many specialists do not provide comprehensive service, and often no professional is available to provide a total view of a client's needs. Third, when specialization combines with solo practice, services become diffuse. A client of health services must often travel from one place to another to receive complete service. Fourth, cost is likely to increase. Because of their expertise and extra training, certified specialists feel justified in charging higher fees.

The legal profession has been reluctant to adopt certification of specialties. One reason is a fear that potential clients will no longer go to the general practitioner. This reason rests on the personal interests of general practitioners. Another reason concerns certification of those professionals who have been practicing for a number of years. A third reason is a romantic conception of the lawyer as omnicompetent, able to advise clients on all aspects of the law.

Specialization develops when a field becomes too large for one person to master. Law and engineering have developed to that point. In practice, lawyers and engineers do specialize. Large law and engineering firms are collections of specialists. They often provide better service for complex or large cases than a solo general practitioner because they can draw upon the many different specialties of their members.

Properly organized, specialization can reduce the cost of service. A lawyer who handles many divorce, workers' compensation, or real estate cases becomes familiar with the relevant law and need not do the extensive research—at the client's expense—that one who only occasionally handles cases in those areas must do. In short, specialization can have the economic advantages that division of labor has in other fields, and it need not lead to a reduction in the quality of services.[50]

The problems of practitioners who have worked in an area for a number of years can be reasonably resolved. They may be "grandfathered" into the specialty. Alternatively, if specialists are not given the exclusive right to practice in fields, then other practitioners can still take routine cases in these fields. More complex cases simply raise the problems of fee splitting discussed earlier.

Engineers have had more practical specialization through education and membership in professional organizations—civil engineering, electrical engineering, and so on—than lawyers have. There are good reasons against certifying these specialties and giving them a monopoly of services in their areas.[51] In Ontario, less than 1 percent of engineers bothered to qualify for specialty designation. Given the cost of administering such programs and the likelihood of disputes as to what services can be exclusively rendered by members of specialties (unauthorized practice disputes), such a program is of little benefit to professionals or clients. These considerations apply to lawyers as well. Thus, permitting professionals other than physicians to designate fields of practice and specialized training should be sufficient. Other norms prohibit them from undertaking work they are not competent to perform.

Even if all the traditional norms of professional ethics were revised, they would not completely solve the problems of maldistribution of services, especially legal and health services. The changes would improve services to the middle class, but they would neither provide for the poor nor solve the geographic maldistribution of services. They would not even make services completely available to the middle class. Thus, by themselves, such changes would be insufficient to realize equality of opportunity. The next section briefly reviews some recent proposals that go beyond changes of traditional economic norms to provide legal and health services equally. These proposals are more directly aimed at the social structure of professional services than the norms considered in this section, which primarily pertain to the conduct of individual practitioners.

PROVIDING MEDICAL AND LEGAL SERVICES

The possible approaches to the provision of professional services are limited only by people's imaginations and their ability to organize activities. Attention here focuses on five methods of funding legal and health services to provide them equally to all. These approaches are not mutually exclusive. Some approaches are more appropriate to one of these professions than to the other.

1. Private insurance mechanisms can be used to fund services.
2. The government can subsidize the costs of services for specific groups.
3. Group practice based on a capitation fee can be used.
4. A national insurance system can be used to finance services.

5. Mandatory national service by professionals can be required for varying lengths of time.

Private Insurance

Insurance is a classic method of pooling risks and spreading costs. Insurance schemes of various sorts have been used or proposed to make professional services economically available. Private health insurance programs have existed for a long time. Rates are somewhat adjusted for risk, although not as much as in life or automobile insurance, and people who are less healthy often pay higher rates. Because the poor, especially the elderly poor, have more than the average health problems, the costs to them are higher and they may be unable to afford it. People in different risk categories pay the average cost of medical services for people in their group plus the costs of administration. In return, they can spread their payments over time and avoid extra expenses should they be greater than average. People still generally pay the costs of the services they receive, and as medical costs have risen, so have private insurance rates.

Private insurance has not existed for legal services except insofar as automobile and other liability insurance provides for legal defense. Private insurance is beginning to be used to make legal services available to the middle class.[52] In the early 1970s, the legal profession did not wholeheartedly support such a development. Concern was expressed about the interposition of a so-called lay intermediary between the lawyer and client. Most of the concern was whether panels are "open" or "closed." In open panels, the insurance pays for a lawyer's services and the potential client may choose any qualified attorney in the area. The argument on behalf of this procedure is that it ensures the client's freedom to choose counsel. In closed panels, a number of lawyers are designated to handle cases for persons in the insurance program. Although clients may choose among these lawyers, they must take one on the panel. Private legal insurance is not designed to attack the problem of costs. It assumes that middle-income people can afford legal services but that they wrongly fear the costs and do not know how to select attorneys. Thus, it does not attack the underlying economic cause of maldistribution of services.

Government Subsidies

As part of its general "War on Poverty" during the 1960s, the U.S. government began to subsidize professional services for the poor. Medicare and Medicaid programs were instituted to provide health care to the elderly and poor. The Office of Economic Opportunity developed legal services programs, which later became the Legal Services Corporation.[53] These programs were not well received by the medical and legal professions despite their ostensible commitment to making services available to all. The medical profession, which had long campaigned against "socialized medicine," resisted more than the legal profession. The lesser resistance by the bar was largely due to the leadership of then ABA president Lewis Powell.

An extended discussion of these programs is not needed or appropriate here, but a few points should be noted. First, they are primarily directed to the poor who previously did not receive services. Second, although professionals did not at first realize it, they promote the economic interests of the professions. Physicians are paid to treat patients whom they previously had not treated or had treated for free. The legal services program does not make payments to the poor or to private lawyers who serve them, but it does increase employment opportunities for lawyers. Also, the Supreme Court decision in the early 1960s requiring that defense counsel be provided for all persons charged with crimes and unable to afford counsel supplied crucial service to the poor and employment for lawyers.[54] Third, these programs are tailored so as not to interfere with services previously provided by professionals. For example, legal services to the poor do not accept cases that lawyers would otherwise take on a contingent fee basis. Thus, the programs do not cut into the existing business of professionals.

Although these programs greatly increase professional services for the poor, middle-class access to services did not improve significantly during the 1970s. Many factors are involved, and somewhat different ones pertain to different services. The basic problem is the increased cost of both health care and legal services. High rates of inflation play a significant part in these increases, but the costs have increased faster than the general rate of inflation. During the late 1970s, the costs of health care increased at $1\frac{1}{2}$ to 2 times the rate of inflation.[55] The net result has been that as health and legal services became more accessible to the poor, they became less accessible to the middle class, especially to those just above the poverty line required for government subsidized services.

Group Services

Group practice has been proposed in conjunction with, or independent of, private insurance to attack the cost problem and make services more available. The idea of professional group practice has existed in the legal profession for more than a quarter of a century.[56] Group practice may be combined with either a fee-for-service or a capitation payment method. With capitation payment, each person pays the same fee for a period of time and is provided all or most services.

The benefits of group practice derive from specialization, preventive services, and concentration. If a group has enough professionals and clients to allow specialization, the benefits discussed in the previous section can be achieved without the undesirable effects of costs and referrals. However, the cost claim assumes all professionals will receive roughly the same income. This assumption is not well founded if there is a shortage of specialists, for then specialists will be able to demand and receive substantially higher incomes than others. If clients pay on a capitation basis, professionals have an incentive to provide preventive services that are often less costly than corrective ones. If payments are on a fee-for-service basis, then mere group practice does not encourage preventive practice. Also, concentration cuts the overhead costs of equipment and support staff and saves clients the costs of traveling from one specialist to another. However, solo practicing professionals already sharing a suite of offices and staff have the cost-saving feature of concentration.

Generally, lawyers are not opposed to group practice; large and middle-size law firms actually are group practices. Large law firms have specialists in various areas—corporate taxes, securities regulations, mergers, and so on—but they operate on a fee-for-service basis and primarily serve corporate clients. A shift to a capitation payment system and group practice for individual clients would be a significant change. Capitation payment would work just like an insurance system; clients would pay a flat fee each year in return for all needed legal services of certain types.

Physicians seem to prefer solo practice more than lawyers do, although medical groups do exist and many lawyers are engaged in solo practice. Many clients are concerned about group medical practice because in some groups they are sent to whichever physician is available at the time. As a result, they lose freedom of choice and a developed relationship of trust. They at least feel they do not receive the individualized attention they desire. But in other medical groups, patients can choose a primary physician whom they will always see unless they are referred to a specialist. People's attitudes about having one primary physician probably differ from their attitudes about having one primary lawyer, because the average citizen has more frequent contact with a physician than a lawyer. People are likely to go to their physician several times a year, but to a lawyer only several times during their life. With either profession, group practice need not prevent client freedom to choose the professional. In large groups, more freedom of selection exists than among solo practitioners in small communities. If group practice preserves this freedom, reduces costs, and improves the quality of service, then a liberal society should promote it to make services more available.

National Insurance

So far, national insurance has been proposed only for health care. A practical problem confronts a similar proposal for legal services. Although all health care is rendered to individuals, most legal services are rendered to companies and corporations. However, were national legal insurance restricted to individuals, such a proposal would be plausible. Borderline cases such as an individual doing business as a company would arise, but programs could be designed to resolve these problems.

There have been many different proposals for funding national health insurance and determining the types of services to be covered. These details are not relevant here. Only two points need be noted about a national insurance system. First, unlike the proposals discussed previously, national insurance would ensure that everyone has access to professional services regardless of financial status. It combines government subsidies for the poor with insurance for the middle class. Unlike private insurance for the middle class, national insurance would cover everyone and realize the value of equal provision of health care for all citizens irrespective of ability to pay. Second, national health insurance need not, as critics frequently claim, limit clients' freedom of choice of professionals and professionals' freedom of choice of clients. Medicare and Medicaid do not significantly limit such freedom of choice, and a comprehensive national insurance plan need not do so either. It does not do so in Canada.

Recently, the primary criticism of national health insurance has been its cost. National health insurance alters only the method of payment, and by itself does not reduce the overall costs of medical care, although it might redistribute them. If everyone paid the same premium, then those people requiring less than average care would subsidize those requiring more than average. Also, were payments proportional to income—for example, by a social security scheme with a progressive tax rate—upper-income groups would subsidize medical care for lower-income groups. Because people's payments would be independent of the amount of care received, they would lack an economic incentive to forgo desired health services. Some authorities believe that demand for medical care would increase. Out-of-pocket expenses would no longer deter people from going to physicians for minor or imaginary ailments. Costs might be reduced in other ways.[57] The basic issue is whether a liberal society is willing to pay the costs of providing health care equally to all. Beyond this, however, not even national health insurance corrects the geographic maldistribution of professional services.

Mandatory Service

By this proposal, professionals would be required to work on government salary for a period of time. Although the time might be a percentage of one's regular working time, say 10 percent, the discussion here is restricted to full-time employment for a number of years. Two variations of this proposal are (1) mandatory service for a few years at the beginning of one's career and (2) a total employment by the government—a national service.

In the American political context, the most plausible suggestion is for a few years of service at the beginning of one's professional career.[58] The professionals would be salaried at a reasonable rate considering their experience and training. Medical residency would not suffice as a professional's service commitment.

Such a program has both advantages and disadvantages. It would provide inexpensive services for those who need them. The costs with salaried professionals are usually less than with a fee-for-service system. Professionals could be assigned to parts of the country where they are needed, and fees could be charged to those who are able to pay but who were previously without services because of their geographic location. In short, it would go a long way toward providing services equally. One disadvantage of such a program is that the professionals would be young and inexperienced and perhaps provide less competent services than those that others in society would receive. The plan would in effect provide job experience for beginning professionals who would then move to higher paying private employment. One should not make too much of these claims, however. Highly motivated young professionals with recent training frequently provide more competent service than complacent, middle-aged professionals who have not kept up with their field. Many young professionals now take government positions in order to gain experience, and one might require that some or all professionals devote two years in later life to such service, although that program would be much more difficult to implement. The primary objection to such a program, however, is the restriction upon the freedom of professionals. What is proposed is simply a draft of professionals. Without a military draft, many people believe it would be hard to justify a draft of professionals. Four reasons can be offered to support such a draft.

1. The government underwrites much of the cost of professional training, especially in medicine, but also in law. The service can be viewed as compensation for the training. As the government also underwrites training in many other professions and fields without exacting a similar repayment, the "deal could be sweetened" by providing more support for students in the health and legal professions.

2. Everyone has an ordinary obligation to contribute his or her fair share to society. Nevertheless, the burden might fall more heavily on those entering the health and legal professions. Some people believe a military draft is appropriate only during a national emergency, and a national emergency does not clearly exist with respect to health and legal services. The restrictions on freedom involved in compulsory service would be justifiable only if there were no other way to solve the problem. If the government were willing to pay enough, it could recruit career professionals to provide the services. However, if a volunteer army is too expensive and inadequate, a similar program in these professions is unlikely to succeed.

3. Professionals can be distinguished from most other people in society by their governmentally protected monopoly privileges of licensing and by the prohibition of unauthorized practice. As they receive benefits from society in the protection provided them, they have a special obligation to compensate society.

4. The compulsory aspect of such service can be overemphasized. No individual would be required to provide such services. One could always avoid it by not entering the health or legal professions. Viewed in this light, the required period of service is more a cost of entering the profession, like the years of education, than a compulsion. No one has a right to be a professional. Rather, it is a privilege, and the period of service is part of the price of that privilege.

These arguments assume that others are not being drafted. If a universal national service is required, as some people have proposed, then no special arguments are needed for requiring such service of health and legal professionals.

The second variation of mandatory service is that, instead of spending a few years, all professionals could be employed by the government on salary, that is, there could be a national health (or legal) service. National health services exist in many countries, such as England and the European socialist countries. Sometimes private practitioners exist alongside the national service system and sometimes they do not. In Britain, physicians in the system are allowed to spend part of their time in private practice. For the legal profession, a large private practice would be needed to provide services to businesses and corporations. Indeed, by far the larger number of lawyers would be so employed.

There are many arguments for and against such a system, and some are quite complex. Such a system has not been vigorously proposed for the United States and is not likely to be adopted in the foreseeable future. Perhaps the major arguments in favor of such a system are the alleged cost efficiency of a salaried system and the ability to ensure the distribution of services easily throughout society. However, it would significantly limit the freedom of professionals. Another argument against it is that it results in less competent service, because professionals lack financial incentives to provide effective service for their clients. This argument assumes that professionals are chiefly motivated by financial gain, something professionals have denied for centuries. Some people claim that clients would be deprived of freedom of choice among professionals, but that need not be the case any more than with group practice. Indeed, freedom of choice by patients need not be any more restricted than at present. Since about as many professionals would be in geographical areas as at present, clients could be allowed to choose the professionals they desire, subject, as at present, to the professionals' willingness to accept them.

The adversarial legal system, based on two opposed sides presenting their cases to be resolved by an impartial third party (judge or jury), makes a national service more questionable for lawyers than for physicians. Attorneys are supposed to represent their clients' interests *against* those of others. If the attorneys on both sides are ultimately paid by, or work for, the same organization, their devotion to their clients might be less. In suits against the government, a special conflict of interest would exist. A similar situation arises with public defenders in criminal cases and lawyers in the Legal Services Corporation. Examination of the general level of efforts by public defenders, even allowing for the fact that they are overworked, suggests that their devotion to clients is less than that of private attorneys. Clients of public defenders get more and longer sentences than comparable clients of private attorneys. Moreover, the Office of Economic Opportunity lawyers had special political difficulties in suits against state governments. Consequently, as long as the adversarial legal system is retained, a national legal service poses a threat to lawyers exercising independent judgment on behalf of their clients.

The point of this section has not been to argue for any particular approach to providing health and legal services equally to all. Instead, it has merely been to review briefly the major proposals and the main arguments for and against them. Some of the proposals appear more plausible than others. A profession as a whole has an obligation to make services equally available to all. As the past organization and practices of the health and legal professions have failed to fulfill this obligation, a new organization and practices ought to be adopted to realize equality of opportunity.

A liberal society should devise a system for delivering health and legal services that both provides them equally to all and preserves as much freedom of choice as possible for clients and professionals. National insurance or service systems are the only ones that ensure service to all. However, a national insurance system fails to correct the geographic maldistribution of services, and a national service system significantly limits the freedom of professionals. A combination of the two, though, would best realize liberal values. National insurance would ensure that no one is denied services for financial reasons. A national service system, much like a college ROTC program, could supply professionals for service in needy areas. In exchange for individual financial support through professional school, persons would agree to serve where needed for a period of years. Such a program would also help poor students who otherwise would not be able to afford professional education. Whatever form the final program takes, however, it must ensure everyone equal medical and legal services to realize welfare, governance by law, and general equality of opportunity.

ACCEPTING IMMORAL CLIENTS

The preceding sections of this chapter have focused on traditional norms impeding equal access to professional services and the possible social arrangements that might provide health and legal services equally to all. One other aspect of making services available should be examined, namely, the freedom of professionals to refuse to serve clients, especially those proposing what the professionals consider immoral conduct. One of the fears physicians have about national health insurance is that they might lose the freedom to decide which clients they will serve. Traditionally, professionals have been free to refuse work offered to them, except for lawyers assigned to cases by courts and physicians, who are obliged to treat people in emergencies. Are there ethical constraints on this freedom?

The general problem of accepting clients whose proposed conduct the professional considers immoral can be broken down into four specific questions.

1. To make services equally available, especially to provide health and legal services, should professionals accept all clients?

2. If they do not have an obligation to accept all clients, is it ethically permissible for them to do so?

3. Under what conditions, if any, do professionals have good reason to refuse to accept immoral clients?

4. If a professional refuses to accept a client whose conduct seems immoral, should the professional refer the client to another professional who will accept him?

These questions are taken up in order.

Should professionals accept all clients subject to their having the time to handle the cases adequately? In the past, professionals, like most other people in society, have discriminated against potential clients on the basis of race, religion, and sex. Equality of opportunity implies nondiscrimination on such grounds; so it is not ethical for professionals to refuse to accept clients on those grounds. Interestingly, none of the codes of professional ethics contains such a norm. Perhaps they do not do so because it is an ordinary norm applicable to all businesses, or perhaps because to so discriminate is now illegal.

Suppose a professional has a plausible reason for thinking a client's proposed conduct is immoral. The first example in this book, of the teenage woman who desires an abortion from a physician ethically opposed to them, is an example. This type of situation may seem rare, but it really is not. Accountants are likely to have clients ask them to manipulate books so that they have larger gains, or greater losses, than might otherwise appear. Engineers are sometimes approached by companies to design projects that the engineers consider contrary to the public good; the proposed projects may be cheaply constructed and unsafe, detrimental to the environment, require residential areas to be destroyed, or be otherwise harmful to the public. For example, the United States government refused to help Egypt construct the Aswan Dam because it thought the overall effects would be harmful to the people of Egypt. Lawyers are approached to draft wills cutting out faithful relatives (e.g., a son who resisted the war in Vietnam) or to sue people for malicious purposes.

The argument for professionals being permitted to refuse such clients is on the grounds of their freedom.[59] To require professionals to serve any and all clients who come to them, even subject to their having the time and, perhaps, to the clients' ability to pay, eliminates their freedom of choice as to whom they may serve. Their work would largely be dictated by others. Most people in society are in this position—they do not have complete freedom to do the work they wish (they are often assigned disagreeable tasks by supervisors), but they are free to quit their jobs. A professional's freedom to accept or reject clients is a similar freedom to accept or not accept employment. Besides, in a pluralistic society, another professional who does not view the client's conduct as unethical is often available. For example, although many physicians believe abortions are wrong except to save the life of the woman, many others ethically approve of abortions upon request.

This argument is not as persuasive as might first appear. Consider the case of an eighteen-year-old college student in Boston who became convinced that, due to overpopulation of the world and the responsibility involved, he did not want to have any children. He decided that a vasectomy would be the most prudent and effective contraceptive measure. All the physicians he contacted in the greater Boston area refused to perform a vasectomy on him. A similar case was a poor twenty-three-year-old nursing assistant in a small town in the 1960s who had three children and two miscarriages and wished to have a tubal ligation. Her physician refused, and as a result she had two more children. In both of these cases, the physicians believed sterilization was unwise for the particular patients; they may have thought it was unethical. Although the wisdom of sterilization in these cases is debatable, a decade or two later few people think it unethical. In this way professionals can prevent clients having access to services that the clients believe are morally justified.[60] In a pluralistic society, professionals are imposing their own morality upon clients, perhaps to the detriment of the clients.

Nonetheless, this last argument is not strong enough to support a norm requiring professionals to accept all clients subject to time to serve and, perhaps, ability to pay. The freedom of professionals would be greatly restricted, and the restriction is more detrimental than the few cases in which clients would be deprived of appropriate services. The argument does imply that professionals should give clients the benefit of the doubt and provide services unless they are strongly convinced that the clients' course of conduct is ethically wrong.

Assuming that society reasonably pursues liberal values, is it ethically permissible for a professional to accept any client whose proposed course of conduct is legally permissible? Charles Fried argues that a lawyer may always do so. For clients to be unable to achieve their ends due to ignorance or misinformation about the law would violate their rights. Consequently, assisting clients to achieve their legal rights is, he claims, "always morally worthy."[61]

This argument faces several difficulties. First, it mistakenly assumes that because conduct is not legally prohibited, one has a right to pursue it. This confuses legal and ethical rights. Moreover, one does not have a legal right to pursue all conduct that is not legally prohibited. A legal right to conduct implies that others have a duty not to interfere; the fact that conduct is not legally prohibited establishes only that the conduct is permissible, that one has no duty not to engage in it. It does not establish that others have a duty not to interfere, and certainly not that one has a positive right to assistance in performing it. Second, sometimes conduct is not made illegal because legal enforcement would be difficult, unduly punitive, or otherwise cumbersome. Some such conduct may be grossly unethical and a professional may be quite justified in refusing to accept a client proposing to engage in it.

Finally, Fried's argument rests heavily on the role of the legal profession in protecting clients' rights. If people have rights to health care, then the argument may have some limited applicability to health professions. Even there, it would be restricted to services providing for the health of the client. Just as a right to Medicaid-funded abortions would not extend to nontherapeutic ones, so a right to health services does not extend to nontherapeutic services. For the other consulting professions, the argument has no force at all. In them, equality of opportunity implies only that services be equally available. That services are not available for unethical purposes does not prevent their being equally available. Even if some accountants in one part of the country assist clients in juggling books in a legal but unethical fashion, equality of opportunity does not require that others do so elsewhere. It is only equality of opportunity for ethically permissible purposes that is required.[62]

Under what circumstances do professionals have a good ethical reason to refuse a client whose proposed course of conduct they consider immoral? This issue is too complicated to consider in detail here, so the opposing positions are only briefly outlined.[63] The "moral integrity" view holds that if another professional will provide the services because he or she does not consider the proposed conduct wrong, then it is better for that person to perform them and the ethically opposed professional has good reason to refuse. The ethically opposed professional would be violating his or her moral integrity, whereas the other one would not. Violating one's own moral integrity is likely to have negative personal effects such as guilt feelings. However, if no other professional is available, as in the example of the physician in Alaska asked to perform an abortion, then making services equally available sometimes justifies providing the service. This last consideration primarily applies to medical and legal services because there is a positive right to them, whereas accountants, engineers, and architects are unlikely to practice in a region where no other professional is available.

The contrary "no difference" view maintains that professionals violate their moral integrity only if it is wrong for them to provide the services. However, if another professional will provide the services, then it is not wrong for them to do so and they would have no reason for guilt. The wrong occurs if the client succeeds in completing his or her course of conduct, for example by constructing a plant that damages the environment, filing a harassing law suit, or having an abortion. As this wrong occurs regardless of what the professional does (for by hypothesis another will do it if he or she does not), the professional's conduct makes no difference to the occurrence of the wrong. If it makes no difference, then it is not wrong. Consequently, the professional has no good reason to refuse to provide the services so long as another will. If the client cannot obtain another professional to provide the services, then the first professional's conduct does make a difference. If the professional provides the services, then the wrong occurs; if he or she does not provide the services, the wrong is prevented. Thus, if no other professional will provide the services if he or she refuses, the professional should refuse because that will prevent the wrong from occurring.

The last argument assumes that another professional definitely will or will not provide services, and usually that is not completely clear. This consideration cuts both ways, for on the moral integrity view it is also relevant to what the professional ought to do. Thus, the uncertainty affects both views, and it cannot be an argument for one over the other.

An objection to the no difference view is that it implies one should cooperate with a Nazi society. Suppose a professional in a Nazi society is asked to prosecute a Jew, perform euthanasia on a Gypsy, or design a gas chamber to look like a shower stall. Could not professionals argue, as many did, that if they do not do it, someone else will?

The reply is that the no difference argument assumes that the professional is not justified in taking steps to coercively prevent the prospective client pursuing the course of conduct he or she desires, as by holding a pregnant woman hostage until she delivers. However, in some cases that is not correct. In the Nazi examples, professionals were justified in using coercion (joining the resistance) to overthrow the government. After all, it was the antithesis of a society based on liberal values. Similarly, sometimes a professional is justified in using coercion to prevent a prospective client from performing certain actions. For example, a psychiatrist is justified in having a psychotic committed if he or she is likely to kill someone.

Finally, if professionals refuse to provide services because they consider the prospective client's proposed conduct immoral, should they refer the prospective client to another professional who will provide them? This issue arises only on the moral integrity view, for on the no difference view, whenever a professional has good reason to refuse, no other professional is reasonably available. Although many people think professionals should refer such clients, they cannot consistently do so. If a professional is convinced that the conduct is unethical, he or she must think that referring the prospective client is assisting in wrongdoing. No one would think it proper for an individual to refuse to assist in the commission of a crime, such as armed robbery, but then refer the would-be robber to someone who would assist him. Consequently, if a professional sincerely believes the prospective client's conduct is strongly unethical, he or she cannot consistently refer the person to another professional.

SUMMARY

This chapter has focused on the implications of equality of opportunity for making professional services equally available to all citizens. Because of the central importance of legal and health services in achieving general equality of opportunity as well as legal justice and welfare, people have a positive right to expect these services to be provided equally to all. Other professional services need only be made equally available. Legal and health care services have been maldistributed economically, racially, and geographically.

A number of traditionally accepted professionally economic norms have contributed to denying the equal availability of professional services. Monopolistic prohibitions of unauthorized practice have prevented services being offered by nonprofessionals. Such restrictions are justifiable only if no reasonable person would want an unlicensed person to provide services or if an unlicensed person doing so might burden the public. Fee schedules and prohibitions of competitive bidding have restrained competition and kept the price of services high; they are illegal violations of the anti-trust laws and are ethically objectionable for the same reasons they are illegal. Fee splitting for referrals is not justifiable, but professionals should be permitted to charge a modest fee for them. Contingent fees in all professions except law are usually unethical, and even those in law could be reduced if legal services handled such cases. Restrictions on advertising and solicitation have been greatly reduced during the last decade. Restrictions on advertising are justifiable only to prevent false, deceitful, and misleading claims. Norms restricting solicitation are justifiable for situations likely to involve overreaching and undue influence. Finally, licensed specialization, except in medicine, is not worth the effort and might unduly increase costs.

Various proposals for providing legal and medical services equally to all were quickly surveyed. Private insurance does not address the economic maldistribution of services. Government programs for the poor still leave the middle class, especially the lower middle class, with inadequate services. Group services can help make services available at lower cost, but they do not address the geographic maldistribution. National insurance does address the economic maldistribution and can preserve client and professional freedom of choice, but it does not significantly solve geographic maldistribution. A general national service unnecessarily limits the freedom of professionals, although a limited service is justifiable as part of the cost of the privilege of practicing law or medicine. However, the best scheme would be national health insurance supplemented by a voluntary service program to rectify geographic maldistribution.

Questions arise concerning the ethics of professionals refusing to accept clients whose conduct they deem unethical. It would unduly restrict the freedom of professionals to require them to accept any and all clients on a first-come, first-served basis subject to time to take cases, and, in some professions, ability to pay. Because this means clients might sometimes be unable to pursue ethically permissible but unwise courses of conduct, professionals should give clients the benefit of the doubt about the ethics of their proposed conduct. Even in a society reasonably pursuing liberal values, it is not ethically permissible to assist clients in all legally permissible conduct. The law does not prohibit all unethical conduct. Two views exist as to when professionals have good reason to refuse to accept clients whose course of conduct they think is unethical. The moral integrity view is that they should refuse if another professional will provide services, but probably should not refuse if no other professional is available. The no difference view is that professionals do not have a good reason to refuse to accept such clients if other professionals will provide the services anyway, but they do if no one else will provide the services and they can then prevent wrong from occurring. Finally, if a professional refuses to accept a client on ethical grounds, he or she cannot ethically refer the client to someone else who will provide the services.

NOTES*

1. AMA, *Principles of Medical Ethics,* sec. 1; ABA, *Code of Professional Responsibility,* Canon 2, EC 2–16, EC 2–26.

2. *Row* v. *Wade,* 410 U.S. 113 (1973).

3. *Beal* v. *Doe,* 423 U.S. 438 (1977); *Maher* v. *Roe,* 423 U.S. 464 (1977).

4. "Medicaid Abortions: Federal Court Overturns Hyde Amendment," *Hastings Center Report* 10 (April 1980):2; "High Court Upholds Hyde Amendment," *Intercom* 8 (July 1980):2f; *Harris* v. *McRae,* 100 S. Ct 2671 (1980).

5. ABA, *Code of Professional Responsibility,* Canon 3; AMA, *Opinions and Reports,* 3.50. See also ABA, Commission, *Model Rules,* 8.4(e); National Society of Professional Engineers, "Code of Ethics," sec. 15, C.

6. Ivan Illich, "Two Watersheds: The American Public Health System," in *Moral Problems in Medicine,* ed. Gorovitz et al., pp. 494–99.

7. "Fee System Limits MDs Nurses Tell Review," *The Globe and Mail* (Toronto), 8 March 1980, p. 10; "Free MDs of Health Tasks Others Can Do: Coalition," *The Globe and Mail* (Toronto), 7 April 1980, p. 13.

8. Patterson and Cheatham, *Profession of Law,* p. 372.

9. Llewellyn, "The Bar Specializes," p. 190.

10. Llewellyn, "The Bar's Troubles and Poultices," pp. 244–245.

11. Orkin, *Legal Ethics,* p. 249.

12. Patterson and Cheatham, *Profession of Law,* p. 370.

13. Ibid., p. 371.

14. Benjamin N. Branch, "Out-Patient Termination of Pregnancy," in *New Concepts in*

---

*See the bibliography at the back of the book for complete references.

Contraception, ed. Malcolm Potts and Clive Wood (Baltimore: University Park Press, 1972), p. 183.

15. College of Nurses of Ontario, *Standards of Nursing Practice: For Registered Nurses and Registered Nursing Assistants* (1976), p. 17n.

16. Lieberman, *Crisis at the Bar,* pp. 124–125.

17. Thomas D. Morgan, "The Evolving Concept of Professional Responsibility," in *1977 National Conference on Teaching Professional Responsibility,* ed. Goldberg, pp. 283–284.

18. 421 U.S. 733, 780 (1975).

19. In *Bates* v. *State Bar of Arizona,* 433 U.S. 350, 363 (1977), the Court held that a state ban on fee advertising is not subject to attack under the Sherman Act.

20. Sec. 11, c.

21. *National Society of Professional Engineers* v. *United States,* 435 U.S. 679 (1978).

22. ABA, *Code of Professional Responsibility,* DR 2–107; ABA, Commission, *Model Rules,* 1.5(e); AICPA, "Rules of Conduct," Rule 503.

23. ABA, *Code of Professional Responsibility,* DR 3–102; but see ABA, Commission, *Model Rules,* 5.4; AICPA, "Rules of Conduct," Rule 505.

24. Orkin, *Legal Ethics,* p. 153.

25. Morgan, "Concept of Professional Responsibility," note 17, pp. 292–294.

26. ABA, Commission, *Model Rules,* 1.5(e) (1).

27. Sec. 5.

28. See Chapter 4; AMA, *Opinions and Reports,* 5.71.

29. ABA, *Code of Professional Responsibility,* DR 2–106(C); ABA, Commission, *Model Rules,* 1.5(c); AMA, *Opinions and Reports,* 4.04; AICPA, *"Rules of Conduct,"* Rule 302; Engineers' Council, "Suggested Guidelines," 5, e.

30. Sharswood, *Essay on Professional Ethics,* pp. 160–161.

31. This claim has empirical confirmation. See Rosenthal, *Lawyer and Client,* p. 91.

32. Alger, Christensen, and Olmstead, *Ethical Problems in Engineering,* p. 58.

33. Patterson and Cheatham, *Profession of Law,* p. 265.

34. AMA, *Opinions and Reports,* 4.41; ABA, *Code of Professional Responsibility,* DR 7–109(C); see also ABA, Commission, *Model Rules,* 3.4(b), comment.

35. Lieberman, *Crisis at the Bar,* pp. 130–132.

36. AMA, *Principles of Medical Ethics* [1957]. (Emphasis added.)

37. ABA, *Code of Professional Responsibility,* DR 2–101, DR 2–102, and DR 2–103; ABA, Commission, *Model Rules,* 7.1–7.5; AMA, *Opinions and Reports,* 6.00; AICPA, "Rules of Conduct," Rule 502; Engineers' Council, "Suggested Guidelines," 5, d, f, g, h; National Society of Professional Engineers, "Code of Ethics," sec. 3, a.

38. *Report of the Professional Organizations Committee,* p. 189.

39. Ibid., p. 192.

40. Patterson and Cheatham, *Profession of Law,* p. 357.

41. See Bayles, *Principles of Legislation,* pp. 85–86; *Virginia State Board of Pharmacy* v. *Virginia Citizens Consumer Council,* 425 U.S. 748, 756–57 (1976).

42. *Bates* v. *State Bar of Arizona,* 433 U.S. 350 (1977); *Virginia State Board of Pharmacy* v. *Virginia Citizens Consumer Council,* 425 U.S. 748 (1976).

43. *Bates* v. *State Bar of Arizona,* 433 U.S. 350, 376–77 (1977).

44. 48 U.S. Law Week 2332 (1979).

45. See ABA, Commission, *Model Rules,* 7.1 and 7.2, which permit lawyers to advertise the comparative quality of services if the comparison can be factually substantiated.

46. Freedman, *Lawyers' Ethics,* chap. 10.

47. *Ohralik* v. *Ohio State Bar Association,* 436 U.S. 447 (1978).

48. *In re Primus,* 436 U.S. 412 (1978).

49. AICPA, "Rules of Conduct," Rule 401; Engineers' Council, "Suggested Guidelines," 5, d.

50. *Report of the Professional Organizations Committee,* p. 200.

51. Ibid., p. 190.

52. For a simple survey of this type of proposal, see Jim Lorenz, "State of Seige: Group Legal Services for the Middle Class," in *Verdicts on Lawyers,* ed. Nader and Green, pp. 144–157.

53. For a general history of the OEO legal program, see Note, "Legal Services—Past and Present," *Cornell Law Quarterly* 59 (1974): 960–988.

54. *Gideon* v. *Wainwright,* 372 U.S. 335 (1963).

55. Walter McClure, "Health Care Cost Commission: Choices for Medical Care," *Minnesota Medicine* 61 (1978): 263.

56. See Llewellyn, "The Bar Specializes," p. 189.

57.4See Bayles, "National Health Insurance," pp. 335–348.

58. See Lowell E. Bellin, "Quality and Equality in Health Care—What Can We Do About It?" in *Moral Problems in Medicine,* ed. Gorovitz, pp. 490–491; and Lieberman, *Crisis at the Bar,* pp. 223–224.

59. Charles Fried, "The Lawyer as Friend: The Moral Foundations of the Lawyer–Client Relation," in *1977 National Conference on Teaching Professional Responsibility,* ed. Goldberg, p. 152.

60. Alan Goldman claims that if lawyers accepted only clients whose aims they considered morally legitimate, due to the moral pluralism among lawyers, only clients whose purposes were blatantly immoral would be unable to obtain services (*Moral Foundations,* p. 131). The past practice of physicians makes this claim questionable, although differences in attitudes of physicians and lawyers towards providing services for immoral purposes could be important in this context.

61. Fried, "Lawyer as Friend," note 59, p. 144; Fried, *Right and Wrong,* pp. 181–182.

62. The ABA, *Code of Professional Responsibility,* DR 2–109, prohibits lawyers accepting clients who wish to harass or maliciously injure someone or to present totally unwarranted claims or defenses; see also ABA, Commission, *Model Rules,* 1.16(a) and 3.1.

63. See Bayles, "A Problem of Clean Hands," pp. 165–181.

STUDY QUESTIONS AND PROBLEMS

1. Arthur Brown is a very busy and successful attorney. Ace Retailers has hired him to defend them in a suit by a customer. The complaint was filed twenty-seven days ago and Brown has not yet filed an answer, although he has had the case for over two weeks. When the president of Ace phones Brown, he tells him that he will not file an answer until he receives a $20,000 retainer. State law requires that answers be filed within thirty days or parties will be

considered to have admitted all allegations of fact in the complaint. The president of Ace thinks the fee is high even for a trial, and the case may be settled before going to trial. But since he does not have time to find another attorney, he sends Brown the check by courier. Is Brown's conduct unethical? May professionals ethically withhold services until they are assured of receiving their fee? May hospitals ethically refuse to admit patients until assured that they have insurance or are otherwise able to pay?

2. Reconsider question 3 in Chapter 2. Does the fact that the engineers' no bidding principle has now been declared illegal in the United States make you want to change your answer from what it was before?

3. Management consultant Claudia Debbs contacts Edmond Forbes's accounting firm to suggest a joint venture. She is contacting local businesses to obtain employment. Her proposal is that she will study the businesses and make suggestions for improvements in their methods of operation. If she finds that changes are needed in their accounting procedures, she will recommend Forbes's accounting firm to design and assist in setting up new accounting practices. Forbes will then pay Claudia a percentage of the fee he receives. Would it be ethical for Forbes to make such an arrangement? Why or why not? Suppose Debbs told the businesses of the arrangement when she was hired. Would that make any difference to the ethics of the arrangement? Why or why not?

4. Engineer Gillian Hancock sends a circular letter to all landowners in a certain area. She offers to survey their property for a reduced price if the offer is accepted within thirty days. She explains that the lower price is possible due to savings of surveying adjoining property at the same time. Is this method of solicitation ethical? Why or why not? Is it not part of a profession's duty to make service available? What are the advantages and disadvantages to the property owners from this offer? What are the disadvantages, if any, to the profession?

5. What differences, if any, are there between personal solicitation by engineers, physicians, and publishers seeking manuscripts?

6. Psychologist Ivan Jackson advertised by mail a service to scientifically select and introduce people to marriageable partners. He claimed that the process increases the chances of a compatible marriage. After people were introduced, he was no longer involved and any decision to marry was theirs. Is it ethical for psychologists to so advertise and provide services in such a manner? Why or why not?

7. Would it be ethical for physician Kay Lewitt to advertise in the following manner? She takes a small advertisement in the classified section of the telephone directory. She lists her degrees and schools, office address, that she is in family practice, and that she is the physician to the local university women's basketball team. Is there a difference between physicians listing clients they serve, lawyers doing so, and engineers or architects listing projects

they have designed? If so, what is it? Why does it make an ethical difference, if it does?

8.   Michael Natwick is a counselor at a high school in a remote community. He has a very emotionally disturbed student and the nearest referral center is 150 miles away. Although Michael is not trained for such therapy, he tries to provide it for the student. Is it wrong for him to do so? Why or why not?

9.   Try to design the broad outlines of a national health insurance scheme. What services would be included and excluded? How should the scheme be financed? What objections could be made to your proposal?

10.   Would a draft of physicians and lawyers for two years of service at modest salary be just? State at least two arguments for and against such a proposal.

11.   Computer specialist Octavia Peterson is asked by a large company to design a program containing all possible data about its employees. The company wants to include all health information, supervisor's reports, financial information, and criminal records it obtains, as well as informal information about the employees' families. Should she accept the job? Why or why not?

12.   Lawyer Ralph Stiles is contacted by a divorced woman. She tells him that her exhusband has not paid any child support for the past two years. He has sent her an occasional check but not through the court, so the money has not been credited to him. She realizes that suing for all the back support will drive him close to bankruptcy, but she maintains, "The bastard deserves whatever he gets." Should Ralph take the case? Why or why not? If he does, is it ethical for him not to include the informal payments as credits to the husband?

4 Obligations to Clients

Securing the services of a professional, as difficult as that may sometimes be, is only a preliminary to the professional–client relationship. This chapter considers the ethical nature of the professional–client relationship and the obligations of professionals to clients that arise therefrom. In the compass of this chapter it is impossible to provide a complete and detailed analysis of these obligations, and important differences arise in applying these obligations to different professional situations. Therefore, the emphasis is on the standard or normal situation of a competent adult consumer. Modifications are needed for other situations, such as physicians treating small children and unconscious patients. On the basis of this analysis, a standard is offered to systematize obligations of professionals to clients and general obligations are then briefly developed.

THE PROFESSIONAL–CLIENT RELATIONSHIP

Many analyses have been offered of the professional–client relationship. Some analyses are empirical; they describe the relationship as it normally exists. That is not the purpose of this section. Rather, the purpose here is to develop an ethical model that should govern the professional–client relationship. However, ethical models and norms often assume certain facts. For example, an ethical model of the appropriate relationship between parent and child makes certain assumptions about a child's abilities. A model of full equality would not work for very young children simply because they lack the physical and mental abilities to engage in such a relationship. Thus, although an ethical model of the professional–client relationship is not simply to describe it, a model can be inappropriate because it makes false empirical assumptions about one or the other parties.

The impulse of philosophy is to generalize. The present aim is to develop general statements of obligation that can require different conduct depending on the situation. The obligations to keep promises and make reparations for past injustice remain constant although the required conduct varies with the situation. There is no a priori reason why general obligations of professionals to clients cannot be established even though their application to particular cases requires different conduct in different situations. This does not imply ethical relativism.

To develop an ethical model that has the broadest scope, the model should not be based on unusual situations, such as a defendant charged with a capital crime or an unconscious patient. Unusual situations are so simply because they lack features of the usual or have additional features. An analysis based on unusual situations is therefore likely to distort normal situations. Professional ethics should be based on the usual sort of contact average clients have with professionals. Individual citizens are most likely to see lawyers in connection with real estate transactions, divorces, making wills, and personal injury negligence cases. Lawyers also spend much time drafting commercial contracts and advising about business matters. The average client will probably have a physician's attendance during a fatal illness or injury, but most physician–patient contacts are for more mundane matters such as a bacterial infection or a broken bone. Only gross neglect by the patient or physician—for example, the failure of a patient to take any medicine at all or of a physician to ask whether the patient is allergic to penicillin before prescribing it—is apt to turn these matters into seriously life-threatening illnesses or injuries. Engineers are apt to be consulted by companies or governments that want a project designed. Similarly, certified public accountants are most often hired to audit the books of a corporation. Both accountants and architects also deal with individuals for such purposes as income tax preparation and designing houses.

The central issue in the professional–client relationship is the allocation of responsibility and authority in decision-making—who makes what decisions. The ethical models are in effect models of different distributions of authority and responsibility in decision-making. One may view the professional–client relationship as one in which the client has most authority and responsibility in decision-making, the professional being his employee; one in which the professional and client are equals, either dealing at arm's length or at a more personal level; or as one in which the professional, in different degrees, has the primary role. Each of these conceptions has been suggested by some authors as the appropriate ethical model of the relationship. Each has some commonsense support.

Agency

According to this view, the client has most of the authority and responsibility for decisions; the professional is an expert acting at the direction of the client.[1] The client hires a professional to protect or act for some interest; the professional provides services to achieve the client's goal—purchase of a house, removal of a gall bladder, design of a building. According to this conception, not only does the professional act for or in behalf of the client, but also acts under the direction of the client as in bureaucratic employer–employee relationships. This conception is especially plausible for lawyers. In filing a complaint or arguing for a client, a lawyer acts for and in behalf of the client. According to some people, a lawyer is merely a "mouthpiece" or "hired gun." It is not a plausible view of accountants performing public audits, for they are supposed to provide an independent review and statement of the clients' financial conditions.

In some contexts, professionals are prone to adopt the agency view of the professional–client relationship. Professionals are sometimes "identified" with their clients and charged with the client's alleged moral failings. Lawyers offer the defense that in representing clients, they do not thereby ascribe to or support clients' goals or aims.[2] They are merely employees hired to perform a specific task. If the projects are bad or immoral, the fault lies with the clients, or perhaps with the legal system for permitting them.

The agency model most clearly exemplifies what has been called the "ideology of advocacy." This ideology has two principles of conduct: (1) that the lawyer is neutral or detached from the client's purposes, and (2) that the lawyer is an aggressive partisan of the client working to advance the client's ends.[3] This ideology is readily applicable to physicians, architects, and engineers. A physician, for example, should not evaluate the moral worth of patients but only work to advance their health. The second element of the ideology does not apply to accountants performing audits, for they are to present independent statements of clients' financial conditions. It applies in other accounting activities though. For example, an accountant preparing a client's income tax statement should try to take every plausible deduction on behalf of the client.

Some aspects of this ideology appear inescapable in professional ethics. If professionals accepted only clients whose purposes they approved of and did not consider clients' interests any more than those of others, many persons with unusual purposes (such as wanting an architectural style of a building that is completely inconsistent with those nearby) might be unable to obtain professional services. And even if they did, the services might not be worth much, as no special consideration would be paid to their interests.[4] The chief problem with the ideology of advocacy, where it does become an ideology, is that sometimes devotion to a client's interests is thought to justify any lawful action advancing the client's ends, no matter how detrimental the effect on others.

The agency view of the professional–client relationship is unduly narrow. A number of considerations indicate limits to a professional's proper devotion to a client's interests, and consequently to a client's authority in decision-making.

1. As discussed in the next chapter, professionals have obligations to third persons that limit the extent to which they may act in behalf of client interests.

2. The agency view arises most often in the context of defending professionals, especially lawyers, from attribution of client sins. This focus is too narrow to sustain a general account of the professional–client relationship. It best pertains to an adversarial context in which two opposing parties confront one another. In counseling, a lawyer's advice "need not be confined to purely legal considerations. . . . It is often desirable for a lawyer to point out those factors which may lead to a decision that is morally just as well as legally permissible."[5]

3. Professionals emphasize their independence of judgment. Unlike a soldier who is not expected to think for himself but to do things the army's way, professionals should exercise their training and skills to make objective judgments. The agency view ignores this feature.

4. Except in cases of dire need—medical emergencies, persons charged with crimes—professionals may accept or reject specific clients. With a few restrictions, they may also stop the relationship. Consequently, the agency view is too strong. Professionals must also be ethically free and responsible persons. For their own freedom and the protection of others, they should not abdicate authority and responsibility in decision-making.

The strongest possible claim of supremacy has been suggested, namely, that, like the common law doctrine of the merging of the identity of the husband and wife, the attorney and client are similarly merged in the identity of the client.[6] The proposal was made in the context of attempts by the Internal Revenue Service to obtain possibly incriminating documents from a client's attorney. By the Fifth Amendment to the U.S. Constitution, clients need not surrender possibly incriminating documents in their own possession. The IRS contends this Fifth Amendment privilege does not extend to lawyers, just as it does not extend to tax accountants. If the identities of client and attorney are merged, then the rights and privileges of a client would apply to the attorney.

Although this "legal fiction" could be useful in this narrow context, strong reasons are against adopting it. Fictions should be avoided in law and ethics if straightforward arguments lead to similar results. Once admitted, fictions can bewitch the understanding and lead to unjustifiable results in other areas. The analogy with the common law doctrine of the identity of husband and wife is quite weak. Except for dowry and a few other matters, the identities of husband and wife were completely merged for legal purposes. In contrast, the merger of attorney and client identities would be very limited. As the considerations against the agency view indicate, good grounds exist for separating the attorney and client in many contexts. Even with respect to incriminating materials, professionals should be permitted or even required to reveal confidences indicating a client's intention to commit a crime.[7]

Contract

If a client ought not to be viewed as having most authority and responsibility, then perhaps the authority and responsibility should be shared equally. In law, a professional–client relationship is based on a contract, and the ethical concept of a just contract is of an agreement freely arrived at by bargaining between equals. If the relationship is a contractual one, then there are mutual obligations and rights, "a true sharing of ethical authority and responsibility."[8] As it recognizes the freedom of two equals to determine the conditions of their relationship, the contract model accords well with the liberal values of freedom and equality of opportunity.

However, no gain results from treating as equals people who are not relevantly equal in fact or from assuming a nonexistent freedom. The history of contracts of adhesion (the standard forms offered by monopolies or near monopolies such as airlines) indicates the injustice that can result from falsely assuming contracting parties have equal bargaining power. Many commentators have noted relevant inequalities between professionals and clients, especially in the medical context.[9] First, a professional's knowledge far exceeds that of a client. A professional has the special knowledge produced by long training, knowledge a client could not have without comparable training. Second, a client is concerned about some basic value—personal health, legal status, or financial status—whereas a professional is not as concerned about the subject matter of their relationship. The client usually has more at stake. Third, a professional often has a freedom to enter the relationship that a client lacks. A professional is often able to obtain other clients more easily than a client can obtain another professional. Especially if a potential client has an acute illness or has just been charged with a crime, he or she is not free to shop around for another professional. From this point of view, the bargaining situation is more like that between an individual and a public utility.

These considerations are not as important for the usual situation in architecture, accounting, and engineering. The clients of these professionals are often better informed about the subject matter of the transaction than are clients of lawyers and physicians. For example, businesses and corporations have accountants working for them who can give advice about auditors. Often firms hiring consulting engineers have had previous experience working with engineers in that field. Governments, even local ones, frequently have one or two engineers working for them who can advise and help. Moreover, they are freer than the professional to conclude an arrangement with another firm. Thus, in these situations the factual basis for the contract model is most nearly present. However, the consulting engineer or architect has some special knowledge and ability the client lacks, or else a professional would probably not be hired, so the contract model's empirical assumptions do not quite hold even in these cases.

Friendship

Instead of viewing the relationship as one between two free and equal persons dealing at arm's length, some authors suggest that the relationship is more personal. One does not relate to a professional as one does to a grocer or public utility. The personal element is most closely captured by viewing the relationship as one of pals or friends. According to this view, professional and client have a close relationship of mutual trust and cooperation; they are involved in a mutual venture, a partnership.

Perhaps the most sophisticated version of this conception is that proposed by Charles Fried.[10] He is primarily concerned with the legal and medical professions. Fried seeks to justify professionals devoting special attention and care to clients and sometimes seeking ends and using means that they would not seek or use for themselves. Friends are permitted, even expected, to take each others' interests seriously and to give them more weight than they do those of other persons. Fried suggests that the attorney–client relationship is analogous to a one-way limited friendship in which the lawyer helps the client secure legal rights. The lawyer helps the client assert his autonomy or freedom within the bounds society permits. Others have suggested that the physician–patient relationship should similarly be viewed as a cooperative effort of friends or pals to deal with the patient's illness or injury.

The many dissimilarities between friendship and the professional–client relationship, however, destroy the analogy. First, as Fried recognizes, the professional–client relationship is chiefly in one direction; the professional has a concern for the client's interests but not vice versa. Second, friendship is usually between equals. Even in friendships between employer and employee, the employer's superiority in the office is changed to a position of equality in the bar for a drink. As the above discussion of the contract model indicates, professionals and clients are not equals. Third, the affective commitment of friendship is usually lacking.[11] Professionals accept clients for a fee, not out of concern for individuals. Thus, one commentator concludes that "Fried has described the classical notion, not of friendship, but of prostitution."[12] As the factual assumptions of this model are incorrect and the analogy supporting it is weak, its ethical implications are unfounded.

The friendship analogy is not needed to justify a professional paying special attention to a client's interests. The role of a professional is to provide services to clients, and the acceptance of a client is sufficient to justify the special attention. A barber who accepts a customer pays special attention to a customer's hair over that of others who need a haircut more. One need not postulate the barber as friend to justify this attention. It is presupposed by any system of services for a fee.

Paternalism

Once one abandons models that assume the professional and client are equal and accepts that the professional is to some extent in a superior position to the client, one faces the problem of the proper extent of professional authority and responsibility in decision-making. Parents have knowledge and experience that children lack, and it is often ethically appropriate for them to exercise their judgment on behalf of their children. Similarly, as a professional has knowledge and experience a client lacks and is hired to further the client's interests, perhaps the relationship should be viewed as one of paternalism.

Paternalism is a difficult concept to analyze. A person's conduct is paternalistic to the extent his or her reasons are to do something to or in behalf of another person for that person's well-being. What is done can be any of a number of things, from removing an appendix to preventing the person from taking drugs. One can also have a paternalistic reason for acting in behalf of a person—for example, filing a counterclaim or asserting a legal defense. The key element of paternalism derives from the agent, X, acting regardless of the person's, Y's, completely voluntary and informed consent. X's reason is that he or she judges the action to be for Y's well-being regardless of Y's consent to it. Y may be incapable of consent, as when a physician treats an unconscious patient in an emergency, or Y may never have been asked, or may have refused to consent to the act.

Conduct can be paternalistic even when Y in fact consents.[13] For example, if X is prepared to do something to Y regardless of Y's consent, then X's reason is paternalistic even if Y does consent. Parents frequently manipulate a child into assenting to actions, although they were prepared to do them without the child's assent. The key element is that X would have done the action, if he could, even if Y had not consented. Such claims are difficult to establish, but this difficulty is a practical problem and does not affect the conceptual matter. In manufacturing consent, information can be withheld, false information provided, or more emphasis placed on some facts than others. Professionals sometimes manufacture consent when action cannot legally be taken without client consent, such as accepting a settlement or performing an operation.

The concept of doing something to or in behalf of someone includes failure to do something. Suppose Y requests X to do something for him, but X refuses because she thinks it would be detrimental to Y's well-being; for example, a physician refuses to prescribe a tranquilizer for a patient. This also counts as doing something to or in behalf of a person without his consent; Y does not consent to the tranquilizers being withheld.

A voluminous literature exists concerning the justification of paternalism. The brief discussion here will outline only the major arguments. Paternalism requires justification because it involves doing something to or in behalf of another person regardless of that person's consent. It thus denies people the freedom to make choices affecting their lives. They lack the freedom of self-determination. As argued in Chapter 1, the loss of control over their own lives, especially to professionals, is one reason for people's concern about professional ethics. Thus, paternalism is of central importance in professional ethics.

Three arguments are often offered to justify paternalism.

1. The agent has superior knowledge as to what is in a person's best interest. Because the agent knows better than the person what is best, the agent is justified in acting to avoid significant harm to, or to procure a significant benefit for, the person. This argument is perhaps the central one in favor of paternalism by professionals. As noted before, a professional possesses a relevant knowledge the client lacks, so he or she is better able to perceive the advantages and disadvantages of alternative actions. Consequently, the professional rather than the client should have primary authority and responsibility for decisions.

2. The client is incapable of giving a fully free and informed consent. By "fully free" is meant without duress, psychological compulsion, or other emotional or psychological disturbance. By "informed" is meant with appreciation of the consequences of a course of conduct and its alternatives. If people cannot give such consent, then their decisions will not adequately reflect their reasonable desires and will not be expressions of their "true selves." This argument, which in some respects is a subcase of the previous one, is also popular in the professions, especially medicine. It is often claimed that people who are ill have a strong feeling of dependency, are worried by their illness, and are in a weakened state, and so lack their usual mental command. A somewhat similar argument can be made about lawyers' clients. If charged with a criminal offense, a person is fearful and disturbed. Even in civil suits, a client's emotions might be aroused, preventing an objective view of the situation.

3. A person will later come to agree that the decision was correct. Although the person does not now consent, he will later. For example, an unconscious accident victim with a broken limb will agree that a physician was correct to set the bone. Parents often require their children to do things, such as take music lessons, on the ground that later the children will be glad they did— "You'll thank me later!" An engineer might see a way to improve an agreed upon rough design to better serve a client's needs, although it involves a significant alteration from the rough design. She might make the change in the belief that the client will agree when he sees the completed design.

To decide whether these justifications support viewing the professional–client relationship as paternalistic, it is useful to consider when reasonable people would allow others to make decisions for them. First, a person might not wish to bother making decisions because the differences involved are trivial. For example, an executive authorizes a secretary to order any needed office supplies, because the differences between brands of paper clips and so forth are not important. Second, the decisions might require knowledge or expertise a person does not possess. For example, an automobile mechanic knows whether a car's oil filter needs changing. One goes to a mechanic for knowledge and service. Third, a person might allow others to make judgments if he or she is or will be mentally incompetent. Some people voluntarily enter mental hospitals.

The first of these reasons does not directly relate to the arguments for paternalism, but the second and third do relate to the first two arguments for paternalism. Reasonable persons would allow others to make decisions for them when they lack the capacity to make reasonable judgments. However, most clients do not have sufficiently impaired judgment to reasonably allow others to make important decisions for them. This incapacity argument has little or no plausibility for the common clients of architects, engineers, and accountants. Business and corporate clients of lawyers are unlikely to have significantly impaired judgment, even if they are biased. Moreover, even with individuals, the view is not plausible for the common legal and medical cases. A person who wants to purchase a house or make a will, or who has the flu or an infection, is rarely so distraught as to be unable to make reasonable decisions. Consequently, the argument from incapacity does not support adopting a paternalistic conception of the professional–client relationship for most cases, although it supports using that conception in special cases.

The first argument for paternalism, that from superior knowledge, fits with reasonable persons allowing others to make decisions when they lack knowledge. Moreover, clients go to professionals for their superior knowledge and skills; such knowledge and skill is a defining feature of a profession. However, many decisions require balancing legal or health concerns against other client interests. As many authors have noted, crucial professional decisions involve value choices.[14] They are not simple choices of technical means to ends, and even choices of means have a value component. Professionals have not had training in value choices. Even if they had, they might not know a client's value scheme sufficiently to determine what is best for him when everything is considered. An attorney might advise a client that he or she need not agree to such large alimony or child support payments, but the client might decide that for personal relations with the former spouse or the welfare of the children, the larger payments are best. Similarly, a physician can advise bed rest, but because of business interests a client can decide her overall interests are best promoted by continuing to work on certain matters. The client might especially need the income or be on the verge of completing a business deal that will earn a promotion. Physicians sometimes fail to realize that a patient's other concerns, even a vacation trip with the family, can precede health. They write and speak of the problem of patient noncompliance just as parents speak of noncompliance by children. Yet, one does not have everything when one has health. Similarly, a client might want an engineering or architectural design to use one type of construction rather than another because its subsidiary supplies such materials.

Although a professional and client are not equals, sufficient client competence exists to undermine the paternalistic model as appropriate for their usual relationship. Clients can exercise judgment over many aspects of professional services. If they lack information to make decisions, professionals can provide it. Sometimes professionals argue that clients can never have the information they have. This is true, but not directly to the point. Much of the information professionals have is irrelevant to decisions that significantly affect client values. The precise name of a disease and its manner of action are not relevant to deciding between two alternative drug therapies, but the fact that one drug reduces alertness is. Similarly, clients of engineers do not need to know the full weight a structure will bear, only that it is more than sufficient for all anticipated stress. To deny clients authority and responsibility by adopting the paternalistic model is to deny them the freedom to direct their own lives. Clients are not capable of determining the precise nature of their problem, or of knowing the alternative courses of action and predicting their consequences or carrying them out on their own. They need and want the technical expertise of a professional to do so. However, they are capable of making reasonable choices among options on the basis of their total values. They need professionals' information in order to make wise choices to accomplish their purposes.

Finally, when the professional–client relationship is conducted on the paternalistic model, client outcomes are not as good as when the client has a more active role. Douglas E. Rosenthal studied settlement awards in personal injury cases.[15] The actual awards received were compared to an expert panel's judgments of the worth of the claims. The less the client participated in the case by not expressing wants or seeking information from the lawyers, and so on, the more the awards fell short of the panel's estimates of the worth of claims. Not only does the paternalistic model sacrifice client freedom and autonomy, but as a result client values and interests are also often sacrificed.

Fiduciary

As a general characterization of what the professional–client relationship should be, one needs a concept in which the professional's superior knowledge is recognized, but the client retains a significant authority and responsibility in decision-making. The law uses such a conception to characterize most professional-client relationships, namely, that of a fiduciary. In a fiduciary relationship, both parties are responsible and their judgments given consideration. Because one party is in a more advantageous position, he or she has special obligations to the other. The weaker party depends upon the stronger in ways in which the other does not and so must *trust* the stronger party.

In the fiduciary model, a client has more authority and responsibility in decision-making than in the paternalistic model. A client's consent and judgment are required and he participates in the decision-making process, but the client depends on the professional for much of the information upon which he gives or withholds his consent. The term *consents* (the client consents) rather than *decides* (the client decides) indicates that it is the professional's role to propose courses of action. It is not the conception of two people contributing equally to the formulation of plans, whether or not dealing at arm's length. Rather, the professional supplies the ideas and information and the client agrees or not. For the process to work, the client must trust the professional to accurately analyze the problem, canvass the feasible alternatives, know as well as one can their likely consequences, fully convey this information to the client, perhaps make a recommendation, and work honestly and loyally for the client to effectuate the chosen alternatives. In short, the client must rely on the professional to use his or her knowledge and ability in the client's interests. Because the client cannot check most of the work of the professional or the information supplied, the professional has special obligations to the client to ensure that the trust and reliance are justified.

This is not to suggest that the professional simply presents an overall recommendation for a client's acceptance or rejection. Rather, a client's interests can be affected by various aspects of a professional's work, so the client should be consulted at various times. The extent of appropriate client participation and decision-making can be determined by advertence to the reasons for allowing others to make decisions for one. Professionals do not have expertise in a client's values or in making value choices. Their superior knowledge and expertise do not qualify them to make value choices significantly affecting a client's life plans or style. However, they do have knowledge of technical matters. A patient will certainly let a physician determine the dosage of medicines. A client can reasonably allow an engineer to determine the general specifications of materials for a job. A lawyer may decide whether to stipulate facts, object to testimony, or agree to a postponement.[16] Clients allow professionals to make these judgments, because the effects on their values are small and they do not wish to be bothered. In short, client consent and involvement are not necessary when (1) the matter is chiefly a technical one or (2) the value effect is not significant.

The appropriate ethical conception of the professional–client relationship is one that allows clients as much freedom to determine how their life is affected as is reasonably warranted on the basis of their ability to make decisions. In most dealings of business and corporate clients with accountants, architects, engineers, and lawyers, the relationship is close to a contract between equals. As clients have less knowledge about the subject matter for which the professional is engaged, the special obligations of the professional in the fiduciary model become more significant. The professional must assume more responsibility for formulating plans, presenting their advantages and disadvantages, and making recommendations. Because of the increased reliance on the professional, he or she must take special care to be worthy of client trust. Thus, although the fiduciary model is appropriate throughout the range of competent clients and services, the less a client's knowledge and capacity to understand, the greater the professional's responsibilities to the client.

Finally, some clients are not competent to make decisions. In this case, the paternalistic model becomes appropriate. These cases of an incompetent client will almost always be restricted to members of the legal and health professions. Even then it does not follow that the professional should make the decisions. If a client is incompetent, a legal guardian should be appointed to make decisions. When this is done, the professional has a fiduciary relationship to the guardian. Consequently, the appropriate occasions for professionals to adopt a paternalistic role are restricted to those in which a client is incompetent and a guardian has not yet been appointed.

OBLIGATIONS OF TRUSTWORTHINESS

The fiduciary ethical model of the professional–client relationship emphasizes a professional's special obligations to be worthy of client trust. Only if a professional deserves a client's initial and continuing trust has the ideal of the fiduciary conception been achieved. As should be clear from the rejection of paternalism, the sense of trust involved is not that of trusting a professional to make decisions for one. One may always pertinently ask, "Trust to do what?" The answer is trust to fulfill the functions that the average client wants and for which a professional is hired. A client wants a professional to use expertise to analyze the problem, formulate alternative plans or courses of action, determine their probable consequences, make recommendations, or carry out certain activities (audit, surgery) in his or her behalf. A professional's obligations to a client are those necessary to deserve the client's trust that these activities will be performed in a manner to promote the client's interests—including the freedom to make decisions regarding his or her life.

This section presents six general obligations that professionals must fulfill to be deserving of client trust. The criterion for determining professionals' obligations to clients is the standard of truthworthiness, of being worthy of a client's trust. Each obligation can then be justified as one that a reasonable client with ethical purposes would want a professional to fulfill. No hard claim is made that the six obligations presented are exhaustive or mutually exclusive. Although they seem to be distinct, some might be combined; perhaps others should be added. The fiduciary model's ideal of a professional being worthy of a client's trust provides the criterion for determining which obligations should be included or excluded. In short, although no proof is given for the completeness of the obligations presented here, a principle of inclusion and exclusion is used.

The six obligations of professionals to clients can be stated as standards of a good or trustworthy professional. A good professional is honest, candid, competent, diligent, loyal, and discrete. These are the virtues of a trustworthy professional. These obligations can also be viewed as norms of conduct. As such, they present responsibilities. Certain duties require specific conduct to fulfill these responsibilities. However, no list of duties fully specifies any of the responsibilities. Duties are classified under one responsibility, but they are often partially supported or limited by other obligations.

Honesty

Professionals should be honest with their clients. By definition, a dishonest professional is not worthy of a client's trust.[17] As the obligation of honesty being considered here is an obligation to the client, it does not directly require honesty towards others. Professionals can be honest with their clients, and in acting in their behalf be dishonest with others. If so, they do not violate a responsibility to their client but one to others. Nevertheless, in two ways they may weaken a client's reasons for trust. First, their client can be tainted by their dishonesty towards others in the client's behalf. To the extent a professional is an agent of a client, his or her conduct reflects upon the client. How much it appropriately does so depends on the extent of the client's knowledge and authorization of the professional's dishonesty. Second, honesty is not an easily divisible character trait. One can be dishonest in certain respects, such as not putting money in parking meters, and still honest in others. Nonetheless, one who acts dishonestly towards others in behalf of a client is more likely to be dishonest with a client. If dishonesty towards others increases the likelihood a professional will be dishonest towards a client, it renders him or her less worthy of the client's trust.

One duty of honesty is not to steal from a client. A clear form of professional theft is an accountant or lawyer appropriating client funds for personal use. This is one of the more frequent forms of lawyer dishonesty towards a client, and the bar has not generally been very active in punishing such dishonesty. Disciplinary committees rarely act against a lawyer who returns embezzled funds.[18] This lack of action is both detrimental to the status of the bar and prejudicial to future clients of that lawyer. To make restitution, the lawyer might use funds entrusted to him or her by other clients or become financially hard pressed and so more tempted to appropriate the funds of future clients.

Such blatant theft is often not possible for professionals. Physicians rarely handle funds of patients. Nonetheless, forms of theft such as kickbacks are open to them as well as to engineers and other professionals. A subtle form of professional theft is the provision of unneeded services. When physicians perform unnecessary tests or surgery, they are being dishonest with their clients.[19] Of course, determining what services are needed is difficult. It would be best to cease speaking of needed and unneeded services, as usually the question is how helpful a service might be. A title search going back fifty years is adequate for most purposes, but better protection is provided by one going back seventy-five years. Similarly, some engineers' or physicians' tests are apt to be more useful than others. How far professionals go on these matters depends on their attitudes toward risk and other factors. If they believe that a service is probably of little value but they might as well perform it and be safe because the client can pay, dishonesty is involved. As a check on motives, professionals can ask themselves, "Would I want it done were I in the client's (financial) position?"

Candor

Although closely related to honesty, candor is different. One can be truthful but dishonest. Whether one can be untruthful but honest is less clear. The following conversation between a waitress and a customer suggests that one might be untruthful but honest.

Waitress: Would you lie to me?

Customer: Yes.

Waitress: Well, at least you're honest.

Being truthful appears to be a subclass of being honest, because deceit is often used to obtain a financial advantage. However, lying by professionals is often not for the professional's own benefit but for what the professional believes to be the client's well-being. Hence, not all instances of untruthfulness are easily assimilable to dishonesty as fraud. In any case, candor includes more than truthfulness, namely, full disclosure. One can avoid lying by keeping silent, but in so doing one fails to be candid.

The responsibility of candor is at the heart of the professional–client relationship. If the relationship is fiduciary rather than paternalistic, then the professional respects the judgments of the client and acts on important matters only with the client's consent. A client may consent to a professional undertaking a range of activities in her behalf, yet this range is limited. She may consent to a professional making judgments in her behalf if the matters do not significantly affect her values or are primarily technical, such as the size of heat ducts to adequately heat a structure. However, as the relationship is a fiduciary one, the client also trusts the professional to consult her and respect her informed judgment in all important decisions. Since a client enters the relationship to receive information from the professional, if the professional withholds information he has reason to believe would influence his client's judgment, he alters the agreement. He manipulates the client's information so that the client's judgments conform to his own. The professional thus acts on his own judgment of the client's interest regardless of the client's fully informed and free consent, and the relationship is paternalistic.

One form of such manipulation is what lawyers call "cooling the client out."[20] For example, suppose that in negotiating a settlement the other side offers $5,000. The attorney thinks $5,000 is a reasonable amount but the client unreasonably expects $10,000. She tells the client that the offer was for $3,000 but that she might be able to get $4,500. In a few days the attorney phones back and says she managed to bargain the opposing party into offering $5,000 and recommends that the client accept. This example is a clear case of paternalistic manipulation of information to obtain client consent. The motivation for such cooling out is not always so paternalistic; the attorney may desire to reach an early settlement simply to obtain a sizeable fee for little work.

This example involves a professional deliberately lying to a client. A lie can be distinguished from withholding information. The paradigm of a lie is intentionally telling someone what one believes to be false. The intent is to deceive. Withholding information need not be intended to deceive, to produce a false belief, but merely to keep a person in ignorance. The conceptually difficult cases are those in which information is withheld in order to create a misapprehension on the part of another—for example, not indicating by a note to a financial statement that certain property has greatly depreciated in value. Although these cases are conceptually difficult, they are not morally difficult. The wrong in lying is the intent to deceive. From a client's point of view, she has hired the professional for information on which she can rely, and deceit defeats that purpose whether it results from false information or the mere withholding of it.

The element of trust involved in the professional–client relationship makes truthfulness even more important than in relationships that do not involve such trust.[21] If one purchases a used car, although more truthfulness is now legally required than previously, one does not put full faith in all the dealer's claims. In a relationship involving trust, one is more apt to do so. Therefore, a lie is apt to result in greater harm. Moreover, as the relationship itself is one of trust and a lie indicates that the other person cannot be trusted, the relationship is likely to be irreparably destroyed.

Few people have ever claimed that lying can never be justified. If a great harm might befall a person or others as a result of a truthful disclosure, then lack of candor is justifiable. Although a lie is prima facie wrong, it can be the lesser of two evils.

Physicians frequently believe that an obligation not to harm their patients outweighs that of full disclosure. The most frequently discussed situation is failure to inform a patient that he has cancer. The argument for nondisclosure is that the information would be harmful to the patient's mental well-being. A serious problem affects this argument. To use the traditional principle that a physician's first obligation is to do no harm merely moves the issue back one step. The issue then becomes whether the psychological distress is harm. While a patient could be psychologically depressed by the information, he could also want to know. To determine whether the distress is greater than the benefits of being informed involves a complex value judgment for which physicians have not been trained and for which they frequently lack relevant information.[22] One study found that most doctors who did not tell patients that they had cancer, even when the patients explicitly asked to be told, believed that patients did not really want to be told the truth.[23] Such a belief is unfounded in the face of the best possible contrary evidence. A recent study found that physicians' attitudes and practices in informing cancer patients of their disease has altered dramatically. Whereas in 1961, 90 percent preferred not to inform patients, by 1977, 97 percent preferred to inform patients.[24]

A more likely example of justifiable nondisclosure is the following. A forty-year-old divorced woman with two children has a vision impairment that is a somatic reaction to stress resulting from her divorce, a move to a different community, and a new job. In cases like this, vision does not usually improve. If she is told the impairment is probably permanent, her stress will be increased, the chances of recovery decreased, and further impairment made more likely. An ophthalmologist delays informing the patient of the prognosis until he is fairly sure no improvement is possible.

Lack of candor is justifiable in this case in part because disclosure directly affects the cause of the patient's disease. In contrast, mental stress is not the cause of cancer, and untoward results of disclosure depend on rash conduct by the patient. In short, in the ophthalmologist's case, harm is more certain because of the more direct causal link between the information and the anticipated harm. Moreover, the information is not permanently withheld. In this case, a responsibility of candor to the patient is overridden by an obligation to protect and promote the patient's health.

Failure to fully disclose information also occurs in legal practice. In interviewing a client, a lawyer wants to determine the facts so that she can construct the client's case. A client asks for specific information about the legal status of certain evidence. Informing the client of the legal significance might encourage him to "remember" the facts in a way most favorable to his side. For example, suppose a man is charged with murder and the weapon was his pocket knife. In an interview, an attorney asks the client whether he usually carried the pocket knife. Suppose the client asks, "What difference does it make?" The significance is that if the man did not usually carry the knife, then his having it would be evidence of premeditation; if he usually did carry it, then it is more plausible that he acted in a fit of passion and is guilty only of manslaughter. If the attorney provides this information before the client answers, the client is not likely to say he went and got the knife to have with him on this specific occasion.

Similar situations arise in other professions. For example, a university professor takes a leave of absence to teach at another university for a year as a visiting professor. If she wants a regular position there, she can have it. She consults a tax accountant to see whether she can claim her expenses for the year as a tax deduction for a job away from home for less than a year. The accountant asks about her intention to remain, and the professor asks why he wants to know. The reason is that if she intends to return, then the expenses are deductible, but if she intends to remain, they are not. If the accountant explains this to the professor, she will almost certainly say she intends to return and generally act in ways to support this claim, even if she has practically made up her mind to accept the new position.

In such situations, failure to inform a client of the significance of facts would not be justified by some other obligation to the client. Instead, it would be by an obligation to others—the government and society. What is at stake is encouraging or contributing to fraud. Withholding the information is not paternalistic, for it is not for the client's benefit but to prevent harm to society.

Failure to explain the significance of such facts to a client might damage the professional–client relationship. A client could feel his attorney or accountant is not being open and is letting the client do himself in. Part of this effect on the trust relation can be mitigated. Unlike the physician's refusal to inform cancer patients of their diagnosis, a lawyer or accountant can explain the significance of facts after she gets the client's statement. She need not withhold the information forever. If providing the information is likely to encourage the client to engage in unethical conduct, a professional is not obligated to disclose the information at that time. These cases must be distinguished from those in which the client simply wants to know the consequences of two alternatives in order to decide what to do. The tax accountant example borders on a case of that sort, although it is unlikely the professor would refuse a new job simply for the tax considerations.

Competence

Although it is not a moral virtue, competence is perhaps the most crucial characteristic. It creates an ethical problem if professionals hold themselves out to do or accept work they are not competent to handle. No matter how honest, candid, diligent, loyal, and discreet professionals are, if they are incompetent they are unworthy of trust, for they cannot do well the job for which they are hired. Of course, clients' beliefs about professionals' competence may not be correct. Reputations for competence, like all reputations, are fickle. Very competent professionals may not have a reputation among potential clients for competence, and incompetent ones may. Generally, the most reliable judgments of competence are those of other professionals.

Almost all professional codes require that professionals undertake only that work they are competent to perform and to continue learning to keep abreast of the field.[25] Many professions do not require periodic examinations of competence. When a professional is licensed to practice, the license is good for life unless disciplinary action is taken. A professional's knowledge that was current twenty years ago might not be so now. The pressures of professional work make it very difficult to keep up in a field, especially one in which changes are occurring rapidly. Professionals would be hard pressed to read the flood of periodicals even if that was all they did. As almost all professionals specialize, they may realistically be expected to remain current in their specialty, whether ceramic engineering, tort law, or pediatrics.

How do professionals know when a client's problem is beyond the limits of their expertise? This problem is especially acute when specialization is not certified or persons without a specialty or certification are not prohibited from providing services. For example, general medical practitioners are usually legally free to perform surgery, and many of them do relatively simple procedures. Should a civil engineer undertake the design of a building's electrical system or should she have an electrical engineer as a consultant? Merely stating that a professional should associate another when indicated or when she is not competent in an area does not settle the problem.[26] Clients are rarely capable of determining when a specialist (or a different type of specialist from the one they consult) is needed in borderline cases. They must trust professionals not to undertake work they are not competent to perform. However, as noted in discussing fee splitting in the previous chapter, professionals have a financial reason for handling cases themselves if possible.

Another aspect of the problem is that although professionals are not very familiar with an area, they can often learn enough to handle a case. Professionals frequently have to research a particular problem. If sufficient time is devoted to a problem outside their usual practice, they can often do a competent job. However, should a client have to pay for a professional's education, especially if he could obtain a trained specialist for less? At this point, at least the responsibility of candor applies, and the professional should explain the situation to the client. It is the client's money and work to be done, so he should decide the question.

Diligence

A responsibility of diligence or zeal is closely related to, but distinct from, that of competence. One can be supremely competent but not diligent, or diligent and zealous but incompetent. A person who is not diligent may neglect significant matters and turn out a substandard "product." A poorly drafted will, mistaken diagnosis, or badly designed project can result from carelessness or incompetence. Thus, these two considerations are sometimes confused or lumped together.[27] A client is often unable to determine whether the unsatisfactory result in her case was due to neglect, incompetence, or unavoidable error.

A responsibility of diligence clearly follows from the criterion that a professional be worthy of a client's trust. A reasonable person would not entrust his important affairs to someone he thought would not actively and carefully handle them. Diligence is especially necessary when time is important, as it often is in professional activities. Many legal clients have lost cases because their lawyer failed to file claims in time, respond to a complaint, or appear in court. Similarly, if one is ill, one wants diagnosis and treatment sooner rather than later. Also, clients often want engineers to design projects quickly, and many wait until the last minute before taking their income tax to an accountant. Journalists almost always work under severe deadlines. Diligence does not require immediate action but allows for reasonable delays, as for test results or space on a court docket.

Professionals perhaps violate the responsibility of diligence more frequently than any other. Most complaints against lawyers are for neglect.[28] And whether justified or not, one of the most common complaints about physicians is that they do not devote adequate time to patients. One may wonder how many missed diagnoses are due to physicians' lack of diligence in ruling out less likely but more serious diseases. Engineers sometimes consider a problem to be a standard one without thoroughly checking it; and college teachers often fail to prepare for class and to return student papers promptly.

A common complaint by, and defense of, professionals is that they lack time to provide each client the attention they think ideal. This defense is questionable. Professionals can usually make time. It only requires saying "No!" when asked to undertake yet another task. If they really are too busy to devote adequate time to clients, they can reduce the number of clients or other activities. This will result in decreased income if the professional is paid on a fee-for-service or capitation basis. But, if the professional does not provide diligent service, the fees are not justified anyway and violate the responsibility of honesty.

One can always devote more time to a specific client, but beyond some point further consideration and attention are unlikely to be justified by expectable benefits. Hence, some professionals' complaints about lack of time are simply claims that further time or attention to a case would not be justified. Is this decision one for the professional or client? As it is essentially a value choice of possible benefits and burdens to the client, the fiduciary model implies that the decision is that of the client. At least when hired on a fee-for-service basis, a professional should make clear to a client that further time could be spent on research or examination, but that it would cost a certain amount and have such and such a likelihood of uncovering anything significant. Since the client bears the risks, she should have the option of deciding whether the extra assurance is worthwhile.

Some physicians practice "defensive medicine" and perform tests not likely to provide useful information simply in order to protect themselves against possible malpractice suits. Were a physician to clearly put the choice of a further test to a patient and she declined, the physician would also have a good legal defense. "Defensive medicine" could thus be based on talking to patients, which would both be less expensive and fulfill the responsibility of full disclosure.

In one type of situation it is justifiable to provide a client less attention than a professional considers ideal. If an insufficient number of professionals is available to provide appropriate attention to each client without some potential clients being denied service, then a professional must balance an obligation to provide diligent service with that to make services equally available. This consideration primarily applies in law and medicine, for people have positive rights to such services. In the other professions, client's rights are only to equal availability and this is not denied if services are provided on a first-come, first-served basis. Physicians in rural communities and emergency rooms and lawyers in public defenders' offices are often in such situations. The issue is one of balancing obligations to clients and to society. The time and attention devoted to the client is less than might be appropriate if conditions of practice were more adequate, but they are appropriate for the context. The professional rather than the client should judge the adequacy of time in this context. Otherwise, self-interested clients might deprive many others of scarce resources. However, professionals must take care that their motivation is in fact making services available rather than their own pecuniary well-being.

Loyalty

Clients ask professionals to act in behalf of some of their interests. A professional is sometimes hired to further a client's interests only to the extent of making a proper and accurate representation of the client's position to another person. Accountants hired to perform public audits, and lawyers hired to make an independent evaluation to be provided to someone else serve a client's interests only to the extent that a correct statement is in the client's interest.[29] A professional who disloyally "sells out" a client's interests is not worthy of the client's trust.

Even when professionals represent clients' interests against those of others, there are limits to the loyalty clients can properly expect from professionals. They may expect only a loyalty that does not violate a professional's other responsibilities. A client is certainly not justified in expecting a professional to commit illegal acts; the value of protection from injury by others in society would be greatly infringed were this allowed. The most difficult problem is determining the boundaries between a professional's loyalty to a client and other responsibilities.

Sometimes other responsibilities must give way to loyalty to clients, and sometimes loyalty must give way to other responsibilities. (These conflicts are discussed in detail in Chapter 5.) Factors other than responsibilities can affect a professional's loyalty to a client, and a major part of some professional codes of ethics pertains to these factors.

The responsibility of loyalty faces conflict from a professional's self-interest and the interest of third parties. One largely unavoidable conflict is that between a professional's interests in income and leisure and a client's interest in services. If professionals are paid on a fee-for-service basis, then (unless they have an overabundance of clients) they have an interest in providing services. Higher rates of elective surgery occur when physicians are paid on a fee-for-service rather than on another basis. Rarely would a physician consciously think that although surgery is not indicated, he or she needs some extra money for a new car. Instead, self-interests unconsciously affect physicians' perceptions of patients' needs. A similar consideration applies to engineers designing projects and being paid a percentage of the project costs. The more expensive the project, the greater their fee.

Alternative systems of paying professionals do not remove the conflict but merely reverse the effect on the client. In a capitation payment system, professionals have an interest in having as many clients as possible to maximize their income and in performing as few services as possible to minimize their costs. On a salary system or a flat fee for a case, professionals receive the same income no matter the number of clients or services performed, so they have an interest in minimizing clients or services. These payment systems thus encourage professionals not to perform useful services. Shortages of professionals or clients have effects similar to these payment systems.

This fundamental conflict of interest between professional and client cannot be removed. It is inherent in the professional–client relationship. At best, it can be minimized by making a firm agreement with the client after initial consultation as to what will be done and its total cost. Such an arrangement is possible only for cases in which the total professional work can be reasonably estimated. Although engineers, accountants, lawyers, surgeons, and dentists perform much work on this basis, physicians rarely do so. Physicians might try a modified fee-for-service system approximating that of lawyers. Instead of a fee for each discrete service, they might fix a fee for treating a type of illness, disease, or injury. For example, a standard fee for a bronchial infection might cover any needed office visits and possible complications.

An important identity of professional and client interests also exists. Generally, in doing a good job for their clients professionals enhance their professional reputation.[30] One must distinguish between professional and nonprofessional reputation, especially for lawyers. A lawyer who does an excellent job for an unpopular client can lose her reputation in the community while enhancing her reputation among other lawyers. The public does not view favorably lawyers who skillfully win cases for unpopular clients. This consideration also applies to some other professionals; for example, nuclear engineers are not very popular with a significant segment of the public.

Besides the irremovable general conflict of interest between professional and client with respect to payment, conflicts of interest are possible with respect to specific professionals, clients, and problems. Such conflicts can usually be avoided or removed. Many professional obligations in codes are aimed at avoiding these conflicts.

The key element of loyalty to a client in specific matters is independence of judgment. Most professional codes mention such a responsibility.[31] The reasons for the obligation of independence of judgment go to the nature of professionalism and the professional–client relationship. Professionals should apply their special skills and knowledge to make judgments on which their clients can rely in protecting or promoting their interests. If these judgments are biased, clients do not receive the type of advice and assistance they are seeking and actions taken on the basis of such judgments may be detrimental.

Independence of judgment can be lost or interfered with in many ways. An important but often ignored way, especially for psychiatrists, psychologists, physicians, and lawyers, is over-identification with a client. Beginning professionals especially have this difficulty. Over-identification with a client's interests can lead to mistaken judgments and actions that jeopardize the client's and even the professional's interests and violate responsibilities to others. An example of a lawyer indicates the problem.[32] An unemployed client had bought a used car that needed many repairs. After making some free repairs, the dealer charged $400 for the last repairs and refused to release the car until the client paid. The client had no money to pay the bill. Pretending to be a prospective buyer, her lawyer went to the dealer and asked to take the car for a test drive. He then drove the car to the client's house and gave her the keys.

The objectivity that a professional must maintain frequently leads clients, especially of physicians, to view the professional as cold-hearted and uncaring. Sometimes these opinions rest not on the substance of professionals' attitudes but on the manner in which they provide advice and comments. Sometimes an attitude of unconcern is necessary for professionals to maintain their own mental stability; for example, pediatric oncologists (physicians specializing in the treatment of cancer in children) simply could not bear the psychological pain if they identified with their patients. Physicians' concern with "bedside manner" indicates awareness of the impression of callousness they may give patients. Despite this aspect of style, however, caring requires a nonidentification of interests in order to retain independent, objective judgment.

A professional's personal interests can also lead to a lack of independent judgment. For example, a lawyer could own property affected by a client's proposed actions or could be likely to be called as a witness. An accountant could own stock in a client's competitor. A physician could wish to conduct an experiment for which the patient is a potential subject, or could have developed a technique or therapy he wants to promote. Requirements of informed consent of experimental subjects are designed to ensure that the client is aware of these interests and agrees to participate. Fewer conflicts arise for physicians than for other professionals because a patient's health does not usually adversely affect the interests of others, including physicians.

At the very least, professionals have a duty to inform clients of their own personal interests that might affect their independence of judgment. Clients trust professionals to exercise independent judgment, and they should be aware of anything that might adversely affect the basis for this trust. Professionals have a responsibility to minimize the influence of such interests on their professional judgments.

One can question whether client consent is sufficient to permit a professional–client relationship in such cases.[33] Given the superior knowledge of professionals, the opportunities for even unintentional exploitation are great. Perhaps clients should be protected from these risks regardless of their consent. Such a policy would not be straightforward paternalism, for the fear is that clients will be misled into consenting to professional employment and thus be exploited or defrauded. Although client freedom of choice is desirable, freedom not based on proper information is a mirage. Client consent is not a sufficient justification, but it is necessary. If the conflict is not great or is only potential, and the client consents, then it is permissible for a professional to undertake a case.

Business dealings between professionals and clients other than for professional services can affect loyalty. For example, an engineer might own a supply company for materials the client uses, and a new production design might eliminate the need for those particular materials. If a lawyer sold her house to her client, it would be unwise for the lawyer to do the title search and contract for the client. Ideally, if everything were fully explained, a mutually satisfactory agreement might be reached. However, should any difficulty arise, the pressure on the lawyer or engineer to conceal information from the client or to misadvise him is nearly overwhelming. The above argument against the sufficiency of consent applies even more strongly here.

A second factor affecting independence of judgment and loyalty to a client is a conflict of interest between clients. This problem can be divided into two types of cases—those in which two or more clients are involved in the same transaction or activity and those in which they are involved in separate transactions or activities. The first type of case is the most obvious. In general, a lawyer ought not represent clients whose interests might conflict. Even though no conflict exists when two or more clients ask for representation, if their interests in the case might conflict, a lawyer ought not represent both. Two persons charged with committing the same crime may believe their interests do not conflict, but the defense of one could be contrary to defense of the other. A husband and wife purchasing a house probably do not have interests that would conflict in the particular case, although a conflict might arise with respect to whether ownership should be joint or in only one of their names.

In a divorce, a husband and wife do clearly have conflicting interests. As a general policy, conscientious lawyers avoid representing both spouses in fault divorces. A leading text claims professional standards have not yet developed to deal with no-fault divorces.[34] While no-fault lessens conflicts, interests in the property settlement and child custody can conflict significantly. Nonetheless, to avoid the costs of two lawyers, a couple might decide to permit one lawyer to handle their divorce. To prohibit such an arrangement would unduly limit the clients' freedom. They could legally secure a divorce without a lawyer; to prohibit them obtaining legal services to ensure the divorce's validity prevents them minimizing risks of an invalid divorce as they see fit.[35]

An obvious requirement is that a professional fully disclose to both clients a possible conflict of interests.[36] Unfortunately, full disclosure is not such an easy matter. First, sometimes full disclosure might require the revelation of confidences of the other party.[37] If full disclosure is not possible, then an attorney should not accept both clients or an engineer accept payment from two or more parties for a project. A requirement of disclosure to the extent discretion allows is insufficient, for the very facts that cannot be disclosed might be most important. Without full information, client consent does not adequately represent a client's desire to assume risks.

Second, must lawyers disclose what their position will be should an actual conflict arise? They cannot at that point act as an advocate for each. Their options are to act as mediator, arbitrator, counselor as to the legal effects or alternatives, or to withdraw. If a serious conflict were to arise and the lawyer to withdraw, the parties would be subject to even higher legal fees than they would have paid had they originally retained separate lawyers. If clients are not informed of the position an attorney will assume should a conflict arise, then they have not been fully apprised of the consequences of alternatives and their consent is not fully informed.

Physicians do not have as many conflicts of interest between clients as lawyers, because the health of one does not ordinarily adversely affect the health of others. Such problems do arise in a few types of situations. For example, a family physician recommending a form of contraception to a couple must consider the possible side effects, say, a vasectomy for the male versus a tubal ligation or birth control pills for the female. A more significant conflict arises in organ transplants if the same physician treats both patients. For example, suppose a physician attends both a potential recipient and a potential donor for a kidney transplant. The potential recipient's interest lies in receiving an organ from the best tissue match, usually a relative. However, the removal of a kidney is a health risk to the donor. In such cases, a physician other than the recipient's should discuss the situation with the donor.[38]

Also, legal firms face many problems of potential conflicts of interest between clients not immediately involved in the same case. Various corporations eventually end up in litigation with each other. Other professions confront this problem much less often, because, for example, an architectural or engineering project for one client is unlikely to be contrary to the interest of a subsequent client. Also, as illustrated at the beginning of Chapter 1, a law firm can find itself representing two different clients in separate cases and taking opposite sides on the same point of law. Even if different members of the firm work on the cases, can a firm simultaneously take opposing positions in separate cases and retain independence of judgment? A direct conflict could emerge should both cases be appealed and consolidated. Perhaps the best that can be done is to monitor cases for potential conflicts, disclose the possibility of conflict, and leave the decisions to clients. If a client believes a conflict exists, then for all practical purposes one does.[39]

Finally, a professional's loyalty and independence of judgment can be adversely affected by interests of third parties. The legal and to some extent the accounting professions have tried to insulate their members from third party influences by forbidding them to practice with people not in their particular profession or in a firm in which people not in their particular profession participate.[40] One fear is that nonprofessional interests and considerations will influence their actions. The financial interests of nonprofessionals, however, do not justify such a strong rule, because professionals also have an interest in maximizing profit. Consequently, the justification for such a restriction must rest upon laypersons directing cases in nonprofessional ways. That concern could be and is met by less stringent rules prohibiting nonprofessionals directing professionals' judgments in behalf of specific clients.[41] A significant effect of these restrictions has been to prevent the formation of firms of lawyers and accountants that could offer clients more efficient combined services.

Professionals have a responsibility to ensure that third party payers do not influence their professional judgment in behalf of specific clients. It is unrealistic to require that professionals not be paid by nonclients. Parents must pay for medical care for children. With parents paying for services for children, potential conflicts of interest are relatively small. Although parents are usually concerned enough with their children's welfare to want a professional to exercise independent judgment in their children's behalf as much as they would want the professional to do in their behalf, that is not always the case. For example, parents of retarded children sometimes want them sterilized, which may be contrary to the interests of the children.

When a third party pays for professional services for an adult, as when an insurance company pays for services, a couple of duties involved in the responsibility of loyalty can be formulated.[42] First, the professional should receive the informed consent of the client. Since the arrangement can affect the professional's independence of judgment, the client should know of the possibility and who is making the payments. Otherwise, the client is not justified in trusting the professional's judgment. With physicians, this condition is usually met, for clients know who their medical insurer is. Second, professionals have a duty to inform the people paying them that they cannot direct or regulate their professional judgment or conduct. That is, professionals should make their employment conditional on their acting solely on the basis of personal and their clients' judgment of the clients' best interests. They must then, of course, live up to this condition if the payer tries to influence their judgment. Doing so may require considerable personal courage, because they may lose future business from a payer such as an accident insurance company.

This situation applies in reverse to accountants providing audits and lawyers preparing independent evaluations. In those cases, the client has hired them to provide information to third parties. The client can have interests (not disclosing financial losses or pending law suits) that are contrary to the professional's independent judgment. In these cases, a client in effect occupies the position of a third party payer and must not be allowed to direct or regulate a professional's independent judgment.[43] To do otherwise risks allowing a client to injure those for whom the statements are prepared.

This problem is especially acute for employee professionals, such as nurses. A nurse's client rarely pays the nurse directly. Instead, another organization (hospital, physician, public agency) does so. Consequently, a nurse is often caught between the demands of the employer and what the nurse considers best for the client. For example, nurses in an institution might be told to give inmates a mood-altering drug, primarily to keep the inmates quiet, when the nurses believe the inmates' problems could be solved more effectively without the drug. No simple solution exists for this problem, as it raises issues about the scope of nurses' competence and autonomy as well as loyalty to clients.

Discretion

The responsibility of discretion is one of the hardest to reconcile with a professional's obligations. Writers on professional ethics usually speak of "confidentiality" rather than discretion. Discretion is a broader concept than confidentiality, including material that is not confidential. The ordinary sense of confidentiality primarily refers to facts and information learned from a client.

The underlying value is privacy, the control of information about oneself that others have. One may intrude upon another's privacy without violating confidentiality. For example, many actions lawyers take in behalf of clients are a matter of public record. However, clients would not be able to trust professionals who constantly spoke to others about actions that they took in their behalf. Clients usually do not want their lawyer or realtor to freely discuss the terms of their divorce settlement or house purchase at cocktail parties, even though the settlement or purchase is a matter of public record. Although such disclosures do not violate any legal right of privacy, the moral basis of privacy is freedom to pursue one's business without scrutiny by others unless one consents or they have a need to know. Being the subject of cocktail party gossip does not satisfy a legitimate need of others. The public may have some legitimate interest in the private affairs of public figures, such as movie stars and politicians. But for the average citizen, the point of a public record of divorce proceedings and house purchases is to provide an authoritative record should any subsequent inquiry arise. Thus, even though the record is public, the purpose and intent is limited to legitimate concerns, and consent to disclosure should be construed as limited to these functions. Professionals who fail to recognize such points exhibit a lack of respect for their clients. They might also carelessly let other strictly confidential information slip.

A more usual element of the responsibility of discretion is confidentiality. It is basic to professional-client relationships. For professionals to make the best possible recommendations and take appropriate actions, they need all possibly relevant information. Clients are often reluctant to discuss matters of a personal nature, whether they affect the body, possibly illegal or simply stupid actions, or business secrets. They might not fully appreciate the significance of facts. This last point is dramatically illustrated by an old lag convicted of burglary and appearing before a judge for sentencing at the Old Bailey in London. When the judge asked him whether he had anything to say before being sentenced, the man replied that it was unjust and unfair that he be sentenced for the crime, that he was completely innocent, and he could prove it. The skeptical judge inquired how he could prove it. The man responded that he could not have done it because he was in prison on the day the burglary occurred. When the startled judge asked why he had not mentioned this before, the defendant replied that he thought the jurors would have a poor opinion of him if they knew he was an exconvict! To obtain as much information as possible from clients, professionals need to assure clients that what they say will remain confidential.

At the very core of the responsibility of discretion is the professional privilege of client communications. This privilege is a legal doctrine providing that professionals cannot be required to reveal client confidences in a court of law. A major issue in modern law, which cannot be adequately considered here, is the proper extent of this privilege. Most professions do not have such a legal privilege, so it primarily relates to lawyers and to physicians in some jurisdictions.

The most sensitive area of the privilege relates to lawyers. Because of the essential involvement of lawyers in the legal process and their function of representing their clients, they must have some privilege. If all the information a lawyer obtains from a client could be required to be presented in court, clients could not trust their lawyers with any information which they believe might damage their case. In that situation, except for a few minor matters of procedure and admission of evidence, lawyers could be only literal mouthpieces for their clients.

Three kinds of reasons can be given for a professional violating confidentiality: the best interests of (1) the client, (2) the professional, or (3) other persons.[44] Codes often state that confidential information may be disclosed when the client consents. Such disclosure does not break confidentiality, for confidentiality means permitting the client to control to whom information is given, and that condition is met if the client consents.

Other instances of disclosure for the benefit of a client need not be with his consent. For example, in negotiating in behalf of a client, it may be advantageous for a lawyer to disclose information to the other party. Similar situations are even more common in the health care professions. A psychologist or psychiatrist might obtain information that would help a patient's regular physician treat him, or vice versa. However, as argued in the first section, the professional–client relationship should conform to the fiduciary rather than paternalistic model. If professionals were to disclose confidential information whenever they thought it in the client's best interest, they would be using a paternalistic model. The client's consent and judgment would be ignored. Nevertheless, the threat of very serious injury to a client justifies violation of confidentiality. Consider the case of a nurse who is told by a patient that he is taking a powerful pain killer, but is explicitly asked by the patient not to tell the physician. Suppose the nurse knows that this medication has affected clinical findings (such as blood pressure) making a misdiagnosis likely and can also interact with another medication the patient is taking. Should the nurse preserve the patient's secret?

Such examples make it unwise never to permit a professional to violate confidentiality. Nonetheless, one must guard against permitting the professional to violate confidentiality simply whenever doing so is likely to benefit the client, even if only minimally. Two rules are possible. First, for some situations (nursing, lawyers negotiating), an understanding can be reached with the client that professionals will disclose confidential information for limited purposes when they believe it is in the client's interest, except for items the client explicitly indicates should not be disclosed. Second, in other cases, professionals may disclose information if they sincerely believe failure to do so will probably result in very serious harm to the client's interests. When failure to disclose would merely amount to a missed opportunity to benefit the client, disclosure would not be permissible. Clients have good reason to accept these norms, for confidentiality is secured except when a serious threat of injury to them exists.

Disclosure of confidential information for the sake of the professional is justified in only two kinds of situations: when it is necessary for professionals (1) to collect a just fee or (2) to defend themselves against a charge of wrongdoing. In the first situation, a client should not be permitted to use confidentiality to cheat or defraud a professional. To substantiate the value of their services, professionals often have to explain in some detail what these services were and why they were performed. In the second situation, clients might not wish to have information disclosed for it would show their complicity in wrongdoing. The more difficult problem is when the client has not done anything wrong but does not consent to a professional's disclosure of information. For example, an engineer might be accused of having stolen a production process from a former client, and his present client might refuse to allow information about her new and different process to be disclosed. In these cases, however, protection of the innocent is a more basic value than protection of a client from embarrassment or financial loss.

Finally, disclosure of confidential information can be justifiable because of the interests of others. No one disputes that confidential information may be disclosed when the law requires a professional to do so. The difficult questions are when the law should require disclosure and whether there are other situations in which the interests and values of others ethically justify disclosure although the law does not require it. These issues cannot be considered until professionals' obligations to third parties have been elucidated.

SUMMARY

This chapter has concerned the obligations of professionals arising out of the professional–client relationship. Five ethical models of the professional–client relationship were discussed—agency, contract, friendship, paternalism, and fiduciary. The primary issue between them concerns the respective authority and responsibility of professionals and clients in decision-making. The agency model falsely assumes that a client has sufficient knowledge to direct a professional in most matters, and it encourages professionals to ignore ethical obligations to others. The contract and friendship models both falsely assume that clients have sufficient knowledge to be full partners in the activities. Although this condition is sometimes approximated when organizations employ accountants, architects, or engineers, it rarely holds for individuals employing lawyers, physicians, architects, and accountants. The paternalistic model deprives clients of freedom to direct their own lives and falsely assumes professionals are able to make complex value judgments in behalf of clients.

The fiduciary model presents the best ethical ideal for the professional–client relationship. It recognizes the superior knowledge that professionals have and imposes special obligations upon them in virtue of that superior knowledge, yet it permits clients to make the decisions that importantly affect their lives. Clients must rely on professionals to analyze problems, formulate alternative courses of action, determine the likely consequences of the alternatives, make recommendations, and use their expertise in helping them carry out their decisions. Because clients must rely on professionals, the professionals must be worthy of clients' trust in performing these tasks.

The fiduciary model's implication that professionals must be worthy of client trust provides a criterion for determining professionals' obligations to clients. Six responsibilities of professionals to clients are honesty, candor, competence, diligence, loyalty, and discretion. By definition, a professional must be honest to be worthy of trust. Professionals can be dishonest towards clients by suggesting and providing services that are not useful, as well as by outright theft. Candor is closely related to honesty but includes full disclosure to clients as well as truthfulness. Although lying to clients can probably never be justified, as it effectively destroys a trust relationship, information may be justifiably withheld from clients if necessary to prevent direct harm to them, and if they are told as soon as possible.

Competence raises ethical issues for professionals in deciding when they are not competent to undertake tasks and ensuring that they have kept up with their fields. Diligence is the requirement that a professional work carefully and promptly. Professionals cannot properly argue that they lack time to adequately consider each client's case unless a shortage of professionals means some people would be denied services to which they have a right.

As professionals are hired by clients to protect and promote their interests, they must be loyal to their clients. For accountants performing audits and lawyers making independent evaluations, however, this responsibility is primarily to third parties. A professional's loyalty can be affected by conflicts of interest between the client and the professional, other clients in that transaction or in other cases, or third party payers. Client consent to a professional acting in his or her behalf after disclosure of an actual or possible conflict of interest is a necessary but not sufficient condition to justify a professional accepting a case. The professional must also be able to exercise independent judgment in behalf of the client.

Finally, discretion rests upon the clients' value of privacy in not having information about them conveyed to others without their consent. Even discussion of a client's public activities can be indiscreet. Confidential information about a client may be disclosed for the client's sake if (1) the client has been informed that the professional will do so when he or she judges it to be in the client's best interest and the client has not explicitly refused permission, or (2) disclosure is necessary to prevent significant harm to the client. It may also be disclosed by a professional in order to collect a fee or in self-defense against a charge of wrongdoing. Confidential information may be disclosed to protect others from injury when required by law.

NOTES*

1. See Veatch, "Models for Ethical Medicine," p. 5. Veatch calls this the engineering model of the physician, but this assumes it is appropriate for engineers.

2. See ABA, Commission, *Model Rules,* 1.2(b).

3. Simon, "The Ideology of Advocacy," p. 36.

4. Simon's proposed alternative to the ideology of advocacy suffers these defects to some extent. He does not allow for professional roles. Thus, all professional obligations are at best specifications of ordinary norms. "The foundation principle of non-professional advocacy is that problems of advocacy be treated as a matter of *personal* ethics. . . . Personal ethics apply to people merely by virtue of the fact that they are human individuals. The obligations involved may depend on particular circumstances or personalities, but they do not follow from social role or station." Ibid., p. 131.

5. ABA, *Code of Professional Responsibility,* EC 7-8; see also ABA, Commission, *Model Rules,* 2.1 and comment.

6. Grace, "Invading the Privacy of the Attorney–Client Relationship," p. 47.

7. ABA, *Code of Professional Responsibility,* DR 4-101(C) (3): ABA, Commission, *Model Rules,* 1.6(b).

8. Veatch, "Models for Ethical Medicine," p. 7.

9. See, for example, Masters, "Is Contract an Adequate Basis," p. 25; May, "Code, Covenant, Contract, or Philanthropy," p. 35; Englehardt, "Rights and Responsibilities," pp. 16–17; Richard Wasserstrom, "Lawyers as Professionals: Some Moral Issues," in *1977 National Conference on Teaching Professional Responsibility,* ed. Goldberg, pp. 120–122.

10. Charles Fried, "The Lawyer as Friend: The Moral Foundations of the Lawyer–Client Relationship," in *1977 National Conference on Teaching Professional Responsibility,* ed. Goldberg, pp. 129–158; and Fried, *Right and Wrong,* chap. 7; see also Veatch, "Models for Ethical Medicine," p. 7.

11. Edward A. Dauer and Arthur Allen Leff, "The Lawyer as Friend," in *1977 National Conference on Teaching Professional Responsibility,* ed. Goldberg, p. 164.

12. Simon, "The Ideology of Advocacy," p. 108.

13. Cf. Joseph Ellin, "Comments on 'Paternalism and Health Care,' " in *Contemporary Issues in Biomedical Ethics,* ed. Davis, Hoffmaster, and Shorten, pp. 245–246.

14. See, for example, Glenn C. Graber, "On Paternalism and Health Care," in *Contemporary Issues in Biomedical Ethics,* ed. Davis, Hoffmaster, and Shorten, p. 239; Buchanan, "Medical Paternalism," p. 381; and Goldman, *Moral Foundations,* pp. 179–186.

15. Rosenthal, *Lawyer and Client,* chap. 2.

16. See ABA, *Code of Professional Responsibility,* EC 7-7; but see ABA, Commission, *Model Rules,* 1.2, 1.4.

17. AMA, *Principles of Medical Ethics,* sec. 2.

18. ABA, Special Committee, *Problems and Recommendations,* p. 117.

19. AMA, *Opinions and Reports,* 5.71.

20. Rosenthal, *Lawyer and Client,* pp. 110–112.

21. Bok, *Lying,* pp. 214, 219.

22. See Buchanan, "Medical Paternalism," pp. 376–383.

23. Oken, "What to Tell Cancer Patients," p. 1123.

---

*See the bibliography at the back of the book for complete references.

24. Novack et al., "Changes in Physicians' Attitudes," pp. 897–900.

25. ABA, *Code of Professional Responsibility*, EC 6–1; ABA, Commission, *Model Rules*, 1.1; AMA, *Principles of Medical Ethics*, sec. 5; AICPA, "Rules of Conduct," Rule 201; Engineers' Council, "Code of Ethics," Canon 2.

26. AMA, *Principles of Medical Ethics*, sec. 5; ABA, *Code of Professional Responsibility*, DR 6–101 (A) (3).

27. See ABA, *Code of Professional Responsibility*, Canon 6, DR 6–101(A) (3), and DR 7–101.

28. Martin Garbus and Joel Seligman, "Sanctions and Disbarment: They Sit in Judgment," in *Verdicts on Lawyers*, ed. Nader and Green, p. 54; and Whitney North Seymour, Jr., *Why Justice Fails* (New York: William Morrow, 1973), p. 17.

29. See ABA, Commission, *Model Rules*, 2.3.

30. Patterson and Cheatham, *Profession of Law*, p. 78.

31. ABA, *Code of Professional Responsibility*, Canon 5; ABA, Commission, *Model Rules*, 2.1; AICPA, "Rules of Conduct," Rule 102; Engineers' Council, "Suggested Guidelines," 4, a–f; AMA, *Principles of Medical Ethics* [1957], sec. 6.

32. Bloom, ed., *Lawyers, Clients & Ethics*, pp. 30–35.

33. ABA, *Code of Professional Responsibility*, DR 5–101(A), permits client consent to justify such a relationship, but ABA, Commission, *Model Rules*, 1.7(b), does not allow it to do so if a lawyer's independence of judgment would be impaired.

34. Patterson and Cheatham, *Profession of Law*, p. 223.

35. See generally Thomas D. Morgan, "The Evolving Concept of Professional Responsibility," in *1977 National Conference on Teaching Professional Ethics*, ed. Goldberg, pp. 300–301.

36. See, for example, ABA, *Code of Professional Responsibility*, DR 5–105(C); Engineers' Council, "Suggested Guidelines," 4, c.

37. Hazard, *Ethics in the Practice of Law*, pp. 36, 76.

38. Cf. AMA, *Opinions and Reports*, 5.51(3).

39. Hazard, *Ethics in the Practice of Law*, p. 83.

40. ABA, *Code of Professional Responsibility*, DR 5–107(C); cf. ABA, Commission, *Model Rules*, 5.4; AICPA, "Rules of Conduct," Rules 504, 505.

41. ABA, *Code of Professional Responsibility*, DR 5–107(B); ABA, Commission, *Model Rules*, 5.4(a); AICPA, "Rules of Conduct," Rule 504.

42. See ABA, *Code of Professional Responsibility*, DR 5–107(A) and (B); ABA, Commission, *Model Rules*, 1.8(f); Engineers' Council, "Suggested Guidelines," 4, c.

43. ABA, Commission, *Model Rules*, 2.3.

44. See ABA, *Code of Professional Responsibility*, DR 4–101(C); ABA, Commission, *Model Rules*, 1.6, 2.3, 3.3; AICPA, "Rules of Conduct," Rule 301.

STUDY QUESTIONS AND PROBLEMS

1. What is the relation between an ethical model and empirical conditions? What is the purpose of an ethical model?

2. Annette Beaudais is a wealthy real estate developer. The building next to hers has bought airspace from a city landmark entitling it to construct an apartment building that will block the view from her building. She wishes to

stop this construction by challenging the planning commission's approval. Her attorney, Charles Dunkirk, has developed three arguments for a suit, the strongest one being that the landmark law violates the state constitution. However, Annette does not want to use this argument because she plans to purchase some air rights from a landmark and believes the law is a good way to preserve historic buildings. A lawyer friend advised her that no legal provision has been made for someone other than the chair of the planning commission to preside at meetings, and since the vice chair presided during the hearing about the sale of air rights to the building next to hers, she wants to challenge on those grounds. Dunkirk believes such a challenge to be silly.

Which arguments should be used? Who should make the decision on such matters? Why? What model of the professional–client relationship underlies your answers?

3.   Ernest Friedman, a physician, has a patient, Georgia Hendricks, a young black woman with sickle cell anemia. She has recently delivered a baby girl. Her attacks have been fewer and less severe in recent years. However, Dr. Friedman has recently read an article indicating that if one discounts a few unusually low-risk women, women with sickle cell disease have an almost 10 percent chance of death during pregnancy. He has suggested sterilization to Georgia, but she has previously refused. This new evidence about mortality makes him even more sure that she should be sterilized to avoid another pregnancy. He thinks that if he put the argument to her dramatically, she could probably be convinced to be sterilized. Should he ethically do so? Why or why not? What type of professional–client relationship would be involved should he decide to do so?

4.   Is the contract model of the professional–client relationship appropriate whenever the client is a business firm? Why or why not? Does it make any difference what profession and business are involved? Why?

5.   What are the reasons for journalists keeping news sources confidential? How do they compare with the reasons for confidentiality of attorney–client and physician–patient information? Who is a journalist's client—the source, publisher, or reader? Why? Does your answer affect your views about a journalist's confidentiality of news sources?

6.   Irvine Jacobwitz, an engineer, is hired by Kristine Lovell to make some additions to a project he designed and completed a few years ago. In going over the previous work, he discovers some mistakes in the original design that make it less safe than is desirable. He can correct those mistakes as part of the additions without telling Lovell of the original errors. Should he correct them? Is it ethical not to tell Lovell of the original mistakes? Why or why not?

7.   Morris Newhouse, a physician, was treating Opal Pierce for a number of years. Opal had been bedridden and treated for cancer. During her treatment Dr. Newhouse had prescribed a barbiturate sleeping pill for her. After the active treatment, it became clear she had become addicted to the barbiturate. Consequently, Dr. Newhouse arranged for Opal's pharmacist to prepare pills

that progressively had less barbiturate and more sugar as a substitute, until now Opal is completely off the barbiturate. However, Opal is receiving the placebo (sugar pills). Dr. Newhouse is charging a nominal sum for prescribing the pills and the pharmacist is charging the regular cost of the barbiturate although the actual cost is greater. Was it ethical for Dr. Newhouse to prescribe the placebos to remove Opal's dependency? Opal is paying for medication that she does not biologically need. Is it ethical for the physician and pharmacist to continue to prescribe and give the sugar pills without informing her? Give reasons for your answers.

8. The local newspaper ran a story saying that the city council had passed an ordinance requiring all bicycles to be licensed. This story was incorrect, for the bill had simply come up for first reading and did not require licensing but only provided for voluntary licensing. For the next two days City Hall was deluged with phone calls about the "new ordinance." On the third day, the newspaper ran another story about the rash of phone calls, stating the correct facts about the proposed ordinance. It did not mention the errors in the original story or run a correction notice. Was the newspaper's conduct ethical? Did it have an obligation to acknowledge its mistake? Why or why not?

9. Psychologist Quentin Ross prepared a written report on his patient Sara Thomas stating that she did not have epilepsy. At the same time, Sara was under psychiatric care, and electroencephalograph tests showed the presence of epilepsy. Quentin had not specialized in clinical psychology. Did he unethically take on a question he was not competent to consider? Why or why not?

10. Lawyer Upton Vickers was handling an automobile injury plaintiff's case. Over the past two years, the case had been put on the trial docket four times, and each time it was postponed at the request of the defense counsel. When the case came up the fifth time, he was quite busy on other business. Believing that if the case was reached it would probably be postponed again, he did not go to court until 11:30; trial call was usually at 10:00. Much to his surprise, he discovered that the case had been called. Since no one appeared for the plaintiff, the case had been dismissed with prejudice so that it could not be brought again. Did Upton act unethically? Why or why not? What happens to his client? What should the client be able to do? Why?

11. When county engineer Wanda Xanthasis got married, the equipment dealers and contractors with county contracts got together and pooled their money. They then bought Wanda and her husband a number a gifts, some of them expensive, and a representative gave them to the couple. Is it ethical for Wanda and her groom to keep the gifts? Why or why not?

12. Yves Zorach, an accountant, is contacted by an employee of an existing client corporation. The employee, Adrianne Bates, tells him that she and other personnel of the corporation are going to form a new company to compete with their present employer. They would like him to serve as their accountant. Can Zorach ethically do so? Why or why not? Should he preserve Adrianne's confidence or should he inform his present client? Why?

13. Elaine Fedder, a sixteen-year-old pregnant woman who wants an abortion, visits the local planned parenthood organization. She requests that they not notify her parents. Nurse Clyde Davis phones Elaine at home. When Elaine's mother answers, he does not leave his name or that of the planned parenthood organization, but he does leave the phone number asking Elaine's mother to have her phone them. Elaine's mother phones the number and discovers it is the planned parenthood organization. She confronts Elaine and forces her to have the baby and marry the baby's father, a seventeen-year-old high school student. Was nurse Davis unethical in leaving the phone number? Why or why not? Do parents have an ethical right to be informed of medical treatment for their children? Was the young woman able to consent to the abortion?

14. George Howard is an activist lawyer with political ambitions. A couple of years ago he handled a suit that struck down racial and sexual discriminatory practices of a local corporation. He is also vice president of a local environmental organization. The corporation's factory is now being forced to close due to new local regulations on pollution. The local black organization, which considers him its lawyer, wishes to join the corporation's management in attacking the local regulations on pollution so that the factory can remain open. George would represent the blacks who obtained jobs as a result of his earlier case. The suit would probably be opposed by the environmental organization to which he belongs. Would it be ethical for George to take the case? Would there be a conflict of interest? Would it be unethical for him to refuse the case? Could he ethically remain as general counsel to the black organization and refuse the case? How much, if at all, should his political ambitions affect his decision?

15. Iris Jordan, an accountant and professor at the state university, is preparing an audit case for the use of her students. Is it ethical for her to use the actual audit reports of a client that were submitted as evidence in a court case? Why or why not? In teaching, how much effort must be made to disguise actual cases? When should persons be disguised? Do patients in teaching hospitals automatically consent to the use of their cases for teaching purposes?

16. Mary Niles sees a young junior high student, Karl Long, in her job as counselor. Karl is inclined to brag about his exploits. Today he claims he has a bad hangover as a result of drinking almost a fifth of vodka the previous night. Upon questioning by Mary, he reports that it was at the house of a friend whose parents were away for the evening. During the last month, he proudly asserts, he and his friends have gotten drunk on at least three other occasions when the parents of one of them have been away. Mary knows that Karl has been having trouble with his parents, but he trusts her. Should she inform Karl's parents about his drinking? If not, what should she ethically do? If so, what can she say to Karl?

5 Obligations to Third Parties

Many of the most interesting, important, and difficult problems of professional ethics concern conflicts between a professional's obligations to a client and to others. For a number of reasons, discussions of these problems often appear to sacrifice society's interests to those of individual clients. Many discussions are written by professionals who have been trained to put client interests first and whose arguments tend to reflect that perspective. Codes of ethics focus on obligations of individual professionals to clients, and many discussions unquestioningly accept the existing codes as ethical premises. Also, the American cultural tradition is highly individualistic, emphasizing individual rights more than rights of the public or an individual's obligations to others.

Conflicts between obligations to clients and to others are central to professional ethics. The professional–client relationship requires that a professional devote a special concern to clients that is not given to others. Such responsibilities to clients as loyalty and confidentiality and the weight given to these responsibilities stem from the professional role in relation to clients; the norms are functional. Most of a professional's obligations to others are ordinary norms; they do not stem from a professional role, because there is no special relationship with others. (The chief exceptions to this claim are the relationships of lawyers to courts and of accountants as auditors.) Consequently, when conflicts arise between a professional's obligations to clients and to others, the issue is generally that functional responsibilities to clients must be limited by ordinary responsibilities to others. These responsibilities must be weighed against one another and more precisely defined. In weighing these responsibilities, it is crucial to produce a balance that best preserves and promotes liberal values in society. Sometimes this balance will make it possible to formulate rules that help specify the professional role, but sometimes it provides only general guidance. Before one can attempt to reconcile obligations to clients with those to others, obligations to others must be made explicit.

THIRD PARTIES

The obligations considered in this section are those a professional has to other persons (third parties) when acting for a particular client. According to the agency model of the professional–client relationship, a professional has few if any obligations to others except those established by law. A professional, as a neutral agent of a client, is absolved of responsibility for a client's immoral but legal actions. However, the agency model has been rejected in favor of the fiduciary model, which states that a professional is not completely directed by the client but offers independent advice and service. To the extent professionals are free moral agents, they are responsible for effects on third parties and subject to obligations to them.

The general argument for professional obligations to third parties stems from the role of professions in society. Professions are licensed or informally authorized by society to provide certain types of services promoting basic values such as health, legal justice, financial integrity, and safe structures. The granting of a license and privilege in effect creates a trust for professionals to ensure that these activities are performed in a manner that preserves and promotes liberal values in society. Consequently, professionals always have some obligation to consider whether their activity is compatible with the realization of liberal values by others.

These considerations arise at two levels. One is the level of professional norms; the other is that of particular actions by professionals. In acting in behalf of a client, a professional is permitted to act in a way that best promotes the client's interests within the framework of professional norms. These norms should preserve and promote liberal values, and so doing requires recognition of obligations to third parties. Governance by law, protection from injury, equality of opportunity, and so on cannot be fully realized in society if professionals are permitted to act towards others in any manner they or their clients wish. In arguing against proposed changes in recognized norms, professionals often mistakenly assert that they should act in the best interests of their clients and that proposed changes in norms would hinder their doing so. But the issue is what those norms should be; that norms would hinder professionals doing the most possible for clients does not necessarily indicate improper hindrance of their promoting client interests. To claim otherwise is to assume that the extant norms are correct and thus begs the question.

Truthfulness is one ordinary obligation that professionals have to third parties. As professionals do not have a special relationship of trust to third parties, an obligation of candor is too strong; ordinary citizens are not obligated to fully disclose all information to each other in all their dealings, especially in such situations as bargaining. Although professionals are as justified in withholding information as their clients are, clients are not ethically entitled to lie or deceive. Because their authority stems from that of their clients, professionals cannot be justified in taking actions their clients are not justified in taking. Liberal values are not promoted by institutionalizing a role whose function is to perform immoral actions for citizens that citizens ought not perform themselves. The obligation of truthfulness includes a requirement to provide information that would obviously mislead others should it be withheld.

Another responsibility of a professional is not to injure third parties. A fundamental value of liberal society is to protect people from injury by others. No social role can be justified that permits people to generally injure others. The crucial notion is that of injury. The actions of a lawyer, engineer, management consultant, or realtor in behalf of a client often result in a financial or opportunity loss for another person. Such conduct does not injure that person provided certain conditions are met. In a competitive society, a gain for one person often means a failure to gain by another. The nonbenefit of the latter is not immoral or unjust provided it resulted from fair competition. Social rules define fair competition, and as long as competitors act within them, losers are not wronged by winners. Thus, the fundamental obligations of professionals towards third parties are truthfulness, nonmaleficence, and fairness.

The application of these obligations to third parties is relatively straightforward for physicians. They have a duty to protect others from dangerous patients. Obviously, they should isolate or quarantine patients with dangerous communicable diseases, but more controversial situations also exist. For example, psychotherapists have been held to have a legal duty to warn third parties if their patients are apt to cause them serious physical injury.[1] The difficulties with this situation do not concern the ethical principle. Psychiatrists and the state may invoke involuntary commitment for the mentally ill who are a danger to others. The central problems are whether something less than commitment suffices and the strength of evidence a psychiatrist should have before warning others.

Similarly, a physician who has good reason to believe that a patient's illness poses a danger to others in his employment has a duty to warn the employer. For example, a school bus driver or airline pilot subject to unpredictable blackouts should be reported to an employer. At a more mundane level, when prescribing drugs that seriously impair reactions, physicians should warn patients not to drive. Physicians have an obligation to the patient in such cases, but they also have one to third parties who might be injured.

Physicians also have duties of truthfulness toward third parties. For example, they should not lie on various health forms such as life insurance examination forms. The more difficult problems concern withholding information from third parties, especially at the request of the patient. A patient might request that the patient's spouse not be told that an illness is fatal. How can a physician respond to the spouse when asked how the patient is? Another example is a physician who provides an examination of a man applying for work with the city garbage collection. The employment form asks whether the patient is a heavy drinker, which is defined as someone who has more than six beers a day. The patient does, but the physician knows that many of the employees of the sanitation department also do. If the physician indicates this patient is a heavy drinker he will not be employed. Truthfulness seems to require noting that the patient is a heavy drinker, but one might argue that in this context (for the purpose of determining whether the patient can be as reliable an employee as most others), he is not.

Physicians have to worry about effects on third parties only in some cases, but engineers and architects must almost always do so. In engineering codes of ethics, obligations to third parties are the most fundamental.[2] Almost all architectural and engineering projects have a potential for injuring people. Whether the design is of an automobile, building, electric power system, or sewer system, a faulty design can result in injury to others. Nor should engineers lie to prospective purchasers about the capabilities of equipment they sell.

For accountants, the responsibilities of truthfulness and fairness predominate, since most of the injury they cause others results from a lack of truthfulness or fairness. Auditors certify that financial statements present data fairly, in accordance with generally accepted accounting principles. Failure to be truthful can cause others to make unwise investments. Similarly, lack of fairness in preparing income tax information and forms can injure the government, and thus society.

Lawyers must also usually consider effects on third parties. Lawyers represent clients in their relations to others. Even in drafting a will, the beneficiaries and relatives of the clients will be affected by it. Consequently, lawyers must always take into account the obligations of nonmaleficence and fairness, and often the obligation of truthfulness as well.

The traditional ethics of the legal profession have not emphasized obligations to third parties. Lawyers do recognize an obligation not to aid clients in illegal activities, but if the clients' courses of conduct are legal, they recognize few further obligations towards third parties.[3] The rationale for this position rests upon the adversary system of law. In court, two parties oppose one another and each side marshals the facts and arguments as best it can to support its claims. The court determines which view is correct. Attorneys need not be concerned for the interests of an adverse party, because they will be represented to the court. In a nonadversary system, a trial may be a cooperative activity directed by the judge towards a determination of the truth.

In the adversarial context, the obligations of nonmaleficence and fairness are mitigated. About the only applicable elements of nonmaleficence are those not to bring suits merely to harass others and not to maliciously badger witnesses.[4] Fairness to the opposing party consists in simply abiding by the rules of the tribunal with respect to the conduct of a case; if this is done, the lawyer bears no responsibility for whatever the adverse party may lose. Of course, if the judge or jury makes a bad decision, the losing party is injured by them, but not by the opposing lawyer.

Most writers on legal ethics treat obligations to the court or tribunal as distinct from those to third parties, but in fact they are simply a subclass of them. The obligation of truthfulness applies to the courts, and lawyers should not lie or mislead judges, and they should correct misapprehensions about the law.[5] Traditionally, lawyers have not been thought obligated to disclose facts adverse to their client's case. Modern rules of discovery, which permit the opposing party to request and obtain information, partially eliminate this difficulty, provided the opposing party knows enough to ask for the relevant information. However, a lawyer ought to reveal factual information to the court or opposing party if they are clearly misled by a false factual assumption—for example, a judge giving a suspended sentence because he mistakenly believes the defendent has no prior record.[6] A host of duties of fairness, such as not to bribe witnesses and jurors, also pertain. Probably the most debated question is whether attorneys must report to the opposing party or tribunal if they should discover that a fraud has been perpetrated upon it and their client refuses to correct the matter.[7] Some commentators claim that this rule breaches the confidentiality of the professional–client relation. In one sense it does, since the client's confidence is not preserved. The issue is whether it is justifiable.

In recent years, various commentators have attacked the use of the adversary model for determining the obligations of lawyers.[8] In the nineteenth century most legal work occurred in the adversary context of the courtroom, but during the twentieth century the focus of legal work has shifted to office counseling about prospective conduct. Many authors now distinguish obligations appropriate to the adversary context from those appropriate to the counseling context.[9] In the latter, other affected parties are not present, and unless the lawyer (or the client) considers their interests, they will not be considered at all.

This issue has recently become a center of controversy for lawyers and accountants in securities practice. The Securities and Exchange Commission claims that its limited staff is inadequate to supervise all of the work done in preparing stock prospectuses and other materials. Consequently, it has decided to hold accountants who prepare financial statements and lawyers who prepare opinion letters liable not only for the statements and opinions but also for reasonable attempts to ensure that the facts supplied by clients are accurate.[10] The point is to protect the investing public from stock fraud involving misleading or inaccurate claims presented in prospectuses. Some commentators consider this requirement to be a reasonable application of accountants' and lawyers' obligations to third parties in nonadversary situations.

Two general arguments have been offered against this requirement for lawyers.[11] One argument is that it violates confidentiality of the professional–client relationship. It does violate the provisions of the ABA *Code,* but as the question is the justifiability of those provisions, appeal to them begs the question. The second argument rests upon the adversary system. The claim is that the distinction between adversarial and nonadversarial contexts cannot be maintained, because even in a counseling context a lawyer must act to prevent the client from being disadvantaged in any possible future litigation.

This argument is also deficient. First, it fails to distinguish between adopting a position and ensuring that courts will uphold one. Drafting an instrument so that one's position will be upheld by the courts is one thing; adopting an unfair position is another. Second, one must distinguish between preventing a client from being at a disadvantage (taken advantage of) and taking advantage of another party. Third, when drafting a contract that will be reviewed by attorneys for the other party, one is still in a sort of adversarial context. And the opposing lawyer will examine the contract from his or her client's point of view. Not all contracts or instruments are so reviewed. In drafting installment contracts to be used for the purchase of automobiles, an attorney knows that most automobile purchasers do not take the contracts to their lawyers for review; no bargaining occurs over any contract terms except price. The same applies to the preparation of legal opinions for the issuance of stock certificates. The adversarial model simply does not fit these situations.

The strongest position is that the securities attorney, like an accountant, is an independent expert and either owes no obligation to a client or must view all parties, including potential purchasers, as clients.[12] As indicated in the previous chapter, in such situations a lawyer, like an accountant, is primarily providing information and advice to the third party rather than to the client. In effect, the client takes the role of a third party payer and the third party (in this case a prospective stock purchaser) has the role of client. This being so, the obligations of full disclosure and diligence primarily pertain to those who will rely on the opinion (or financial statement in the case of accountants). These obligations reinforce those of truthfulness and fairness to third parties in requiring lawyers and accountants to take reasonable precautions to prevent corporate clients committing fraud on the public. However, in most cases this peculiar role reversal does not pertain and a method is needed to reconcile professionals' responsibilities to third parties with their responsibilities to clients.

CLIENTS VERSUS OTHERS

The central problem of reconciling obligations to clients and to others must now be confronted. The traditional professional position is that so long as conduct is legally permissible, responsibilities to clients take precedence over ordinary responsibilities to others.[13] Due to their obligations to clients, proper conduct for professionals often differs from that for nonprofessionals. The frequency with which the following comment of Lord Brougham (from the early nineteenth century) is approvingly quoted testifies to the strength with which this view is held.

> An advocate, in the discharge of his duty, knows but one person in all the world, and that person is his client. To save that client by all means and expedients, and at all hazards and costs to other persons, and, amongst them, to himself, is his first and only duty; and in performing this duty he must not regard the alarm, the torments, the destruction which he may bring upon others. Separating the duty of a patriot from that of an advocate, he must go on reckless of the consequences, though it should be his unhappy fate to involve his country in confusion.[14]

Taken literally, Brougham's comment would be the strongest possible claim to violate ordinary morality, for he does not even restrict the means used to legal ones. However, in the original context of a thinly veiled threat to expose the king's adulterous affairs should charges be brought against his client, the queen, Brougham implicitly restricted the means to legal ones. And almost everyone agrees that professionals should restrict themselves to legal means, except for rare acts of civil disobedience such as courtroom disruptions.[15]

The problem of reconciling responsibilities to clients and to others can be broken into more discrete issues. One issue is how the *law* should balance professionals' obligations to clients and to others. Should accountants who are not auditors be legally required to report cases of fraudulent corporate balance sheets? Should engineers be legally required to report poorly designed products to consumer protection agencies? Should physicians be legally required to report cases of child abuse, gunshot wounds, and venereal disease to authorities? Ought lawyers be legally required to report confidential information received from clients, such as where murderers have left their victims' bodies or their clients' intentions to commit crimes? Simply stating that professionals must act within the law provides no guidance as to what the law should be.

A second issue concerns balancing obligations when the conduct is within legal limits. Can any legally permissible means be used to assist clients, regardless of how well these means conform to the dictates of ordinary norms? Since the conduct of lawyers in assisting their clients almost always affects others, whereas the conduct of other professionals is less likely to do so, these issues are more pressing for lawyers. Nonetheless, all consulting professionals occasionally face them.

One difficulty in analyzing these problems concerns the basis for claiming that conduct is contrary to ordinary norms. If it is illegal, at least a community has clearly judged that it ought not to be engaged in. If it is not illegal, in a pluralistic society, a generally accepted judgment of its morality might not exist. However, the question is not whether the conduct is contrary to what most people believe to be wrong, but whether it is contrary to a rationally defensible ethics applying to nonprofessionals. Furthermore, this aspect is often not in question, because the conduct is detrimental to others and thus violates an ordinary norm not to injure others. In a few cases, such as abortion, that is disputed, but it does not affect the issue under consideration—whether professionals are sometimes exempt from ordinary ethics whatever it requires.

A few brief examples will illustrate the type of problems involved in reconciling ordinary responsibilities to others with special ones to clients. Suppose a consulting engineer discovers a defect in a structure that is about to be sold. If the owner will not disclose the defect to the potential purchaser, ought the engineer do so? Suppose a lawyer learns that a client intends to commit perjury on the witness stand. Should the lawyer report the client's intentions to the authorities? May the lawyer morally put the client on the stand? Suppose a physician diagnoses a man as having Huntington's chorea, a fatal genetic disease usually not manifested until after the age of thirty. Further suppose that the man tells the physician that he does not want his wife to know, because he wants to have children and she might not be willing if she knew they could be affected with the disease. Should the physician respect the patient's request?

One argument is that a professional, especially a lawyer, must distinguish between the wrongs permitted by a reasonably just legal system and personal wrongs.[16] A lawyer ought not commit personal wrongs such as lying to a judge or abusing a witness. However, in asserting a technical point, such as a statute of limitations to defeat a legal claim, a lawyer is acting as a representative of the client, for the act is legally defined. When lawyers act as representatives and not personally, they are insulated from responsibility.[17]

Several difficulties confront this view. A major problem is distinguishing between representative and personal acts. That distinction might be based on how the acts are defined. Filing motions and making objections are acts defined by the legal system, while lying and abusing persons are not so defined but have meaning independent of the legal system. This distinction is not clear-cut, however; lying to a judge can be defined independent of the legal system, but the act can also be described as committing a fraud upon a tribunal. A judge is defined by a position within a legal system, so even "lying to a judge" is not completely specifiable independent of a legal system. Humiliating a witness can also be described as cross-examining a witness, which is a legally defined act. Conduct can be properly described in more than one way, and some descriptions of an act might refer to a legal system and others not.

Even if it can be made, the distinction between wrongs a system permits and those done personally has limited applicability. It best applies to an attorney in a trial situation. In counseling or negotiating, fewer of an attorney's acts are defined by reference to the legal system. Indeed, as negotiation also occurs completely outside a legal context, probably no acts of negotiation are necessarily defined by the legal system. The distinction is also perforce restricted to lawyers. The acts of architects and most other professionals are not defined by similar systems of rules. The analysis will not apply to professional ethics generally, or if it is applied, will confine other professionals to all the requirements of ordinary norms.

More fundamentally, even granting the distinction, why should the way an act is defined have conclusive weight in determining the morality of conduct? Presumably the reason is that the legal system allocates rights in order to peaceably settle disputes and that objections to injustice the system permits should be corrected through the political process. But many ethical constraints limit conduct that is not beyond the realm of legal tolerance; it would be a morally deficient society in which everyone pursued his or her claims to the extent of the law. No argument is given why acts performed in a representative capacity are subject only to legal constraints and not also ethical ones. This analysis places legal rights above ethical considerations. No reasons exist to so exalt legality.

Difficulties ensue from distinguishing between the conduct of a person in a professional role and as a private citizen. "Costs" are involved in ascribing an amoral character to a lawyer's activities in the professional role.[18] Arguments like the above for allowing such conduct assume that the legal system is just. To the degree the legal institution is not just or wise, such role-differentiated norms can be undesirable. A lawyer's character will also be adversely affected. As lawyers, they need to be competitive, aggressive, ruthless, and pragmatic. Such traits cannot be readily confined to the professional role. These character traits usually affect most conduct and are relatively permanent.

At this point a way is needed to resolve conflicts between a professional's obligations to clients and to others. Just as religious obligations are limited by ordinary ethical norms and law when they adversely affect persons outside the sect, so professional responsibilities to clients must be limited by ethical responsibilities to others. A balancing of these responsibilities cannot be done solely on a case-by-case basis, for many detrimental effects of general professional practice do not result in single cases. In short, the issue is how one determines the norms of professional roles. This issue cannot be settled within the perspective of professionals, because it is the one that is to be determined. Reference must be made to the broader framework of liberal values.

The approach here is to adopt a consumer perspective and consider what balance would most protect and promote the values of a liberal society. In particular, the proposed test is to ask what balance of responsibilities a reasonable person who may be in the role of client or affected person would find best promotes a society with the values of governance by law, freedom, equality of opportunity, prevention of harm, welfare, and privacy. The balancing is between what people would want done for themselves as clients and the effect of such conduct upon themselves as affected third parties.[19] The proposed test subjects professionals to ordinary ethical norms. It evaluates professional responsibilities by the values of society and ordinary citizens, yet ordinary citizens make allowances for the particular functions professionals play in society.

The procedure has three important steps. First, one must identify and weigh the values of the client against those of others who will be affected. Unlike a standard utilitarian analysis—determining the rightness of actions by their producing the greatest balance of happiness over unhappiness—this evaluation is not done simply on the basis of the happiness of the persons affected. Second, one must consider the general probability of one being in either position—client or affected third party. This consideration is especially important for issues in which many persons are affected. Third, one must remember that one is considering rules for professional roles; one is not deciding a particular case and one will not be able to give a different answer for a later similar case. In general, the procedure is designed to foster asking whether one would rather live in a society with professionals governed by one set of norms or another. Consideration of examples will clarify the procedure.

The simplest case is that in which only three parties are involved—a professional, a client, and one affected party. An example is a consulting engineer who has found a structural defect in a building that the client, a seller, has not revealed to the prospective buyer. The engineer's report was confidential, and should the prospective purchaser learn of the defect, the price would go down. The client's values involved are confidentiality and financial interests. The prospective purchaser's affected values are financial but can also be physical safety. If the defect makes the premises unsafe, then any occupant could be injured or killed.

To apply the recommended procedure, one should ask whether one would be willing to risk the financial loss and injury for financial gain and confidentiality. Due to the importance of physical safety, a reasonable person would conclude that knowledge of the defect as a purchaser is more important. Therefore, a reasonable person would support a rule that obligates the engineer to inform the prospective purchaser of the defect.

To show the significance of the weighing of values, one can compare this case with one in which an engineer has determined that modification of a structure to the owner's desired use would be prohibitively expensive. In this situation, a prospective buyer would not risk physical safety; however, knowledge of the engineer's report would give the buyer a bargaining advantage over the client. The values to be compared are financial interests and confidentiality for the client and financial interests for the prospective purchaser. A reasonable person would prefer a norm by which the engineer respects confidentiality in this case. Purchasers are capable of protecting themselves from financial loss as they need not offer more for something than it is worth to them, even though a seller might have been willing to sell for less.

More complex cases arise when a large number of persons might be affected by a client's conduct. In these cases, the values of the affected persons must be weighted by the number of persons involved. One way to do this is to weight the values by the general probability of being a client or affected party. An example will clarify this point. Suppose a business consultant hired by the management of a corporation learns that the balance sheet, although done according to accepted accounting procedures, gives a deceptively favorable impression of the financial strength of the corporation. The management's values are financial interests, including job security, and confidentiality. The affected parties include all stockholders as well as potential stock purchasers. Although the financial loss to management of the actual financial position becoming known is probably greater than for any particular stockholder, there are many more stockholders. Consequently, to apply the recommended procedure, one must use the general probability of being a stockholder versus that of being a member of management. As ordinary people are much more likely to be stockholders, at least through a retirement system, they will prefer a norm requiring disclosure to one requiring the preservation of confidentiality. Thus, the consultant should break confidentiality in this case.

Perhaps the most discussed issue of reconciling a professional's responsibility to keep client communications confidential and ordinary responsibilities to the public is whether criminal defense attorneys ought to inform on clients who commit perjury. Monroe H. Freedman contends that a lawyer's responsibility of confidentiality overrides the public's values of conviction of criminals and avoidance of perjury. He maintains that if a lawyer knows a client is going to commit perjury, he or she ought not reveal either the intention to do so or that it has been done.[20] Freedman emphasizes the problems of alternatives. If the attorney does not guarantee confidentiality, then the client will not confide in him. If the attorney seeks to withdraw from the case or ignore the testimony, the judge or jury will infer that the client lied. Nonprofessionals arguably have an obligation to report such conduct and even if they do not, it is surely permissible for them to do so. Thus Freedman's view clearly places professionals under a set of norms different from the ordinary ones.

Freedman assumes a full-blown adversary model of the legal system. Although that model fits the criminal trial context better than others, even there it need not be unmitigated by considerations of ordinary morality. Such considerations could limit confidentiality by prohibiting the performance of, or assistance in, acts that are unethical or illegal. The basic issue is the extent to which the adversary model should be applied, even in criminal cases. Freedman's assumption begs that question.

By the proposed test, the question is whether reasonable people would forgo the increase in convictions should lawyers be obligated to inform in order to be able to perjure themselves without their lawyer informing on them. Many people might immediately respond that lawyers should inform on clients, because they (the responders) would never be criminal defendants and would have nothing to fear from such a policy. That is not the appropriate test, however. One must instead imagine that one is choosing between the values for oneself, that one must sacrifice one set of values for another. Thus, the procedure was specified as using the general probability of one being in positions, that is, the general probability of a member of the population being a criminal defendant.

Given that clarification, one must realistically examine the consequences of alternative policies. Requiring lawyers to inform on clients will only slightly increase convictions. Most convictions are guilty pleas to reduced charges. That also means few occasions for perjury exist. Few people dispute that attorneys in civil cases should reveal their client's perjury. The reason is either that a specific person is injured by the testimony or that the defendant has less at stake—only financial interests rather than liberty. Although the effects are less direct and affect unidentified individuals, the harm from criminal offenses is surely greater than from civil cases, which counterbalances the greater loss to the defendant. Nor does it follow that a defendant can get a mistrial by simply committing perjury. An attorney might be required to complete the trial (either arguing or not arguing a defendant's perjured testimony) and to inform authorities afterwards for purposes of prosecution.

The value choice is avoidance of conviction of the innocent and adequate legal defense versus conviction of the guilty and preservation of the legal system from corruption. As lying does not significantly help prevent conviction of the innocent, a reasonable person would hold that lawyers should inform. Such a system might mean more clients would lie to their attorneys, but the alternative is to permit attorneys to knowingly assist clients in lying to the court. No clear reason exists for a reasonable person to prefer the latter to the former.

The same general considerations that apply to the criminal defense attorney whose client wishes to commit perjury apply to other cases of unethical or illegal conduct by clients. For example, an accountant or engineer might learn of illegal activities of a client such as deliberate violations of building codes. The strongest claim to confidentiality is of a criminal attorney with his client, for liberal norms of criminal justice strictly preserve the right not to incriminate oneself. As the claim of confidentiality is weaker in these other situations, release of confidential information is justified by preventing greater injuries to third parties. Often the illegal or unethical conduct will be that of an employee in a client firm, in which case a professional might be able to prevent the wrongdoing by informing the employee's supervisor. If the supervisor will not rectify the situation, then one must take the matter to the next higher authority. Eventually, if the matter is serious enough—a significant violation of a law or government regulation—the matter might have to be taken to corporate stockholders or government authorities.[21]

One final complex example will be given. Consider whether physicians should report wanted criminals who come to them for medical treatment. Such a situation arose in 1972 when the FBI published in the *Archives of Dermatology* a wanted notice of a woman indicted for conspiracy in interstate transportation of explosives.[22] Because the woman had a skin disease, the FBI hoped that she would see a dermatologist for treatment and the dermatologist would then report her. Subsequent discussion concerned whether a medical journal should publish such a notice, but the underlying issue is whether a physician should report such persons to authorities. If they should, then informing them about wanted persons by such notices is appropriate. If they should not, such notices would do little good if physicians acted ethically. (Of course, notices might tempt them to act unethically.)

No ethical objection would arise were a nonprofessional to spot the woman and report her. Wanted posters used to be in the post office for all to see. The only likely objections to publishing wanted notices in *Reader's Digest* or *Time* are apt to be concern for the effectiveness of the technique and the dangers resulting from the general public looking for criminals. If professionals ought not to report their clients, their ethical obligations differ from those of ordinary citizens due to an overriding responsibility to their clients.

The question is whether a reasonable person with liberal values would prefer a system in which physicians reported patients wanted by authorities to one in which they did not. If patients were reported, then law enforcement and crime prevention might improve. However, many wanted persons would forgo medical treatment rather than risk being apprehended. The number reported and apprehended would thus be fewer than the number who would see physicians without a reporting requirement. Suspects would suffer greater harm as they would not receive medical attention.

Many people might immediately respond that patients should be reported, that they (the responders) would not mind because they themselves would never be criminal suspects. As indicated above, however, that is not the appropriate test. Instead, one should consider the probabilities of either happening so that one is trading a probability of a loss of confidentiality for a probable increase in protection by better law enforcement.

Given this clarification, a reasonable person's view would probably vary with the crime of which a person is suspected and the seriousness of the person's medical problem. A rule that suspects' confidentiality be preserved if they have a serious medical condition but not otherwise is unworkable. The rule allows physicians so much discretion that suspects would be unable to predict whether they would be reported. Suspects would have to be able to diagnose their own ailment to determine whether a physician should report them. As a result, many suspects would fail to see physicians and both goals—treatment of serious injuries and apprehension of suspects—would be defeated.

Consequently, only the seriousness of the crime provides a workable rule. A plausible rule is that physicians should report only persons suspected of crimes of violence. As conspiracy is not a violent crime, in this case the rule suggests that the woman ought not be reported. If conspiracy is justifiably a criminal activity, perhaps physicians should also report persons for conspiracy to commit violent crimes. The value promoted by reporting persons suspected of violent crimes is protection of life and physical well-being. As that value is also at stake in conspiracy to commit violent crimes, the same justification applies to it, except for differences in the likelihood of injury occurring. In short, as life and physical integrity are at stake in violent crimes, a reasonable person would prefer avoidance of personal harm over medical treatment and protection of confidentiality as a suspect. When a lesser value of a potential or real victim is at stake, a reasonable person may not have such a preference.

This discussion has not attempted to distinguish between those professional norms that should be legally enforced and those that should be left to the realm of other techniques. To make that distinction, one needs to consider such matters as costs, effectiveness, and fairness of enforcement. Instead, the purpose has been to illustrate an intellectual procedure for determining the substantive content of professional norms. The point of considering these specific cases has not been to provide definitive solutions but to illustrate the proposed test for balancing professionals' obligations to clients with obligations to others. Professionals are not completely exempt from the constraints of ordinary norms, but the functions of their professions in society must be taken into account in the balancing process. Even then, the balancing should not be done on the basis of the values peculiar to particular professions but from the perspective of a reasonable nonprofessional in society judging by justifiable liberal values. Consequently, even the special weight that professionals may give to client interests is ultimately justified by considerations of ordinary ethics. Ordinary norms apply to everyone, but the various situations and roles of people in society sometimes require somewhat different conduct for the sake of achieving liberal values.

SUMMARY

This chapter has concerned professionals' obligations to third parties, people other than their clients. These obligations are those of ordinary norms, because professionals have no special relationship to third parties. The three fundamental obligations of professionals to third parties are truthfulness, nonmaleficence, and fairness. Candor, with its requirement of full disclosure, does not pertain, because the professional does not have a special trust relationship to third parties.

Conflicts between functional responsibilities to clients and ordinary obligations to third parties are at the heart of professional ethics. The proposed test for reconciling these conflicting responsibilities is to identify and weigh the values of the client against those of third parties who will be affected, consider the general probability of being a client or affected third party, and remember that one is developing a rule to be applied to all similar cases. The result of such a procedure will frequently be a rule that reconciles the considerations in conflicting responsibilities. The procedure does not guarantee that all reasonable persons will arrive at the same conclusion; reasonable people with liberal values may disagree due to subtle differences in weighing values, attitudes toward risk, or differences about factual matters. Nonetheless, great differences will be eliminated and a basis provided for reasonable discussion.

NOTES*

1. *Tarasoff* v. *Regents of the University of California,* 17 Cal. 3d 425, 551 P. 2d 334, 131 Cal. Rptr. 14 (1976). See also Comment, *"Tarasoff* and the Psychotherapist's Duty to Warn," pp. 932–951.

2. Engineers' Council, "Code of Ethics," Canon 1; National Society of Professional Engineers, "Code of Ethics," sec. 2.

---

*See the bibliography at the end of the book for complete references.

3. One of the advantages of the American Bar Association, Commission on Evaluation of Professional Standards, *Model Rules of Conduct* over the American Bar Association, *Code of Professional Responsibility,* is its greater emphasis on obligations to third parties. See, for example, *Model Rules,* 3.3(d), 3.4, 3.9, and 4.1.

4. ABA, *Code of Professional Responsibility,* DR 7–102 (A) (1); American College of Trial Lawyers, *Code of Trial Conduct,* 15(e).

5. ABA, *Code of Professional Responsibility,* DR 7–106 (B) (1); ABA, Commission, *Model Rules,* 3.3(a) and (b).

6. ABA, Commission, *Model Rules,* 3.3(a) (2) and 4.1(b) (1).

7. ABA, *Code of Professional Responsibility,* DR 7–102 (B) (1); ABA, Commission, *Model Rules,* 3.3(b).

8. The strongest and most broad-ranging attack is Simon, "The Ideology of Advocacy," pp. 29–114.

9. See Cheek, "Professional Responsibility," p. 620; the ABA *Code of Professional Responsibility* comes close to making the distinction in EC 7–3; and it is explicit in the structure of the ABA, Commission, *Model Rules.*

10. See Cheek, "Professional Responsibility," p. 597; Joseph A. Califano, Jr., "The Washington Lawyer: When to Say No," in *Verdicts on Lawyers,* ed. Nader and Green, p. 194; Donald J. Evans et al., "Responsibility of Lawyers' Advising Management," and Arthur F. Mathews, "Liabilities of Lawyers under the Federal Securities Laws," in ABA, National Institute Proceedings, "Advisors to Management," pp. 13–40 and 105–155, respectively, esp. p. 31, on this point.

11. "ABA Statement of Policy Regarding Responsibilities and Liabilities of Lawyers in Advising with Respect to Laws Administered by the SEC," *Business Lawyer* 31 (1975): 543–544; and Freedman, "Civil Libertarian," pp. 287–288.

12. Stuart Charles Goldberg, "Policing Responsibilities of the Securities Bar: The Attorney–Client Relationship and the Code of Professional Responsibility—Considerations for Expertizing Securities Attorneys," in *1977 National Conference on Teaching Professional Responsibility,* ed. Goldberg, pp. 19–66. The ABA, Commission, *Model Rules,* 2.3, essentially takes this position.

13. According to Geoffrey C. Hazard, Jr., the ABA *Code* holds that lawyers owe clients almost unqualified loyalty and owe others only what is compatible with that obligation; see Hazard, *Ethics in the Practice of Law,* p. 8.

14. Quoted in Freedman, *Lawyers' Ethics,* p. 9.

15. See AMA, *Principles of Medical Ethics,* sec. 3; Lieberman, *Crisis at the Bar,* pp. 168–169.

16. Charles Fried, "The Lawyer as Friend: The Moral Foundations of the Lawyer–Client Relationship," in *1977 National Conference on Teaching Professional Responsibility,* ed. Goldberg, p. 153; see also Fried, *Right and Wrong,* pp. 191–193.

17. Fried, *Right and Wrong,* p. 183.

18. Richard Wasserstrom, "Lawyers as Professionals: Some Moral Issues," in *1977 National Conference on Teaching Professional Responsibility,* ed. Goldberg, pp. 116–118.

19. This test differs from Alan Goldman's proposed test of asking whether impartial contractors would agree to permitting lawyers to violate the moral rights of third parties so that they might do the same in one's behalf; see Goldman, *Moral Foundations,* p. 144. First, the reasonable person is not assumed to be impartial but only to have limited benevolence and to hold liberal values. Second, the proposed test is to help determine what rights should be recognized by appealing to underlying interests and values, whereas Goldman assumes certain rights. The issue is, however, what interests or rights of third parties should be recognized to override conflicting obligations to, or interests of, clients.

20. Freedman, *Lawyers' Ethics,* chap. 3, esp. pp. 27, 40. See also ABA, *Code of Professional Responsibility,* DR 4–101 (C) (3), DR 7–102 (A) (4), and DR 7–102 (B) (1); ABA *Opinion* 314 (1965); and ABA, Commission, *Model Rules,* 3.3 and comment.

21. See ABA, Commission, *Model Rules,* 1.13 (b) and (c).

22. See Gaylin, "FBI Poster," pp. 1–3.

STUDY QUESTIONS AND PROBLEMS

1. Asher Bausch and his wife, Ashkenazic Jews, went to the local genetics unit to be tested for the chances of having a child with Tay Sachs disease. This recessive genetic disorder is untreatable and produces blindness, motor paralysis, and other symptoms leading to death, usually before the age of three. The tests showed that Asher was a carrier but his wife was not. While he and his wife were not at risk of having a child with the defect, Asher's brothers had a 50 percent chance of being carriers, and if they married an Ashkenazic Jew, the chances were 1 in 30 that she would be a carrier and so the odds were 1 in 60 that they would have an affected infant. When Dr. Cloe Dunlop explained these facts, Asher became upset. Dr. Dunlop asked Asher to send his brothers a letter the genetics unit had prepared suggesting that they be tested for the carrier status. Asher refused. He felt ashamed and could not bring himself to tell his brothers. Would it be ethical for Dr. Dunlop to write the brothers and recommend that they have genetic screening? Why or why not?

2. Edgar Farr is representing his client who has been convicted on a criminal charge. They are now before the judge for sentencing. The judge asks the clerk if Farr's client has a criminal record, and the clerk says he does not. However, Edgar knows that his client does have a record. While he is trying to decide what to do, the judge says, "As this is your first offense, I shall give you a suspended sentence." What should Farr do? Why?

3. A clinical psychologist, Gerri Hudson, is treating Irwin Johnson, who was referred to her as being near a nervous breakdown. After a few sessions, Irwin confesses to having murdered someone. Gerri does not think Irwin will murder again and thinks that she can assist him whether or not he turns himself in to the police, as he is thinking of doing. What should she ethically do? Why?

4. Engineer Katherine Lowell works for the Bright Lights Power Co. In examining the plant of a subscriber, Widgets, Inc., she discovers that Widgets can save considerable money by making a few inexpensive modifications at its plant. Should she inform Widgets or Bright Lights of this fact? Why?

5. As President of Global, Inc., Malcolm Nevis has aggressively promoted the company. He has taken over various other companies and significantly increased Global's earnings. He has insisted that Global's accountants follow liberal methods so long as they conform to generally accepted accounting principles. Olive Patterson, Global's chief accountant, is rather worried about

some of the methods Malcolm has insisted on. Global sold a subsidiary for $2,750,000 and Nevis wants to count $1,750,000 as profit for last year, although the subsidiary would not have contributed nearly that much to earnings for several years. He wants to include as earnings for last year oil and gas production payments for the next two years that were sold to another corporation. He also wants to include last year's earnings of three new subsidiaries purchased at the beginning of this year. Finally, President Nevis wants to capitalize over several years the administrative expenses of a subsidiary that would otherwise show a large loss. All of these items are within generally accepted accounting principles. If they are followed, however, will they provide a fair statement of Global's financial condition? Would they mislead potential investors? Is it ethical for the accountants to follow President Nevis's instructions? Why or why not? If not, what should Olive Patterson do? Why?

6. Attorney Quincy Reynolds is representing Trickle, Inc., in a contract negotiation with the Fillers Union. They are only a few cents apart on the wage increase. The union's chief negotiator, Susan Toms, phones Quincy and suggests that Trickle might release ten employees who do not belong to the union and who are not essential to Trickle's operations. The union will not support any grievance the employees may file, and Trickle will save more than enough money to meet the union's wage demands. What should Reynolds do? Must he convey the offer to Trickle's president? What should he recommend? Why?

7. Uriah Vishman was hired to audit two state institutions. He discovered serious irregularities and perhaps fraud. He reported his findings to his superior, but no action was taken. He then went to the district attorney, who was a close friend of the governor, who was running for reelection. The district attorney refused to take any action at this time, informally suggesting that he might do so after the election. Ethically, what should Uriah do? Should he make his findings public? Has he fulfilled his responsibilities by reporting to the appropriate authorities? Who are his actual employers?

8. Wilma Xuan is editor of the Clinton *Courier*. She receives a visit from Albert Bateman and a Mrs. Charles Douglas III. The day before, Mr. Bateman's wife had been arrested at a local department store for shoplifting $5.26 worth of goods. She had her four-year-old son with her. At her trial she claimed she had not taken the goods and that her son had probably put them in the shopping bag while she was looking at something else. However, a store detective testified that he had seen her take the items. As a warning to other shoplifters at Christmas time, the judge sentenced Mrs. Bateman to a week in jail instead of the usual $100 fine. Mrs. Douglas tells Wilma that Mrs. Bateman had been her maid for several years after immigrating to this country, was completely honest, and would not do such a thing. She is staying with Mr. Bateman to take care of the children while Mrs. Bateman is in jail. Mr. Bateman asks Wilma not to print any story about Mrs. Bateman's conviction or at least to delete her name. If her name appears, their two young children will be

subjected to harassment by other children; Mrs. Bateman will not be able to face their neighbors, so they will have to sell their recently purchased home and move to another neighborhood. What should Wilma ethically do? If she withholds the name, will she be depriving the readers of information to which they have a right? Can justice operate in secret? Should the innocent children suffer for their mother's wrong?

6 Obligations to the Profession

In the social structure of American society, professionals are at the top—in prestige, wealth, and power within their own communities and the country as a whole. This leading role is partly due to their being among the best educated people in society, which prepares them for leadership outside their profession. Because they make many decisions that significantly affect others, they share responsibility for the realization of liberal values in society.

Most ethical codes recognize a responsibility for the public good.[1] This responsibility belongs to a profession as a whole. In their respective areas, the professions contain almost all the available expertise and have a near monopoly over implementation of social policies. Other people can design and administer health, legal, or construction programs, but professionals provide their day-to-day implementation. For example, legislatures, health system agencies, district councils, and hospital boards—consisting of many or mostly lay members—set many health care policies. Nevertheless, the practical administration of many of these policies is done by members of the health care professions. Many administrators in the medical side of the Department of Health and Human Services are physicians. At the most concrete level, decisions by physicians to order this or that diagnostic procedure or to institute one treatment regimen or another determines whether many policies are effectively implemented. In the legal profession, policy implementation is controlled by judges, prosecutors, and private attorneys. Construction engineers implement consultants' designs, and engineers take a large part in the development and enforcement of safety and pollution control policies. Given their special knowledge and actual services, responsibility for implementing policies for the public good is to a large extent unavoidably a matter for the professions.

Responsibility for public good has three main facets. First are activities of social leadership, such as service with charitable organizations, government commissions, and so on. This participation is due more to professionals' positions in the social structure than to their special knowledge. Such responsibility also devolves upon business people and others occupying prominent positions or having the time to contribute, such as knowledgeable homemakers.

A second facet of responsibility for public good is the improvement of professional knowledge, tools, and skills. For physicians and engineers, improvement of service primarily concerns research; for lawyers and accountants, it chiefly concerns reform. However, all professions have responsibility for both research and reform; only the relative emphasis differs.

A third facet of this responsibility is to preserve and enhance the role of the profession itself. Professionals maintain that the continued high status and respect of their profession is for the ultimate benefit of society. Ethical questions arise when professionals use their talents in the aid of special interests that conflict with, or are contrary to public interest.

The last two facets of responsibility for the public good support obligations of individual professionals to their professions and are the subject of this chapter. These responsibilities are those of a profession as a whole and are not reducible to precisely similar obligations of individual professionals. No one individual professional can be responsible for research and reform, for example; both must be products of the whole profession. Moreover, the freedom of individual professionals would be unnecessarily limited if each were required to participate in, say, research. Such a requirement is unnecessary, though, because all appropriate research could be conducted by some members of a profession.

Nonetheless, individual professionals have obligations to assist the professions in improving skills and in maintaining a position that enables them to fulfill their social role. Although the ultimate beneficiary is the general public, for individual professionals the obligation is immediately to the profession. Unfortunately, individuals sometimes forget that their ultimate justification must be the good of society, just as Richard Nixon's advisers forgot that an obligation to assist a president must rest ultimately upon the public benefit. Professionals are sometimes blindly devoted to the profession regardless of the effect upon liberal values.

RESEARCH AND REFORM

Responsibility for research in their respective fields devolves upon professionals as the only people qualified to perform it. Only they have the necessary knowledge. Reform can be pursued by nonprofessionals, but only with significant assistance from professionals. To undertake reform of automobile insurance or safety law, for example, requires information about the possible alternatives and their likely consequences. Lawyers, insurance agents, and engineers must provide such information as the public and legislators lack experience in these areas.

Other important reasons exist for professionals to carry a significant part of the burden of reform. Knowing social defects in their fields, they are better prepared to pursue reform than nonprofessionals. In their work they frequently discover matters needing reform and for which no organized reform group exist. If reform and enhancement of liberal values are to occur, they must at least advance reform enough to interest a significant group of nonprofessionals in pursuing it.

Implementing the results of research and reform studies is an issue for society in general. The function of professionals in reform is similar to their function with respect to clients. Professionals diagnose the problems, suggest alternative approaches, predict likely consequences, make recommendations, and implement programs. The decision to adopt a program, however, is a value judgment for which professionals have no more training and expertise than particular clients or the public. Thus, these decisions are for the public either at large or democratically elected representatives.

A couple of general questions concern research and reform by professionals. The first question is who does or should carry them out. Not everyone is equally competent at, or interested in, these activities. For the most part, the decision to engage in them should be left to the individual professionals. Nevertheless, professionals who do not actively engage in either have an obligation to promote and support such activity by other members of their profession. In their daily work they can keep their eyes open for areas in which research or reform is needed and call attention to the needs they perceive.

A second question concerns the funding of research and reform activities. Several centuries ago most research was privately funded. Either the researcher or private benefactors supported it. Today, few private individuals can afford to fund research. Most research funds come from society, the government being the major source of research funds.[2] Since the results of research add to society's store of knowledge, that is probably as it should be. Private foundations are another important source of funding for professional research. In part, governments indirectly support these foundations by their tax exempt status. A third major source of funding is private corporations. They do not usually support so-called basic research but only that which has potential for relatively immediate benefits to them. The proportion of funding from these sources varies greatly among the professions. For example, engineers receive much, and lawyers little, of their research funding from private corporations. In contrast to research, most reform efforts are perhaps the result of labor, business, or private voluntary groups. Government studies and reform projects are often begun only after another group has exerted considerable pressure for reform.

The funding of research and reform by private corporations or interest groups raises a crucial ethical issue concerning the professionals' independence of judgment. When corporations fund research, they are usually interested in certain results. For example, drug companies want their drugs proven safe and effective. As the researchers depend on corporation grants for their funding, they might be biased in favor of them. Tests have been designed and results presented so as to appear to support conclusions more strongly than they do. But even if research is unbiased, reformers as well as corporations often present biased interpretations of it.

The primary responsibilities of professionals engaged in research and reform are candor and independence. These are essentially the same as the responsibilities professionals have to their clients and they rest upon similar considerations, namely, the users' needs for complete and unbiased information. Few people would dispute that researchers must be candid and independent in their judgments. The purpose of research is to discover the truth. A lack of candor or independence thwarts this purpose. Some people deny that candor and independence pertain to reform activity. Although these factors are mitigated in the context of reform activity in the United States, they are still relevant. The following discussion considers these obligations and others with respect to research and reform.

Research

Because medical and social sciences are directly concerned with human beings, they often use human subjects in experiments. Ethical issues of human experimentation are far too complex to adequately discuss here. Congress established the National Commission for the Protection of Human Subjects of Biomedical and Behavioral Research, which spent several years exploring different aspects of the topic.[3] After the mandate of the National Commission expired, the President's Commission for the Study of Ethical Problems in Medicine and Biomedical and Behavioral Research was established to continue its work and to consider other problems.

Informed consent is the most fundamental requirement in research with human subjects.[4] Obtaining this consent is part of a responsibility of nonmaleficence. Without the subjects' consent, any harm that befalls them is injury. The elements of informed consent are (1) a capacity to understand and choose; (2) an explanation of the experiment, its alternatives, and the risks and potential benefits of each option; and (3) free and voluntary consent. A responsibility of candor is central to the second element. Unless a researcher is candid with subjects, their consent will be uninformed and the experiment constitutes injury to them.

The underlying ethical value is protection of people from injury by others. A physical or psychological harm does not constitute a wrongful injury if a person freely and knowingly participates in an activity with a risk of harm—for example, plays softball in the neighborhood and breaks a leg. As the choice is the individual's, he or she is responsible for the risk and harm. For this principle to apply, the elements of informed consent must be met. Some people, for example, retarded, very young, or senile persons, lack the capacity to understand the activity or risks involved in an experiment. A problem that arises and cannot be discussed here is the extent to which others should be permitted to consent for a person unable to do so. Should they be permitted to consent to a person's participation in research from which that person will not benefit, or is that unjustly using the person as a means to the ends of others?

Requiring that a person have the capacity to understand and choose is pointless if the person is not given all relevant information for deciding. Crucial information includes what will be done to the person (e.g., blood will be taken on three occasions in a total amount of 30 ml), the risks of the procedure (a drug has side effects such as loss of hair and dizziness), and its potential benefits (a drug may be more effective in curing a disease). Frequent problems that arise with this element are a failure to provide the information in nontechnical jargon a layperson can understand (for example, using "apnea" instead of "temporary stopping of breathing"); a failure to explain the alternatives available, including no treatment;

and difficulty in deciding what counts as a relevant risk (for example, a bruise from the drawing of blood).

Complications concerning informed consent arise when an experiment is double-blind (neither the subject nor the experimenter knows which drug a person receives) or involves a placebo (an inert drug) or deception. In a double-blind format, subjects can be told that they will receive either of two specific drugs. When placebos are used alternately with an active drug, subjects can be told that what they receive could be an inert substance. Experiments involving deception are much more difficult. A classic example was one in which subjects were told to administer electric shocks to another person whom they could not see but could hear.[5] Actually, the other person did not receive any shocks but merely screamed at the appropriate times. The point was to see whether people would obey authority to give shocks at lethal doses. Immediately after the experiment, the subjects were informed of the deception, but was this sufficient for informed consent? If not, should such experiments be forbidden?

Finally, even if everything is explained and subjects understand, they must still voluntarily decide to participate. If, for example, subjects think they will not receive medical care if they refuse, then they do not freely decide to participate. Some of the more difficult problems with this requirement concern whether prisoners can ever freely volunteer, whether students in a course may be required to participate in research by the instructor (in the past a common requirement in many psychology courses), and whether high payment for participation is permissible.

Volumes have been written on these topics, and it is not possible to begin to review all the arguments and problems. The National Commission's published reports and appendixes provide a good starting place for those who are interested in the problems. Nonetheless, even though difficult questions remain, the principle of informed consent to participate in human experimentation is now established in professional ethics. Many other issues about research still exist, however, and the relevant responsibilities have not been widely recognized or discussed.

The value of research is particularly relevant to its ethics. Insofar as society supports research, a responsibility exists not to waste resources. Even when the research is privately funded, society is the indirect funder. Companies obtain their research funds from the prices they charge for their products. Ultimately the consuming public or public at large pays for research. More importantly, if human subjects are involved, to risk their well-being when no significant results are obtainable exhibits a callous disregard of the welfare of others; they are put at risk for no possible significant gain.

An example illustrates a researcher's responsibility to engage in only significant research. One common type of research is testing drug products that will compete with those of other companies. For example, company A markets a high selling eyewash, and company B wishes to compete with it. The eyewashes of both companies have essentially the same chemical ingredients. Should a researcher conduct tests of B's new eyewash? Although it is harmless to the subjects, no social benefit will be derived from it except perhaps slightly lower prices through competition. Trained researchers and healthy subjects will spend time and efforts that could be better spent in other activities. What makes the problem more difficult is that government regulations require B's product to be tested even if it is essentially the same as A's.

One might question whether ethical considerations ever justify preventing a researcher and a fully informed, consenting subject from engaging in a research project. Suppose an adult has a presently incurable and fatal illness that involves progressive mental deterioration. Further suppose a researcher develops a completely untested theory of treatment that involves placing the person in an intensive care unit, sedating him, and reducing his body temperature for a month. The theory is speculative but plausible. Even if the treatment works and an effective treatment of this very rare disease were found, the understanding of its causes and prevention would not be significantly advanced. Moreover, the treatment could make the disease worse. Should such research be undertaken?

Some people argue that if the experimental subject gives an informed consent, then no one has a right to interfere with the freedom of the researcher and subject. Without the experiment, the subject will certainly die; if it is successful, other lives can be saved. This argument, however, ignores the funding of research. Since society is being asked to underwrite the costs of the experiment, it may refuse to support it. As the probability of the treatment being successful cannot even be estimated, it may not be worth the cost, at least until animal experiments have confirmed the theory.

This discussion of the value of research has glided over the main, underlying consideration—the value of knowledge. The professions, especially academics, have traditionally argued that knowledge or the truth should be pursued wherever it leads. Only recently have people seriously considered that perhaps the truth should not be sought in some areas. Some research poses grave risks to society. The defense of research of all kinds has rested upon three contentions. (1) Knowledge itself is valuable, so a prima facie justification for research always exists. (2) Discovering truth can be distinguished from the uses to which it is put. (3) Researchers cannot know the uses to which their results will be put.

Although each of these considerations is important, even together they are not sufficient to justify absolute freedom of inquiry. The intrinsic value of knowledge is quite limited. It can be considered the satisfaction of curiosity, the desire for knowledge for its own sake. People who are curious simply want to know something; they do not have any plan for using the knowledge. No one is curious about many things, such as the color of pen I am using, so much possible knowledge has no intrinsic value. Most of the knowledge people prize, such as the structural properties of a new alloy, is valued for its consequences—the ability to use it in construction. Although such knowledge is frequently gained because a researcher was simply curious, if the knowledge had no instrumental value, the only loss from not doing the research would be frustrating the researcher's curiosity. If the knowledge were to be put to harmful uses, the harm caused might be much greater than the good caused in fulfilling a researcher's curiosity.

Knowledge is distinct from the uses to which it is put, but some knowledge is more appropriate for certain uses. Basic research is sometimes distinguished from applied research. Basic research is primarily concerned with theory construction for the advancement of understanding. Applied research is directed towards uses, although it can have a significant theoretical component. The knowledge of consulting professions is not a mere knowing that; it is also a knowing how, and knowing how is related to uses. A lawyer's knowledge of how to draft contracts and conveyances to prevent racial groups purchasing property in a housing development is more apt to further than to end discrimination. A physician's knowledge of undetectable poisons is more apt for use in committing than preventing murder. A nuclear engineer's knowledge of explosive mechanisms is more apt for war than peace.

Finally, while researchers sometimes do not know the ultimate uses to which their results will be put, that is not always or even usually the case. For example, those scientists who worked on the development of bacteria and chemicals for warfare knew the intended use of their results. And even when researchers do not know to what use their results will be put, they usually know its potential uses. Consequently, they cannot completely escape responsibility for them, because they both know of and have some control over these results.

A recent striking example of these types of concerns was the debate during the 1970s over recombinant DNA research.[6] Recombinant DNA is the technique of manipulating the genes of organisms to produce new ones. This research raises a number of significant questions. First, such research might be dangerous. New strains of viruses or bacteria might be created that are both harmful to humans and resistant to human defense mechanisms or chemical means of destroying them. So one question is the safety of this research for the workers and the general public. Second, such research has potential for both beneficial and harmful uses. One might develop organisms to help clean up oil spills or develop techniques for altering human genetics to prevent or rectify diseases. One might also, perhaps, develop methods for killing people, producing monsters, and so on. So a second question concerns the uses to which the results of such research will be put. Third, both of these concerns raise questions about legal reform to control such research.

This complex and fascinating topic cannot be considered in detail. The issue here is the responsibility of the professionals involved. Much to their credit, some scientists recognized the issues and raised them in the scientific community. A voluntary moratorium on such research was instituted until further study of the problems could be conducted and guidelines developed. Regardless of the merits of the different sides of the debate, the raising of the issues and their consideration is an example of professional responsibility with respect to the value of research and the uses to which it can be put. Of course, the issues are not settled, for researchers must still ask these questions about particular research projects.

This discussion shows that researchers are responsible for the value of their research. They are aware of its potential value and voluntarily decide to undertake it. This responsibility also includes the uses to which the research is or might be put. The extent of responsibility for uses is the extent to which they can be foreseen, as researchers cannot be justly held responsible for what they cannot know. For example, researchers might discover something which thirty years or so later, much to their surprise, is used to create something harmful, such as an agent to defoliate plants in warfare. The fact that research can have harmful uses does not imply that it should not be undertaken. Nevertheless, the possibility of harmful uses must be taken into account. The greater the potential harm of the research, the greater the possible benefits should be and the stronger the safeguards to ensure that it is not used in harmful ways.

Reform

The ethical responsibilities and duties of professionals for reform are best developed with respect to lawyers, as they are most concerned with social reform through the law. Other professions are also responsible for legal reform in their areas of activity; physicians are as responsible as lawyers for health and sanitation codes. Moreover, reform need not result in legal requirements but may result in rules voluntarily implemented by people in the field, such as changes in childbirth procedures to provide a more homelike and psychologically rewarding experience. The responsibility for reform is consequent upon professionals' expertise and, in many cases, monopoly.

Lobbying does not fulfill a profession's responsibility for improving the legal system or promoting the public good. Lobbyists represent interested parties and not the public generally. They are paid to secure passage of legislation favorable to their clients. A leading text on legal ethics states that the general obligation of the lawyer as lobbyist is honesty to both legislator and client.[7] If honesty includes candor, then that is at least a significant responsibility of the lobbyist.

The conditions of lobbying differ from those of advocacy. In court advocacy, the other side will usually have an attorney to present the facts most favorable to its position. In lobbying, there are frequently informal meetings in which only one side is present. When the other side is not represented, if a lobbyist does not present the situation candidly, the legislation will probably be based on incomplete and misleading information. Moreover, in advocacy the law is already established and provides a framework within which a lawyer may argue.[8] In lobbying, the question is what that framework should be, and no substantive principles limit the injustice that can result from securing passage of an evil law. The responsibility of candor becomes more important because a lobbyist does not have the independence of a researcher, does not operate in an adversarial context, and is not limited by a framework of substantive law.

Lobbyists, like researchers, are responsible for the ultimate results of their activities. Although legislators make the final decision concerning the advantages and disadvantages of legislation, an uncandid lobbyist is apt to bias the information upon which legislators' judgments rest. If a lobbyist delays the imposition of safety rules that would prevent accidents, then the lobbyist is partly responsible for accidents. If lobbyists provide accurate and unbiased information, then they have done as much as can be expected and have fulfilled their responsibility. If the legislators still delay imposing safety rules, then they have made the decision and are alone responsible. Of course, they may have made a correct decision, because the ultimate disadvantages of the legislation might have been too great for the good it would have done.[9]

Some lawyers believe that by representing public interest groups or practicing in so-called public interest firms they fulfill their responsibility for reform. If they happen to believe in the causes they represent, they could be doing so. However, in one sense they are representing special interests.[10] For example, when the Corps of Engineers wanted to construct a dam on the Red River in Kentucky, lawyers representing environmentalists opposed its construction. Such representation was not of the public at large, because a number of Kentuckians favored construction of the dam to prevent flooding. As any good lawyers would, the environmentalists' lawyers argued that alternative ways of preventing the flooding existed. In this sense, they took into account the interests of those who favored the dam. However, the lawyers for construction of the dam argued similarly that its environmental impact would not be serious and so took into account the interests of those opposed to the dam. These sorts of considerations occur in any law suit of that nature and do not mean that either side represents the public interest.

Representing so-called public interests is not representing all the interests of people in society. As the dam example illustrates, both sides took account of the interests of people on the other side, but neither could claim necessarily to have the correct view of the public interest. That is a decision to be made by a judge or legislature after hearing both sides. Of course, these latter are not necessarily correct about the public interest either, but their role is to try to arrive at such a decision rather than to make the best case possible for one course of action. Public interest law is advocacy of a selected set of interests, even if these interests are shared by very many people and have not been adequately represented in the past.

Lobbying and public interest activity do not fulfill the responsibility of professions for reform because they are interested rather than disinterested activities. To be disinterested is not to be uninterested. No reformer is uninterested. Being disinterested means that no one group or set of interests is given special weight in determining the best course of conduct. A lobbyist's or public interest lawyer's clients may believe that their position is disinterested, but client corporations and interest groups are not disinterested, no matter how much they think that what is good for them is also good for the public, for they exist to further particular interests.

Public interest lawyers do, nevertheless, help fulfill the responsibility of the legal profession for law reform. They represent interests that have previously been un- or underrepresented in many legal decisions. Almost half a century ago, Karl Llewellyn warned that the legal profession had developed so that its best talents were exerted primarily in behalf of the business and financial side of the law, to the neglect of other aspects.[11] The same note was sounded by Jerome E. Carlin in his study of the ethics of lawyers.[12]

The problem is even deeper, however, than these authors indicate. In some areas interests or people are not organized. For example, victims of negligent accidents and purchasers of property are not and are not likely to become organized as environmental and antinuclear energy groups are. Few lawyers can take a disinterested position on such topics. Informal estimates are that over 60 percent of the bar would have their income substantially affected by abolition of the fault system for personal injury.[13] Yet, only lawyers are likely to be in a position to develop new systems. Simliar considerations apply to engineers, for example concerning aerospace engineers and space policy.

Consequently, reform in these areas depends on professionals who can take a disinterested view of the problems. This requires that their incomes not depend on the current practice or a particular policy. Many of these professionals, such as lawyers specializing in corporate taxation, are not especially qualified to analyze these problems. About the only professionals left to engage in such reform are academics. The government should probably fund their research to support legal reform in these areas. In Canada, the Science Council and various law reform commissions have been established to do research and recommend policies and law reform. In the United States, similar organizations have not generally been officially created, although the National Academy of Sciences does some of this work in science. Academic professionals have to assume a special responsibility to consider and support reform that can be detrimental to the income of other members of their profession, simply because they are often the only people in a position to do so. If they do not, the profession cannot fulfill its responsibility for reform.

RESPECT FOR THE PROFESSION

Professionals usually consider it important for the public to hold both their profession and its individual members in high esteem. Probably no profession takes this consideration as seriously as the law, and everyone rises as robe-clad judges enter the courtroom.[14] Yet, some of the most important authors on legal ethics dismiss public opinion of a lawyer as unimportant. George Sharswood wrote, "Nothing is more certain than that the practitioner will find, in the long run, the good opinion of his professional brethren of more importance than that of what is commonly called the public."[15] A contemporary text continues the theme: "The lawyer, as any professional man, is seldom concerned with the layman's view of his conduct. But he is very much concerned with how his fellow lawyers view his actions."[16] The accepted opinion is that although it is important for the public to have a good opinion of the profession as a whole, public opinion of a particular professional, especially a lawyer, is of little importance. Nonetheless, many professionals are upset when some of their members incur the public's wrath, because they claim it reflects adversely on the profession as a whole.

The first questions, then, are whether, and if so why, professionals should be concerned with the public opinion of their profession. Professionals exercise considerable authority in their respective spheres of activity. The exercise of authority requires willing compliance by those subject to it.[17] If those subject to authority do not respect and trust the authorities, the system will break down. Given the importance of the subjects with which professionals are concerned—health care, legal justice, accurate financial reporting, safe buildings and equipment—the proper performance of their activities is important for the public good. Consequently, the public respect and confidence necessary for the professional role are also important.

Just as one must distinguish between particular professionals being trusted by their clients and their being worthy of such trust, so must one distinguish between a profession having public respect and confidence and its being worthy of them. A profession could receive undeserved respect and confidence. Indeed, professions have often tried to conceal activities by their members when such activities show that respect and confidence are not deserved. Some citizens believe that professionals will not inform authorities of the negligence or misconduct of other professionals because it would be detrimental to their mutual "club" and well-being. This claim is supported by some studies.[18] The responsibility to maintain the public's respect for, and confidence in, a profession is to promote not the wealth and prestige of the members but the well-being of society.

Professionals may confuse their self-interest in the maintenance of respect for, and confidence in, the profession with the ethical reasons for it. Deserved respect rests upon fulfilling the obligations of the profession as a whole, especially those of candor and fairness. Three specific duties usually recognized in professional codes pertain to these obligations. First, professionals should exhibit respect for one another. Only if they respect one another can they expect the public to do so. Exhibiting respect for another professional does not require withholding respectful criticism. In particular, professionals have a duty to testify in courts and other forums about the competence and morality of other professionals.[19] Second, professionals have a duty to provide any information they have concerning the competence and character of applicants for admission to their profession. When on committees or boards considering applicants, they have a responsibility to apply the standard rigorously but fairly. Third, professionals have a duty to bear their fair share of the work in fulfilling the profession's social role. The obligations of the profession as a whole can be fulfilled only by the individual members, and each member owes it as a duty of fairness to the others to do a fair share in fulfilling these obligations.[20]

Although the foregoing matters are rather straightforward, a more complicated issue is also involved with respect for the profession, namely, the identification of a profession, or important members of it, with special interests. As argued in Chapter 1, in a liberal society the privileges accorded a profession as a whole are for the benefit of all citizens, not for the special interest of a few. At different times almost all the professions have been identified, at least in the minds of a significant segment of the public, with special interests. This identification has often resulted from a failure to make services equally available, but it also stems from other sources. In recent years, for example, physicians have been thought to be closely tied to drug companies and to prescribe brand name medicines when drugs of generic description would do as well and cost patients less. On the whole, however, physicians have been less identified with special interests than other professionals. Civil engineers have been identified with construction interests, disregarding their projects' environmental impact; and accountants are sometimes identified with large corporations and tax evasion.

This sort of identification with special interests arises most for the legal profession. A physician who treats a corporate executive for an illness does not become identified with the executive's business activities. Lawyers, accountants, and engineers, however, serve corporate executives in the conduct of their business, and they are readily thought to be personally committed to the views of such clients. The rub of the problem comes when one considers that every person, no matter how hated in society, is entitled to legal counsel. Even the disliked financier is entitled to legal representation. As discussed in Chapter 3, people are not entitled to be provided other non-medical professional services, although they should be equally available. Moreover, although professionals do and sometimes should refuse to assist clients in pursuing unethical courses of conduct, they should give potential clients the benefit of the doubt. If lawyers refused to serve clients whenever they disapproved of them or their activities, many of those most in need of legal counsel would be deprived of it and the value of equality of opportunity subverted.

The debate over the identification of lawyers with their clients has gone on for well over a century.[21] It was raised with respect to the confirmation of Supreme Court Chief Justice Charles Evans Hughes, who was thought to have served primarily a limited group of special-interest clients. The problem has probably become more acute during the twentieth century, because of the unofficial specialization of legal practice. Lawyers specializing in corporate taxation, corporation law, criminal defense, and so on are almost certain to have a clientele drawn from special interests. The same consideration applies to engineers specializing in such fields as nuclear and petroleum engineering. By specializing, a person appears to identify with special interests.

Two distinctions help clarify the issue. The first distinction is between representing a particular client and the pattern of clients represented. The obligation of the legal profession to provide services to all citizens requires that even the most obnoxious and ruthless persons be represented. Consequently, one cannot attribute to a lawyer the character or interests of a particular client. This consideration applies with less force to a consulting engineer, because engineering services need only be equally available, not provided. However, the pattern of clients an attorney chooses to represent is indicative of his or her character. Lawyers who always represent social radicals, large corporations, or particular industries are responsible for the goals and policies they thereby further. Since American lawyers, unlike English barristers, may refuse to serve clients who ask for their services, they can exercise control over the interests they represent. Similarly, consulting engineers who always work for companies exhibiting the strongest disregard for the environment or public safety may be identified with them.

Although professionals are appropriately identified with the interest of the predominant pattern of their clients, it does not follow that they are not conscientious. If they believe that these interests are generally valuable and support the welfare of society, then their activity does not necessarily indicate a reprehensible character. However, they must stand by and not deny responsibility for the character of the interests they represent. Perhaps the exception here is criminal defense attorneys. Unlike attorneys in most civil fields, they do not have an opportunity to take cases of plaintiff and defense. Although they are often the first to be attacked by unenlightened members of the public, they perform an invaluable task in upholding the value of governance by law. Some law firms specialize in plaintiff or defense work in order to avoid a conflict of interest in representing opposing sides of issues, but by so doing they sacrifice a reputation for independence of judgment and become identified with special interests.[22]

For nonconsulting professionals employed by a firm, similar considerations apply. They should not be identified with all the particular policies and actions of their employer. However, they are appropriately identified with the predominant policies of the company. What makes the problem more difficult for such professionals is that refusal to work for the company can mean a total loss of income (one's job), while for consulting professionals it merely means a partial loss of income—that from a particular case or project or perhaps from a few of them. Thus, personal considerations become much more significant, especially if other employment is not easy to obtain. This consideration does not alter the principle involved. It does make it more important to assure oneself of the ethics of a company before starting work and implies that the unethical conduct must be more serious before one ought to quit for ethical reasons.

The second distinction is between the interests represented and the way in which they are represented. One can represent, say, the coal industry, so as to aid its proper consideration within the legal system. One can also represent it in a manner that totally disregards other interests and values in society. One can expend all energy and every legal technicality to avoid regulation of strip mining, or one can represent strip mining companies so as to secure a reasonable consideration of their interests in balance with interests in a clean and unspoiled environment. Even lawyers representing the government can do so in a way that reflects discredit upon them.[23]

SUMMARY

This chapter has considered some of the obligations individual professionals have to their professions. These obligations rest upon the responsibilities of a profession as a whole to further the values of a liberal society. The responsibilities of a profession as a whole are not reducible to similar obligations of individual professionals, but individual professionals do have an obligation to assist in fulfilling them. The emphasis has been on obligations of research, reform, and maintaining respect for the profession, although these do not exhaust the list of such obligations. For example, there are obligations to provide candid and independent judgment in refereeing articles submitted to professional journals and there are perhaps obligations with respect to professional schools. However, those considered here are the most basic.

The primary responsibilities in research and reform are candor and independence. Researchers must be unbiased and fully disclose their findings. They are responsible for the value and possible use of their research. Useless research should not be undertaken. To the extent one can foresee the possible uses of research, this must be considered and the likely good consequences balanced against the likely bad ones. In conducting research, a researcher has a duty to secure the informed consent of human subjects. For informed consent, the subject must be competent to understand and choose; must be informed of the nature of the experiment, of the alternatives to participation, and of the risks and benefits of each; and must freely and voluntarily consent.

In reform, the obligation of candor requires that relevant information be fully disclosed, whether advantageous or not. Similarly, independence is required to help ensure that the efforts are for the public good. Lobbying and public interest activities do not often fulfill the responsibility for reform. In some areas, academic professionals have a special responsibility for reform because they are the only experts who do not have a financial stake in opposing some possible reforms.

Respect for the profession must be deserved. Respect is important so that professions can properly perform their functions and contribute to the public good. To ensure that respect is deserved, professionals have duties to provide evidence to proper authorities concerning the character and conduct of other practicing professionals and of applicants for admission and to bear their fair share of the work in fulfilling the obligations of the profession as a whole. They are also responsible for the interests and conduct of the predominant pattern of their clients and of the general conduct of their employers and the way they represent or work for them.

NOTES*

1. ABA, *Code of Professional Responsibility,* Preamble; ABA, Commission, *Model Rules,* Preamble; AMA, *Principles of Medical Ethics,* sec. 7; Engineers' Council, "Code of Ethics," Canon 1; National Society of Professional Engineers, "Code of Ethics," Preamble.

2. In Canada, for example, 35 percent of research and development is funded by industry, and most of the rest (at least half of the total funds) comes from governments. Ministry of State, Science and Technology, Canada, "A Rationale for Federal Funding of University Research," Background Paper No. 8, November 1979, p. 1.

3. U.S. Commission for the Protection of Human Subjects of Biomedical and Behavioral Research, *The Belmont Report,* and the various other reports issued by the Commission.

4. 45 CFR Part 46, Subpart A (revised 1/10/78); AMA, *Opinions and Reports,* 5.02, 5.18.

5. See Stanley Milgram, *Obedience to Authority* (New York: Harper & Row, 1974).

6. For a brief history and commentary on the public's role, see Callahan, "Recombinant DNA," pp. 20–22.

7. Patterson and Cheatham, *Profession of Law,* p. 154. See also, Michael Pertschuk, "The Lawyer-Lobbyist," in *Verdicts on Lawyers,* ed. Nader and Green, p. 206.

8. Lieberman, *Crisis at the Bar,* pp. 173–174.

9. Ibid., pp. 174–175.

10. See Hegland, "Beyond Enthusiasm and Commitment," p. 809.

11. Llewellyn, "The Bar Specializes," p. 179.

12. Carlin, *Lawyer's Ethics,* p. 178.

13. Patterson and Cheatham, *Profession of Law,* p. 348.

14. The Michigan Supreme Court found it important to adopt a rule requiring judges to wear robes after a judge in Detroit had not been doing so. Judge Justine C. Ravitz, "Reflections of a Radical Judge: Beyond the Courtroom," in *Verdict on Lawyers,* ed. Nader and Green, p. 256 n.

15. Sharswood, *Essay on Professional Ethics,* p. 75.

16. Patterson and Cheatham, *Profession of Law,* p. 180.

17. Bayles, *Principles of Legislation,* pp. 22, 25.

---

*See the bibliography at the end of the book for complete references.

18. See, for example, ABA, Special Committee, *Problems and Recommendations,* p. 219.

19. AMA, *Principles of Medical Ethics,* sec. 2; ABA, *Code of Professional Responsibility,* DR 1–103 (B); ABA, Commission, *Model Rules,* 8.1 (b); Engineers' Council, "Suggested Guidelines," 1,d.

20. For an account of the duty of fairness, see John Rawls, *A Theory of Justice* (Cambridge: Harvard University Press, Belknap Press, 1971), pp. 111–112, 342–350.

21. See the correspondence of David Dudley Field, a prominent lawyer who handled cases for many nineteenth-century "robber barons," and his son, with Samuel Bowles, a prominent newspaper publisher, in *Problems in Professional Responsibility,* ed. Kaufman, pp. 249–266.

22. Hazard, *Ethics in the Practice of Law,* p. 91.

23. See Alan B. Morrison, "Defending the Government: How Vigorous Is Too Vigorous?" in *Verdicts on Lawyers,* ed. Nader and Green, pp. 242–246.

STUDY QUESTIONS AND PROBLEMS

1. Dr. Amy Best and her associates are aware of problems that may arise in securing informed consent in random clinical trials with placebos. If research subjects are told that they might receive an inert pill that will not help their condition, it can influence both their psychological reaction and reporting of effects. Consequently, they devise a study to test the effects of informing patients that they may receive placebos. In one center, subjects will be told that they have a 25 percent chance of receiving a placebo, that the researchers cannot explain whether they will or not because they will not know, and that this is the only way to determine whether the drug really has a beneficial effect. At another center, the same trial will be run, but neither the subjects nor the researchers will be told that a placebo is being used on some patients. They will simply be told that there is some chance the new drug might not be effective in their case. Is the information provided sufficient to ensure the *informed* consent of the subjects? If this project cannot be carried out, can one ever know the significance, if any, of informing patients that they may receive a placebo? If one does not know whether to discount that information, how reliable will future random double-blind clinical trials be? In the end, is this experiment ethically permissible? Why or why not?

2. Chester Dunbar, a consulting psychologist, is asked by Xandu, Inc., to devise a test for its employees to determine their sympathy for union organizers. The test is to look like one for job competency. Is it ethical for Chester to accept this job? Why or why not?

3. Eleanor Fredricks, a professor of pharmacy at State University, has been asked by Yahoo Pharmaceuticals to test a new parenteral (injectable) formulation of their antibiotic drug. The drug has already been approved for use in oral form, which is more quickly absorbed into the blood system and therefore better than a similar antibiotic manufactured by a rival firm. Both drugs are equally effective over the same range of organisms, and the rival firm's drug is already approved for parenteral use. Yahoo's drug is not better in the injectable formulation, because both it and the rival's are absorbed at

the same rate. Eleanor has doubts about the usefulness of performing the research. Why expose patients to some risk and waste valuable research time when the drug will not add anything to medicine's arsenal against diseases? At best, it will help Yahoo's profits. However, Yahoo's chief of research argues that many physicians currently use the rival's drug when patients must receive it parenterally and then switch to Yahoo's when the patient is capable of taking an oral dosage. If their product is approved in parenteral form, patients will not have to switch drugs. Moreover, competition between the two drugs might lead to a lower price and so benefit the public. Is it ethical for Eleanor to do the trial testing? Why or why not?

4. For several years George Hardy has represented a number of welfare recipients. He has become very concerned about a number of injustices that he sees they are subject to. One day a representative of the Justice for Welfare Recipients organization approaches him. They would like to hire him to represent test cases for welfare reform. They would bring him clients and pay for their representation, but he must press only the issues they want raised. As the representative explains, if he raises various issues that are relevant to the particular client, then the courts will avoid the central issue they want decided. Although some particular clients are likely to suffer, in the long run more welfare recipients will benefit, and will do so sooner, by this tactic. If George agrees, he will do more for welfare recipients than he can by the way he has been practicing. Would it be ethical for George to agree to take such cases? Why or why not?

5. The directors of a state consulting engineering society want to form a political action committee. The committee will accept contributions from its members of up to $5,000. They will use it to support particular candidates who are sympathetic to reform legislation regulating the profession and standards in the industry in which they are involved. Is it ethical for the society to engage in this activity? Why or why not? If so, would members have an ethical obligation to contribute to it as a way of furthering reform? Why or why not?

6. Ivy Jason works as an engineer for a large manufacturing corporation. She has been engaged in a study of the pollution emissions at the corporation's plants. She has discovered that the plants' new process greatly reduces discharges of the major pollutants but that a different chemical is given off in small quantities. This chemical has not been proven harmful, but in one study of an area downwind from where the chemical was introduced into the air for a prolonged period, there was a significant increase in temporary respiratory illnesses. Her supervisor has asked her to testify on the company's behalf before the Environmental Regulatory agency as to the reduced pollution by the new process. When Ivy presents her discovery of the new chemical, her supervisor tells her not to mention it. If the members of the agency ask her about it, then she is to give them a truthful answer, but he is sure they will not ask because no one has raised the issue. Is it ethical for Ivy not to volunteer the information to the agency? Why or why not?

7. Kirk Longman, an attorney, has brought suit against Zeckman Industries on behalf of black and Spanish-speaking persons, challenging its employment practices as discriminatory. On the first day of the trial, he attempts to introduce evidence that the test given applicants is failed more often by minority candidates than whites. This evidence has been received in other trials and has shifted the burden of proof to those using the tests to show that they are relevant to the job. However, the judge rules the evidence inadmissible. The next day, Kirk is interviewed on a local television show and remarks that the judge is unaware of recent legal trends and that it is unfortunate they will have to go through an appeal to get his rulings reversed. A few days later, columnist Melanie Novak, who is also an attorney, writes that the judge is quite ignorant of the law and that his racism shows throughout the trial. His conduct is, she writes, a disgrace to the bar and bench. Were the comments of attorneys Longman and Novak ethically permissible? Why or why not? Does the fact that Melanie is also a journalist make a difference? If she were not a lawyer, would that make any difference to the ethics of her comment? Why or why not? If any of the comments were improper, what, if anything, should be done about them?

8. The nurses, residents, and interns at Northern Hospital go on strike. They contend that the staffing conditions are so deplorable that it is dangerous to the patients. Present staff is overworked and cannot provide adequate care. Ten percent of the hospital's positions are currently vacant, and they claim it is because Northern pays 15 percent less than the other hospitals in the region. The strikers demand an immediate pay increase to bring them up to the average in the region and a 10 percent increase in the staff size. Is it ethical for the nurses, residents, and interns to go on strike? Does it reflect adversely on their professions, indicating more of a concern for their own salary and working conditions than for their patients who are left without care? Why or why not?

9. Otto Proctor is a famous criminal defense attorney known for defending some shady persons. When he defended a notorious reputed crime boss on charges of filing a fraudulent tax return, he pulled one of his best "tricks." The unsuspecting prosecutor let him get a jury three-fourths of which were blacks. On the day the case went to the jury, he invited the star black player from the city's baseball team to come in and meet his client. With the jury in the courtroom, the ballplayer stopped by the defense table, shook hands with the defendant, and loudly remarked that he hoped his good friend would beat the bum rap. After two hours of deliberation, the jury returned a verdict of acquittal. Were Otto's tactics ethical? Why or why not?

7 Ensuring Compliance

Having considered the obligations of professionals, questions arise as to how one ensures compliance with them. How does one prevent misconduct—violation of professional norms—from occurring? If misconduct occurs, what responses are appropriate? Most discussions focus on sanctions (ranging from blame to loss of license to practice) for misconduct, assuming that adequate sanctions deter misconduct by others. That assumption is doubtful, at least at present levels of sanctioning. Avoiding original misconduct is preferable and other policies would help prevent it.

Historically, the professions have been self-regulating. Norms have been established and enforced by the professions. Were that system effective, there would be little reason for suggesting new approaches. The first section of this chapter briefly examines the effectiveness of self-regulation. The second section examines traditional arguments for professional autonomy, especially in establishing and enforcing norms of professional conduct. The last section examines three proposals to help ensure professionals' compliance with ethical norms.

SELF-REGULATION

The control professions exercise over the conduct of their members varies among the professions. The legal profession probably has the most control; with some modifications, the ABA codes are adopted by courts or legislatures and thus have the force of law. The ultimate sanction for violation of the disciplinary rules is disbarment. Within the other professions, enforcement is not as strong. Professional societies can only remove persons from membership for misconduct. Hospital boards can remove physicians' hospital privileges, but loss of privileges at one hospital does not automatically involve loss of privileges at another hospital. State authorities can suspend or revoke a professional's license to practice.

Admission

Two points of self-control exist, namely, admission and discipline (sanctioning for misconduct). In a liberal society, admission to the professions must respect equality of opportunity. The history of the professions in the twentieth century has not reflected favorably on self-regulation as a method of preserving or promoting equality of opportunity in admission. Between World Wars I and II the legal profession rather widely discriminated against ethnic minorities, especially Jewish and Catholic persons of recent immigrant origin from Southern or Eastern Europe.[1] Among the methods used were increasing educational standards for bar admission, integration of the bar (making everyone belong to the state bar association), and, in Pennsylvania, a system whereby all new attorneys had to secure another attorney to allow them to serve a six-month clerkship. The reasons for these changes were not simply to discriminate; they also had the worthy aim of increasing professional competence for the sake of clients and the public. The medical profession greatly strengthened medical education just prior to World War I, resulting in a significant improvement in the quality of medical care. However, another immediate effect was to close six of the eight black medical schools in the country.[2]

One might respond that after World War II this type of discrimination rapidly ceased. However, it is widely recognized that discrimination against women and blacks continued until at least the 1970s. For example, in 1972 women generally comprised a small percentage of the professions (see Table 7.1). Although some

Table 7.1 Women and minorities in the professions

Profession	Percentage of Membership			
	1972		1978	
	Female	Black	Female	Black
Accountants	21.7	4.3	30.1	7.5
Dentists	1.9	5.6	1.7	4.3
Engineers	0.8	3.4	9.4	5.5
Lawyers	3.8	1.9	9.4	2.6
Nurses	97.6	8.2	96.7	11.7
Physicians	10.1	8.2	11.3	9.7

SOURCE: Statistical Abstract of the United States, 100th ed. (Washington, D.C.: U.S. Department of Commerce, Bureau of the Census, 1979), p. 416 (No. 687).

improvement had occurred by 1978, the respective percentages were still not large, and the percentages of women and blacks who were dentists had actually decreased. Of course, these percentage gains represent gains in the entire membership in the professions, and a large number of practicing white male professionals already existed. Therefore, great gains in the percentage of women and blacks admitted into a profession will not immediately result in as large a percentage increase in the membership of the profession as a whole.

Efforts to increase female and black enrollments in professional schools has resulted in widespread ethical and legal discussion of the merits of affirmative action admission programs. Too much has been written on this complex issue to even summarize the arguments here. The issue concerns the proper interpretation and implementation of equality of opportunity in a liberal society. Those favoring affirmative action argue that to compensate for past discrimination and provide equality of opportunity, special efforts must be made to enroll women and blacks. Those opposed to affirmative action argue that white males lack equality of opportunity if they are denied admission in favor of academically less well qualified female or black applicants.

After years of controversy, the Supreme Court of the United States partially settled the constitutionality of affirmative action programs by its decision in the *Bakke* case.[3] The medical school of the University of California at Davis had two admission programs, one for regular applicants and one for members of minorities to which 16 of the 100 slots for new students were allocated. Allan Bakke twice applied for admission under the general admission program and was rejected, although applicants in the special program with Medical College Admissions Test scores significantly lower than his were admitted. He filed suit alleging that he was discriminated against. In a complex decision, the court held that a special (quota) admissions program is unconstitutional but that race may be taken into consideration in the admissions process. The division in society over this issue can be seen by the split in the court in its opinion. Justice Powell wrote the opinion. He was joined by four justices in holding that the special (quota) admissions program is illegal, but these four justices disagreed with the holding that race could be taken into account. Four different justices joined Justice Powell in holding that race could be considered in admissions, but they would also have permitted the special (quota) admissions program.

After having been admitted to and graduated from professional school, in some professions one must still become licensed in order to practice. A significant issue concerns the requirements for licensing and admission to the profession. Should an applicant's moral character be a standard for admission? If so, what aspects of moral character should be considered?

The argument for restricting admission requirements to competence rests on the liberal values of governance by law and presumption of innocence. Applicants for admission should receive due process—that is, an appropriate hearing and the opportunities to present evidence in their behalf, to hear and counter evidence against them, and to appeal. This much is not disputed. The significant question is whether applicants should be presumed to be likely to act in an ethical fashion, as average citizens are presumed not to have broken the law, or should they be required to present evidence of good moral character. In many professions, applicants will not have had an extended period of practice upon which their ethical conduct can be judged. (This claim does not hold for those professions, such as engineering, which require a period of practice before licensing.) Unless there is evidence of unethical conduct, applicants should be presumed to be likely to act in an ethical fashion.

The argument to the contrary is that admission to a profession is not a right but a privilege. Without previous practice by applicants, they may be required to provide evidence that they will act in an ethical fashion. The point of licensing is to protect the public (future clients) from unethical and incompetent professionals. Therefore, not requiring evidence of good moral character for admission would thwart the purpose of licensing. Consequently, not only must applicants have good moral character and so be likely to act in an ethical way, but they also may be required to shoulder the burder of proof of their moral character, as of their competence.

Even if one requires good moral character, one must determine what that ambiguous phrase means. Without clarification, the phrase permits much discrimination on the basis of personal prejudices. Obviously, any qualification for admission to a profession should be related to the abilities required to perform the tasks of that profession ethically. Indeed, this is constitutionally required.[4] The central character traits required for the ethical performance of a profession are those that correspond to the responsibilities identified in the previous chapters—a concern to serve, an interest in reform or research (or more generally, to assist the profession in fulfilling its responsibilities), nonmaleficence, fairness, honesty, candor, diligence, loyalty, discretion, and competence. As character traits are relatively enduring dispositions to act in certain ways, presumably a person who has good ones upon admission will continue to act appropriately.

Nevertheless, disputes exist concerning the revelance of certain traits. For example, at first glance homosexuality seems not to be relevant to professional practice, at least as compared to a tendency to forcible sexual conduct. After all, heterosexuals also have sexual inclinations towards some of their clients. Nonetheless, one might argue that a person who engages in homosexual conduct where it is illegal has a disposition to violate a criminal statute and thus lacks an appropriate character for being a lawyer.[5] Yet, the concern should be with character traits that affect a professional's relations with clients or third parties, for licensing exists to protect them. There is no reason to believe that a homosexual is more likely to show an unethical disregard for clients or third parties than a heterosexual. Thus, even if a homosexual applicant might frequently violate a criminal statute, that is not in itself sufficient to refuse admission, even to the legal profession.

Discipline

Even if persons have the requisite character traits for admission, they might not continue to possess them. This raises the issues of enforcement of professional norms, especially by sanctioning professionals for violation of them. The client is often the person who suffers most from professional misconduct. The "natural" penalty for professional incompetence falls upon the client rather than the professional. Incompetent lawyers lose cases; incompetent physicians misdiagnose or mistreat diseases and injuries; incompetent engineers build structures that collapse; and incompetent accountants mess up books. Their clients bear the consequences! Of course, many failures do not indicate incompetence. Someone must lose a law suit, and medical and engineering knowledge is not sufficient to guarantee a cure or an indestructible building.[6]

Due to rapidly changing laws and knowledge, competence is probably the most easily lost trait of new professionals. Despite this, most professions do not have strong checks on the continuing competence of their members. Physicans are usually required to participate in some continuing education, and lawyers are developing more continuing education than previously. But periodic examinations, say, every three or five years, to ensure continuing competence are not required. The mistaken assumption persists that competence is an enduring character trait.

Many types of sanctions are socially imposed on professionals. Courts can impose at least eight different types of sanctions for lawyer misconduct.[7] The following is a more general list:

1. Other professionals or nonprofessionals blame a professional for misconduct. In society at large, blame is the chief sanction for unethical conduct.

2. Social or professional ostracism and boycott can occur. Clients might refuse to consult unethical professionals, and other professionals might not refer clients to them.

3. Professionals can be excluded from membership in a professional society.

4. Professionals can be sued for malpractice. Although most malpractice indicates momentary carelessness rather than misconduct, some malpractice does involve misconduct.

5. A professional's license to practice can be suspended or revoked.

Suspension and revocation differ significantly, but both deny permission to practice for a period of time. Where specialization exists, certification in a specialty can be withdrawn without depriving a professional of a right to practice. Revocation of certification will not even deny the right to practice a specialty if general practitioners are also permitted to perform the work, such as general surgery. For example, a local society of periodontal dentists removed the certification of one dentist. Much to its members' chagrin, the dentist simply broadened his practice to do more than periodontal work and had an even more thriving business than before.

The professions have historically evaluated the ethical conduct of their members and applied the semiformal sanctions (3) and (5) above. Nonprofessionals are minimally involved. The licensing of physicians often ultimately stems from a nonmedical public authority, yet review and determination of misconduct is almost always performed by other physicians.

The fundamental issue is whether this self-regulation by professionals is justified. For a liberal and democratic society to permit professional self-regulation, either professional and public interests must be congruent or the disadvantages of nonprofessional regulation must exceed the expectable public benefits in terms of increased compliance and furtherance of liberal values. If professional and public interests are not congruent, then professional self-regulation is unlikely to promote liberal values adequately. Professional interests will bias self-regulation to favor professional over public interests.

Public and professional interests are not always congruent. A professional is a subgroup of a population whose members have certain common interests. These common interests can be divided into three sets: (1) self-interests in promoting the economic well-being of the profession, such as the fees and employment of architects; (2) technical interests in the development of the craft and techniques of the profession, such as methods of construction with concrete or space shuttle craft; and (3) other directed or cultural interests, such as the health, legal justice, or safety in the community.[8] For public and professional interests to be completely congruent, the other directed interests of a profession would always have to predominate over its conflicting self-interests. Disparate interests are almost never without some influence, even if they are no more than an altering of the perception of the predominant interests. The rhetoric of professional devotion to the public good hides this pervasive coloring of the perception of public interest. The public interest is at best congruent with the other directed interests and with those economic and technical interests that fortuitously conform to the public interest.

A couple of examples illustrate the incongruity of public and professional interests. Limited access to a profession protects the economic well-being of its members. Despite numerous studies indicating a developing shortage of physicians, during the late 1950s and early 1960s, the American Medical Association persistently denied the existence of such a problem and opposed attempts to increase the supply of physicians. By 1971, medical degrees were awarded to 8,919 students, but 5,748 new physicians were immigrants, and the next year the number of immigrant physicians reached 7,143.[9] The need to have so many immigrant physicians declined during the 1970s as medical education was expanded. A shortage enables physicians to charge higher fees than they might otherwise and ensures each physician sufficient patients. As a result, citizens with low incomes or citizens living in areas not attractive to physicians receive inadequate health care.

Lawyers have an economic interest in keeping various transactions and disputes within the legal system. The interests of lawyers as a group most obviously conflict with the public interest in no-fault laws, especially for automobile accidents. As much as 23 percent of each premium dollar of automobile insurance under the fault system goes to the administration of claims, mostly legal fees.[10] Under a no-fault system, the percentage is much lower. The self-interested activity of the trial bar in opposing no-fault automobile accident insurance is widely recognized. In divorce and property law, the economic interests of lawyers also generally conflict with those of the public in a nonlegal or a legally simple system.

Given that professional and public interests are not always congruent, nonprofessional regulation might still be unwise if self-regulation were successful. But professional self-regulation has not been successful at any level. It has not ensured that professional norms take sufficient account of public interests. The consideration of professional norms in Chapters 3-6 has repeatedly indicated instances in which professional norms, from advertising and fees to third party interests, are contrary to promoting and preserving liberal values of freedom, equality of opportunity, welfare, and prevention of injury. Thomas D. Morgan argues at length that the ABA *Code* puts professional interests first, client interests second, and those of the public last.[11] A recent history of the bar in the United States asserts, "Ever since the beginning of the urban industrial era the bar had adopted a series of compromises to reconcile public responsibility with professional self-interest—and to conceal the distance between them."[12]

Nor has self-regulation proven more successful in enforcing the norms that were adopted. In his study of the New York City Bar, Jerome E. Carlin found self-enforcement of norms ineffective. He estimated that only 2 percent of lawyers who violated ethical norms (based on their self-reports) were officially processed, and fewer than 0.2 percent were officially sanctioned by censure, suspension, or disbarment. He concluded that the likely function of formal controls is forestalling public criticism and control rather than preserving the moral integrity of the profession.[13] During 1975–76, of the 5,000 complaints to the California State Bar, only 937 were investigated and only 53 resulted in disbarment or suspension. California has 50,000 lawyers.[14] A report in New York City concluded that discipline had become more lenient after a 1970 ABA report generally condemning the profession for lax enforcement.[15] Similarly, in his detailed study of the medical profession, Eliot Freidson found that formal self-regulatory mechanisms did not predominate even in hospitals and were not very common in most medical work settings. Even when deviant conduct was observed, it was not always attended to, less often communicated to others, and rarely subject to regulation.[16] From January 1970 through June of 1977, the American Institute of Certified Public Accountants disciplined only 121 members.[17] The situation is no better in engineering where, of the approximately 60,000 members of the National Society of Professional Engineers, in 1975 it was reported that only about 150 cases of unethical conduct are heard each year and that 20 of the 52 member societies had never processed a single disciplinary case.[18]

Finally, even when action is undertaken against professional misconduct, it rarely comports with the expectations of the public. Names of professionals charged with misconduct are usually withheld from the public until all possible appeals have been exhausted. No sanctions are imposed before then. The ABA Special Committee on Evaluation of Disciplinary Enforcement reported:

> The public is unable to comprehend why an attorney convicted of stealing funds from a client can continue to handle client funds; or why an attorney convicted of securities fraud can continue to prepare and certify registration statements; or why an attorney convicted of filing a fraudulent income tax return can continue to prepare and file income tax returns for clients; or why an attorney convicted of conspiracy to suborn perjury can continue to try cases and present witnesses; or why an attorney convicted of bribing officials of an administrative agency can continue to practice before the very agency he has corrupted; or indeed, why an attorney convicted of a serious crime of any nature can continue to hold himself out as an officer of the court obligated to uphold the law and to support the administration of justice.[19]

As the Committee made clear, the public's inability to comprehend these matters is not due to mental deficiency. Similar points can and have been made about the enforcement of professional norms for physicians, accountants, and other professionals.

Consequently, the claims for professional self-regulation do not withstand critical scrutiny. The interests of the professions are not congruent with those of the public. Professional self-regulation has not resulted in norms promoting liberal values or in adequate enforcement of the norms that were adopted. One strong and pervasive claim for professional self-regulation remains, namely, the need, even necessity, for professional autonomy.

PROFESSIONAL AUTONOMY

The claim of professional autonomy includes more than mere self-regulation of misconduct. As noted in Chapter 1, some authors consider autonomy to be a defining characteristic of professions. Autonomy in the handling of particular cases was there taken to be a common feature of professions. Discussion of the appropriate extent of autonomy was postponed to this point, however, so the following discussion considers autonomy in a wider perspective than mere enforcement of professional ethical norms.

One may distinguish two different areas of professional autonomy. One area concerns establishing or enforcing norms of professional membership and conduct; the other is the management of professional activity, either in general operations of a professional organization or firm or in particular cases of clients.

The three traditional arguments for professional autonomy rest upon the following important premises: (1) only professionals have the expertise required to handle particular cases; (2) professional judgment should be independent of extraneous influences to ensure that the client's interests are looked after; and (3) professional autonomy is necessary to ensure confidentiality in the professional–client relationship.

Expertise

The argument from expertise is usually considered to be the strongest. It begins with the assumption that the most important distinguishing feature of a profession is the possession of a body of knowledge attained through an extended period of education. "The profession bases its claim for its position on the possession of a skill so esoteric or complex that nonmembers of the profession cannot perform the work safely or satisfactorily and cannot even evaluate the work properly."[20] Professional practice, the exercise of expertise, involves organizing particular facts into patterns and applying general principles and rules to them, and this requires the exercise of judgment in the absence of certainty. Choosing a drug for a patient, wording a contract for a client, or determining the standards for safe electrical equipment in a building requires expertise involving both knowledge and judgment. Such judgments cannot be evaluated solely on the basis of evidence about the percentage of successful outcomes in a series of cases. Evaluating a particular case requires skill developed through expertise. Thus, laypersons are not competent to judge or direct the work of professionals, since they cannot possibly have the requisite skill.

Despite its attractiveness, this argument is, at best, too broad and, at worst, simply unsound. First, it does not apply to the area of establishing professional norms or the general management of professional activity. Many professional norms are simply restatements of ordinary ethical norms that prohibit bribery, deceit, theft, and so on. The organization of professional activity concerns the types of services to be rendered, the most efficient way to provide them, and the reduction of their costs. Intelligent laypersons can judge and direct this kind of activity as well as professionals. Hospital administrators, lay members of health systems agencies, and many corporation executives are not members of the professions and yet perform such activities every day.

Second, the argument falsely assumes that each case is unique and requires special judgment, ignoring the more frequent, routine professional work, such as treating flu, conveying real estate, preparing an average individual income tax statement, or designing a simple sewer extension. In such work, little discretion is required.[21] Professional expertise is not needed to identify and judge gross mistakes—failures to perform simple, routine tasks adequately. For example, I once complained to a group of first-year law students that a lawyer had not done a good job in preparing my will. Their immediate response was to ask how I, a layperson, was competent to evaluate the lawyer's work. My reply that he had failed to date the will silenced the argument from expertise. Similarly, a surgeon who leaves a sponge in a patient after an operation[22] or an architect who has the stairs to the second floor going out the front door of a house (an actual case!) makes a gross mistake. Engineering failures are often obvious and dramatic, as for example, brakes that burn out after being used a couple of times.

This argument from gross mistakes might be claimed to be irrelevant, especially in the area of enforcing rules of conduct. Gross mistakes usually constitute negligence, but negligence is not the same as misconduct. Everyone makes a gross mistake now and then. Only negligence showing a defect of character relevant to professional conduct, such as incompetence, constitutes misconduct. Furthermore, gross negligence and incompetence are not the difficult cases; the difficult ones involve professional activity requiring judgments in the vague, gray area of professional expertise.[23]

Granted, not all negligence is misconduct, and negligence does not necessarily indicate incompetence. Still, most client complaints against lawyers are for neglect, a form of negligence that is also misconduct.[24] Persistent or frequent negligence is evidence of incompetence. At the least, the notion of a gross mistake further narrows the areas in which the argument from expertise has any plausibility.

Moreover, in one of the most important institutions in society—jury trial—laypersons consider such complicated cases every day. Malpractice cases often involve complicated issues of the appropriate standards of care to which a professional should conform. As is the case in disciplinary hearings, both sides present testimony as to the standard practice and the conduct of the professional. When the question is whether the defendant's conduct was ethical rather than technically competent, laypersons usually have as good a background as a professional. After all, professionals are not usually experts in ethics.

Third, the argument from expertise assumes that professional judgments are either value-free or rest upon indisputable value judgments. If disputable values are involved, then professional judgments are liable to conflict with those of clients or the public. It is hard for professionals not to be systematically biased. Physicians tend to promote the prolongation of human life and physical health at all costs. This bias has led to enough court cases in recent years, such as that of Karen Quinlan, a young New Jersey woman in an irreversible coma and kept on a respirator, not to require further comment.[25] Lawyers have a penchant for legal forms and written agreements. The emphasis upon written agreements in advance is detrimental to flexibility and trust. Business-people frequently find good will and easily alterable verbal agreements more efficient. Domestic relations have historically been of least success in law, because the law's rigidity and formalism are destructive of the mutual trust and flexibility essential for tranquil domestic relations. Engineers tend to favor construction and the development of complex technology rather than no construction and simple technology.

Although it is understandable and perhaps valuable for professionals to have these built-in biases, it is because they have them that professional autonomy in establishing norms results in norms contrary to the public good. A representative body of citizens might devise rules more favorable to promoting and preserving liberal values for the general public. If the value choice in particular cases is for clients, the argument from expertise has weight only for choices of technical matters that do not significantly affect client values. As laypersons can judge the basic ethics and competence of professional activity, and direct its general organization, and as clients make important value choices, the argument from expertise does not support a general claim of professional autonomy.

Independence

The second major argument for professional autonomy is that professionals must be free to exercise their best judgment on professional matters and that involvement of laypersons intrudes upon nonprofessional concerns. As discussed in Chapter 4, almost all professional codes stress the need for independence of judgment. The argument from independence applies primarily to autonomy in managing professional activity. It has little to do with establishing and enforcing professional norms. To so apply it, one would have to argue that the threat of review by a layperson would restrain professionals from exercising their best judgment in behalf of clients.

There are two basic arguments against independence in managing professional activity. First, complete independence assumes that professional ideals are practically absolute and that professionals fearlessly defend them against inimical external influences. However, the values pursued by the professions are not absolute. Other values, such as the prevention of suffering, sometimes outweigh the pursuit of health, legal justice, accurate financial records, and beautiful or durable structures or equipment. Although by acculturation professionals give great weight to the value represented by their profession, the health, legal, or other status of a client is sometimes less important than other values of the public or even the client. Nor are the professions always the best defenders of these values. In medical experimentation, the well-being of individual clients is too often sacrificed for further medical knowledge. Lawyers sometimes sacrifice clients for precedent-setting (and reputation-gaining) appellate decisions. A study of lawyers' conformity to the canons of ethics indicates many lawyers do not strongly resist client pressures to violate them.[26] Engineers and architects have been known to give bribes and accountants to write them off as business expenses.

Second, the strength of the argument from independence varies inversely with the generality of the subject. When decisions concern the general management of an organization, independence is not basic. Professionals are not prevented from doing their best for a client if a lay board decides that a legal services group should not take class action or landlord-tenant cases, that a medical group will not provide cosmetic surgery for signs of old age, that a highway department will plan for access roads, or that buildings in an area should not be over a certain height. These decisions do not prevent professional independence of judgment in the cases and projects actually undertaken.

With respect to particular measures in specific cases, a professional's claim to the exercise of independent judgment becomes stronger. However, provided they are permissible within the framework of public values, important value decisions should be made by clients. Judgments about filing a suit as a class action, having elective surgery, or installing drainage systems in developments seriously affect the interests of clients. Such decisions also affect public values—the cost of court, medical, or storm sewer systems. Although in making such decisions professionals sometimes consult other professionals, this does not free the decisions of professional bias or provide input from the public perspective. Clients can often benefit from the perspective that nonprofessionals provide. Counselors and pastors are frequently consulted in medical situations.

A professional has a strong claim to independence of judgment only for technical decisions not significantly affecting values, in which the element of particular knowledge and expertise dominates. Few people would wish to interfere at this level. Interference is most likely to come from third party payers, such as insurance or finance companies. A parent might wish to deny a dependent teenager an abortion and wish to make her marry, but this concerns the autonomy of the teenager, not the physician. The same point applies whenever third parties intervene.

Confidentiality

The third major argument for professional autonomy is that its abridgement will intrude upon the confidentiality of the professional–client relationship. As noted in Chapter 4, confidentiality is essential for consulting professionals, especially physicians and lawyers. Without it they cannot obtain the information necessary to handle their clients' cases properly. Engineers and architects must know the intended uses of equipment and buildings. Lay involvement, professionals contend, would destroy confidentiality and thereby client trust.

Without denying the importance of confidentiality of professional–client communications, one can seriously challenge the relevance and validity of the argument from confidentiality to professional autonomy. First, the argument is of limited scope. It does not apply to the establishment of norms or to the general management of an organization, because particular clients are not directly involved. Moreover, confidentiality is not wrongfully breached if clients consent to disclosure of information. Thus, the argument pertains only to disclosures of information without client consent in enforcing norms and managing particular cases.

Second, lay employees of professionals have access to the information but preserve confidentiality.[27] Other nonprofessionals can also keep information confidential. Only in the enforcement of norms might confidentiality be a serious consideration. Currently, most complaints, at least against lawyers, are made by clients. A complaining client is usually willing to waive confidentiality, and as discussed in Chapter 4, professionals are entitled to disclose information to protect themselves against charges of wrongful conduct. More aggressive enforcement of norms of professional conduct might involve more cases not based on client complaints. As clients might be implicated in wrongdoing, they might refuse to waive confidentiality. The reason for professional–client confidentiality disappears then, because it is not a protection for criminal or unethical conspiracy. Any protection a client might have should rest upon Fifth Amendment protection from self-incrimination, not confidentiality. Hence, the argument premised upon the necessity for confidentiality in the professional–client relationship does not support the demands for professional autonomy as they are usually articulated.

The three traditional arguments for professional autonomy fail to establish a strong objection to public participation in procedures to ensure compliance with professional norms. Professional autonomy is essential only in the choice of technical matters to achieve permissible client goals.[28] Professionals in other countries lack autonomy in some or all of the other areas in which professionals in the United States have traditionally had it. Eliot Freidson has eloquently stated the bad consequences, for both the public and the professions, of unrestricted autonomy.

> This is the critical flaw in professional autonomy: by allowing and encouraging the development of self-sufficient institutions, it develops and maintains in the profession a self-deceiving view of the objectivity and reliability of its knowledge and of the virtues of its members. Furthermore, it encourages the profession to see itself as the sole possessor of knowledge and virtue, to be somewhat suspicious of the technical and moral capacity of other occupations, and to be at least patronizing and at worst contemptuous of its clientele. Protecting the profession from the demands of interaction on a free and equal basis with those in the world outside, its autonomy leads the profession to so distinguish its own virtues from those outside as to be unable to even perceive the need for, let alone undertake, the self-regulation it promises.[29]

In short, autonomy prevents the professions and professionals treating others in society on a basis of freedom and equality of opportunity and promoting other values of a liberal society. These points have been underscored as the professions have had to be pushed by public agencies and laypersons to modify policies with respect to fee schedules, advertising, provision of services, paternalism, and securing the informed consent of research subjects, to name only a few areas.

As previously practiced, self-regulation has not ensured compliance with professional norms. The arguments for professional autonomy do not support it.

The challenge to liberal society in the last decades of the twentieth century is to develop new ways to better ensure that professionals comply with ethical norms.

NEW APPROACHES

If self-regulation by the professions has not effectively prevented or sanctioned misconduct, one must consider the alternatives. A viable alternative should promise a greater degree of compliance and not cost significantly more in terms of liberal values. The three approaches considered in this section are not mutually exclusive, nor do they require completely abandoning the traditional mechanisms for ensuring compliance. Two of these approaches focus upon sanctioning misconduct. One is for changing the composition of the groups that establish and enforce professional norms to include at least some if not a predominance of laypersons; the other is for improving enforcement procedures. The third approach is directed toward developing motivations to compliance among professionals.

Lay Involvement

Laypersons are competent to judge professional conduct and would provide a public perspective to the development of norms that is presently lacking from self-regulating systems. One might claim that professionals should be judged only by other professionals because otherwise they would not receive a judgment by their peers. This claim is defective because it sets professionals above others in society and implies that laypersons are not the peers of professionals who essentially constitute a nobility not to be evaluated by commoners. It does not comport with due process and justice for a banker charged with unethical conduct or sued for conversion of funds to be brought before a judge and jury of bankers.

To a limited extent, laypersons have been successfully involved in enforcing professional norms. Since 1969, the Michigan State Bar Grievance Board has been composed of seven members, two of whom are nonlawyers.[30] The Grievance Board takes appeals from panels of volunteer lawyers who conduct the initial hearing and pass judgments. An executive director of the Michigan State Bar stated that having laypersons on the Board is "a salutary arrangement." He also said, "Laymen are as competent as lawyers in judging misconduct."[31] Several other states now also have nonprofessionals involved in disciplinary proceedings, but not, as yet, establishing rules of conduct.[32]

In medicine, dentistry, and psychology, institutional review boards for human investigation have nonprofessional members. The requirement of nonprofessional members now includes persons not associated with the institution.[33] Although these committees are concerned with only a small aspect of professional practice, they do enforce ethical rules of conduct and preserve confidentiality. The committees are still dominated by professionals, but the presence of nonprofessionals makes those appearing before them and their professional members more sensitive to ethical concerns. Although there have been many complaints about the operation of such boards, significant, widespread complaint has not been directed at the participation of nonprofessionals.

In general, the involvement of laypersons has been quite limited. In none of the foregoing situations do they predominate; nor are they involved in establishing the ethical norms of the professions. One major exception to these claims was the National Commission for the Protection of Human Subjects of Biomedical and Behavioral Research. The Commission had a majority representation of knowledgeable laypersons and was engaged in establishing norms for professional experimentation. However, the Commission only recommended guidelines for publicly funded research and did not directly establish norms to which any profession was automatically committed. The successor, The President's Commission for the Study of Ethical Problems in Medicine and Biomedical and Behavioral Research, has similar limitations.

Having nonprofessionals as members of groups establishing ethical norms is practiced elsewhere. In Ontario, Canada, laypersons have served on the groups governing professional engineers and lawyers for a number of years. A recent study of the regulation of engineers, lawyers, architects, and accountants found that lay membership was not an issue, only whether the lay members should be designated to represent certain groups, such as clients.[34] A 1976 report of the Association of the Bar of the City of New York recommended lay participation in policy making as well as discipline, and one commentator has suggested that the accounting profession should follow suit.[35]

The mere addition of a few laypersons to groups establishing and enforcing professional norms could be more a public relations effort than a serious attempt to reform professional conduct. If, as has been argued, professional norms are to be evaluated by their promotion and preservation of liberal values, establishing and enforcing norms of professional conduct should rest with the public. This requires that legislatures should adopt the norms or authorize commissions with predominantly lay membership to do so.[36] Enforcement should also be a function of the lay public rather than of the professions. No other monopolies of essential public services are regulated solely or primarily by representatives of the monopoly.

Given the variety of possible sanctions for misconduct, no one enforcement or sanctioning mechanism exists. Blame is an informal system, whereas revocation of licenses to practice is at least a quasi-legal system. In considering the involvement of laypersons, one is primarily considering semiformal systems whether by professional organizations or by government licensing. Without adequate semiformal sanctioning systems, the involvement of laypersons will not be significant.

Effective Enforcement

A second set of proposals for enforcing professional norms is designed to make the enforcement process more effective. There are four main areas of consideration. The first is the substantive grounds for professional discipline. In many states, such as New York, physicians' licenses can be revoked only on grounds much narrower than those the AMA *Principles* and its Judicial Council's *Opinions and Reports* use to judge conduct unethical. Although the ABA *Code's* disciplinary rules are more comprehensive than the AMA *Principles* and certainly more so than the licensure laws for physicians, it has not provided for discipline of lawyers for even flagrant and persistent violation of the ethical considerations. The grounds for disciplinary action should be broadened to cover all forms of professional misconduct, and the ABA Commission's *Model Rules* is to be commended for its doing so. The codes of many other professional groups vary considerably in their comprehensiveness and explicitness. Governance by law requires that professionals not be disciplined without clear norms indicating what is prohibited, and protection of the public from injury requires that all forms of unethical conduct be covered. Thus, many criteria for discipline should be revised to be both more explicit and comprehensive.

A second requirement for more effective enforcement is the reporting of violations. A study of physicians found that they did not attend to unethical practice by others, and when they did, official action rarely occurred.[37] The ABA Special Committee on Evaluation of Disciplinary Enforcement found the same problem among lawyers.[38] The evidence cited above about enforcement suggests the same is true in the other professions. Despite the fact that they should be better able to observe and recognize misconduct, few complaints against lawyers for unethical conduct are made by other attorneys. The Special Committee recommended that sanctions be applied against attorneys and judges who fail to report misconduct. Such discipline would only be enforcing an obligation already recognized by the ethical codes of most professions.[39]

It is especially incongruous for the professions to rely primarily upon client complaints of misconduct, when their case for self-regulation rests on the claim that clients are incompetent to judge misconduct.[40] Reliance upon client complaint also means that sanctions are primarily imposed for violation of obligations to clients. Violations of obligations affecting the economic well-being of other members of the professions, such as the old minimum fee schedules, are frequently reported by professionals. Violations of obligations to third parties and the public are not adequately reported. Thus, the very process of enforcement slights the well-being of the public compared to the well-being of clients and the economic self-interests of other professionals.

The duty to report unethical or illegal conduct should not be limited to other professionals, however, but should also include clients (see Chapter 5) and nonprofessional employers. This is the classic issue of whistle-blowing, and it raises two questions, namely, the responsibility of supervisory and subordinate professionals in a firm, and possible mechanisms to help protect the whistle-blower. The responsibilities of supervisory and subordinate professionals were basically raised, and to a large extent settled, at the end of World War II by the Nuremberg trials of Nazi war criminals. Although the wrongs done by professionals are usually much less serious than those of Nazi war criminals, there is no reason why the same principles should not apply.[41] Essentially, supervisory professionals are responsible for any conduct carried out by a subordinate in pursuance of their orders or directions. Moreover, they are responsible to exercise reasonable care to see that subordinates conform to the norms of professional ethics. Only if they knew, or should have known, of the unethical conduct of a subordinate are they responsible for it. Subordinate professionals are responsible for knowingly violating professional norms even if done at the direction of a supervisor, but they may reasonably rely on the supervisor's direction if the ethical character of the conduct is debatable.

The second issue is more difficult. Some people have suggested that an employee who blows the whistle on his employer should have some form of job guarantee. This proposal is probably unworkable and undesirable. First, it is very difficult to distinguish between the sincere but mistaken employee and the disgruntled employee who merely wishes to embarrass a supervisor or employer. The intent of the proposal is to protect the former and not the latter, but the difficulty of the distinction makes it hard to apply in practice. Second, after an employee blows the whistle on an employer or supervisor, hard feelings are likely to remain. If a supervisor is removed, then there might be no problem. However, often employers or supervisors who remain believe the employee did not exhibit proper loyalty, by which they mean the employee should not have made so much of a fuss and should have worked the matter out privately with the employer. An employee is likely to believe that an employer or supervisor should have reacted more quickly and that the employer or supervisor gave him a difficult time until the whistle was blown. Relations are thus likely to be strained, and continued employment satisfactory to neither party.

A better solution would be to have a committee that is within the firm but that also has significant lay representation from outside, whose function is to receive complaints about unethical conduct. The existence of independent laypersons on the committee should help ensure that significant complaints are not lightly dismissed. Some legal firms have designated one or two senior partners to receive complaints about unethical conduct and to provide ethical advice, but this procedure relies too much on the integrity of a member of the firm who might have a significant financial stake in the unethical conduct, for ethical conduct can mean the loss of an important client. As was argued in the previous section, lay representatives could maintain confidentiality so long as the firm took proper remedial action. If it did not take proper action, then confidentiality would be broken. This is not a serious objection, for confidentiality would probably have been broken earlier by the employee who brought the matter up, and its risk is the price of assurance of ethical conduct.

A third aspect of enforcement is adequate investigation of allegations of misconduct. The ABA Special Committee reported that "lack of adequate financing is the most universal and significant problem in disciplinary enforcement."[42] Adequate investigators are especially needed for matters not based on client complaints, because they often involve collusion between a professional and a client. For example, a physician and patient might agree to hospitalization for tests that could be performed on an outpatient basis but would not then be covered by medical insurance. An engineer might collude with a contractor in using substandard materials, or an accountant with a client in hiding significant losses or taking unjustifiable tax deductions. Increased funding and adequate staffing does sometimes significantly increase the effectiveness of enforcement. The Michigan State Bar revised its funding techniques to set aside a significant part of lawyers' dues to fund enforcement and establish a full-time staff. The result was a quadrupling of disciplinary actions.[43] However, as a result of the Special

Committee's report, many state bar associations increased their funding for enforcement but the number of sanctions imposed has not greatly increased.[44]

A fourth aspect of the disciplinary process concerns procedures and delay. A crucial issue concerns the purpose of discipline. If it is viewed as straightforward punishment, then constitutional standards are apt to apply, for revoking a license to practice could be viewed as deprivation of property by loss of ability to earn a living. Although governance by law requires that due process be accorded in any disciplinary procedure, one need not require that all possible appeals be exhausted before revocation occurs. As noted before, a license to practice a profession is a grant of privilege for the protection of the public. Sanctions are to ensure that the public is served only by competent, ethical professionals. When ordinary citizens are punished for criminal conduct, general rights are removed. Sanctions of professionals do not deny rights that all citizens generally possess but rather deny a special privilege. The removal of a privilege is not ethically the same as the denial of a general right. One can perhaps see the point better by imagining a system in which licenses to practice a profession were granted, like broadcast licenses, for only three-year periods. A refusal to renew a license would not be punishment. Nevertheless, although not punishment in the full sense, sanctions for misconduct can have the purposes of usual punishment—retribution, incapacitation by removal of opportunity to practice, and general and specific deterrence.

Three problems arise in disciplinary procedure. First, sanctions are not applied as swiftly as feasible. The many avenues of appeal often take two years or more to complete, and during that time professionals are usually not suspended from practice. From the public viewpoint, this practice is not justifiable. If a license to practice is a special privilege for the sake of protecting the public, then an initial determination of misconduct and judgment of revocation are sufficient to justify suspension pending the outcome of an appeal. The public good outweighs the professional's interest in continuing practice, once a full hearing and presentation of evidence has resulted in a decision against the professional. After all, injunctions are often issued against businesses suspected of engaging in illegal and deceptive practices even before a final determination is made. As only the economic interest of professionals is at stake, no reason exists to accord them significantly greater rights than businesses.

A related element of delay arises from the fact that court convictions, even criminal convictions for conduct clearly related to professional activity, do not automatically result in suspension of a license to practice. Hearings on fitness to practice are often suspended until the outcome of a court case, and then all issues are reargued in the hearing. Meanwhile, the public is subject to the ministrations of these professionals. At the very least, conviction for some designated crimes should automatically result in loss of a license to practice. No conceivable justification exists for allowing a physician convicted of manslaughter of patients to continue to practice. A study of the twenty disciplinary actions by the American Institute of Certified Public Accountants during the first nine months of 1976 showed that eighteen of them were of people convicted of crimes or who had had their licenses revoked by state boards.[45] One of the remaining two was of a person granted immunity from prosecution for bribing revenue agents. Thus, the sole case in which the Institute needed a hearing was an accountant who solicited business by a letter and used a fictitious name; he was required to take a course in professional ethics!

A second problem of disciplinary procedure is the multiplicity of jurisdictions. Physicians can have their license suspended in one state and still be licensed in another, or they can be denied privileges at one hospital for incompetent or unethical conduct, yet this information may not even be communicated to another hospital at which they practice. National licensing and disciplining would eliminate this problem. During the nineteenth century, when communications and conditions in the states varied greatly, differing state policies were perhaps reasonable. In the last decades of the twentieth century, no justification exists for different professional norms among the states. Professional ethics is not ethically relative, and cultural conditions among the states do not differ sufficiently to support different norms. The existence of national ethical codes testifies to the national character of professional norms. Short of national licensing and disciplining, court and ethics committee decisions in other states should be taken as determinative of the issues so that a professional cannot reargue the same points in another forum.

A third problem concerns the confidentiality of the disciplinary process. Names of professionals charged with misconduct are not often released until all appeals have been exhausted. Such a policy is intended to protect innocent professionals from damage to their reputation and business. Yet, the public has two major interests in an open process. One interest is that of potential clients in information about the ethical character of professionals. That a lawyer has been charged with neglect or misappropriation of client funds is quite relevant to a potential client's decision to employ that lawyer.

Another interest is in public observation of the disciplinary process to ensure that it is fair and just. Sometimes an open hearing is also beneficial to professionals charged with misconduct; this is true, for example, if they are being harassed by other professionals for improperly advertising or holding unpopular views. A Canadian attorney who was president of the Alberta Human Rights and Civil Liberties Association criticized a proposed Edmonton by-law imposing a curfew for juveniles as infringing the civil liberties of parents and children.[46] He also said that if everyone defied the law and pleaded not guilty, its absurdity would become obvious. The law society charged him with attempting to subvert the law. The attorney went to court and asked that the hearing be open to the public and waived his right of privacy. His request was denied on the ground that the right of privacy also extended to the law society. One need not choose between having the process completely open or closed. A reasonable balance of the competing interests would be to withhold names of professionals until the preliminary investigation is completed and a determination made of sufficient evidence to support proceeding to a hearing.[47]

Motivation to Compliance

The approaches of lay involvement and more effective enforcement of professional norms apply after original violations. A third approach aims to prevent original violations through professional education to secure a greater awareness of, and commitment to, professional norms. Education in professional ethics can take several forms. First, in the so-called pervasive method, ethical considerations are built into all or most aspects of a field. For example, a course on criminal law might consider ethical problems of criminal defense attorneys and prosecutors, and one on genetic diseases might consider the ethics of confidentiality. The pervasive technique suffers two chief defects. Not all faculty are knowledgeable about professional ethics and capable of adequately teaching it. Moreover, the diffuse character of the study prevents sustained consideration of the issues and can lead students to believe ethics is a peripheral concern. Yet, the pervasive method is valuable in reinforcing learning from other courses.

The second form is a required course on professional ethics. Although this method enables a more sustained and critical consideration of professional ethics, one course cannot be expected to alter student character. Such courses emphasize conceptual aspects of ethics, while students need to develop dispositions of honesty, candor, loyalty, and so on. As Aristotle noted, such dispositions are learned only by practice.

A third form is clinical education. It allows students more of an opportunity to develop dispositions by having limited practice subject to ethical evaluation. Medical and dental education has always had a large clinical component, but overt ethical considerations have been lacking. In the twentieth century, legal education has not included much clinical practice until the last decade or so. Still, many law students never engage in a clinical program. The other consulting professions, such as engineering and accounting, usually have even less such clinical experience.

Education in professional ethics probably does not significantly affect the frequency of professional misconduct. Sociological studies of both the legal and medical professions indicate that the social setting of professional practice is the chief determinant of compliance with professional norms.[48] Two elements of the social setting are crucial—the degree to which a professional is subject to collegial rather than client pressure and the nature of the collegial pressure. One can distinguish professional practice along a continuum from a solo practitioner economically dependent on client opinion to a professional in a large group practice and economically dependent on colleague approval.[49] The more isolated a professional's practice, the less opportunity other professionals have to observe his or her conduct. When professionals consult clients in the privacy of their office protected by professional–client confidentiality, others cannot observe their conduct and subject it to ethical evaluation. A professional who is economically dependent on attracting clients is very susceptible to client pressures for inappropriate conduct, whether a shady legal deal, the prescription of narcotics for nonexistent medical problems, the falsifying of books, or an inexpensive but unsafe design. At the opposite end of the spectrum, salaried professionals practicing as members of a team have little opportunity or incentive for misconduct. Their colleagues will know of their conduct, and there is no financial incentive to attract clients by unethical conduct.

At this point the nature of collegial pressures becomes relevant. Colleagues can provide peer support for violations of, or for compliance with, ethical norms.[50] Loyalty to the team can make a professional less apt to criticize the ethics of his colleagues and superiors.[51] Involvement of independent laypersons in professional organizations for purposes of ethical review would help ensure that colleague support is for, rather than against, ethical practice.

To emphasize the importance of the work setting for ensuring compliance with professional norms does not imply that the other approaches should be neglected. Layperson involvement might contribute to creating colleague pressure for compliance rather than for violations. Unless professionals have been educated in professional ethics, they will not recognize ethical issues when they arise or be intellectually equipped to work out reasonable solutions. And should they act unethically, effective discipline will protect others. Thus, the three approaches can work together and perhaps have a synergistic effect.

SUMMARY

This chapter has concerned methods for ensuring compliance with ethical norms. The first section considered the actual practice of professional self-regulation and concluded that it has been discriminatory and ineffective. The most pronounced discrimination occurred in admission to professional education and practice during the first half of this century. Professionals, no less and no more than others in society, discriminated against people on the basis of ethnic origin, race, and sex. Efforts to rectify past discrimination by affirmative action programs were briefly examined; both those for and against such programs are concerned with equality of opportunity but see them differently in terms of who benefits and who loses under such programs. The Supreme Court has held that special (quota) admissions programs are unconstitutional, but that race may be taken into consideration.

It is justifiable to require applicants for admission to a profession to demonstrate good moral character, meaning possess those virtues corresponding to the professional responsibilities previously identified. Character traits and conduct do not constitute grounds for denying admission unless they have a close relationship to unethical professional conduct. Various kinds of sanctions can be imposed on a professional for unethical conduct, ranging from moral disapproval to revoking a license to practice. Professional regulation is primarily concerned with membership in societies and licensure. The interests of the profession and of the public are not always congruent, and an examination of the enforcement of norms by professionals indicates that they have not been very active.

Professional self-regulation might still be justifiable because only professionals have the expertise to consider misconduct, lay involvement would interfere with professional independence of judgment in behalf of a client, or lay involvement would violate professional–client confidentiality. None of these reasons is, however, satisfactory. Laypersons can and have satisfactorily judged professional misconduct and a lay perspective would be beneficial in formulating professional norms by giving greater emphasis to public concerns. Lay regulation and supervisory control would not infringe professional independence of judgment in behalf of particular clients, and laypersons can keep matters confidential as well as professionals.

Three new proposals for ensuring compliance were examined. Professional norms should be established and enforced by groups with predominantly lay membership. The method of enforcing professional norms should be modified to be more effective. The grounds for discipline should be both broadened and made more explicit in many professions. Professionals should be held responsible for reporting unethical conduct by other professionals, including supervisors and subordinates, and firms should have committees with independent lay membership to receive complaints from subordinate employees. Funding and personnel for professional association enforcement should be increased. The disciplinary process should be modified in many professions to suspend licenses pending appeals after convictions at first hearings, to establish national licensing and disciplining, and to eliminate secrecy once sufficient grounds have been found for a hearing. Courses in professional ethics should be instituted in all professional schools and ethical questions raised and discussed where appropriate in other courses. Despite these measures, the nature of professional practice is probably the most important determinant of professional compliance with ethical norms. Collegial pressure and support for ethical conduct is the most significant factor ensuring compliance. Hopefully, this book will contribute to the education of professionals and nonprofessionals who will help provide that pressure and support.

NOTES*

1. Auerbach, *Unequal Justice*, chap. 2.

2. Ibid., p. 109.

3. *Regents of the University of California* v. *Bakke*, 98 S.Ct. 3140 (1978).

4. *Schware* v. *Board of Bar Examiners*, 353 U.S. 232, 238–239 (1957).

5. *In re Florida Board of Bar Examiners*, 358 So. 2d 7, 10 (Fla. 1978) (J. Boyd, dissenting).

6. A study of dams indicates that floods in excess of spillway design account for 35 percent of failures, foundation problems for 25 percent, and other causes the remaining 40 percent; see Hayrettin Kardestuncer, "Engineer the Master?" in *Social Consequences of Engineering*, ed. Kardestuncer, p. 9.

7. Patterson and Cheatham, *Profession of Law*, pp. 38–39.

8. See R. M. MacIver, "The Social Significance of Professional Ethics," in *Cases and Materials on Professional Responsibility*, ed. Pirsig, p. 50.

9. Kingsley Davis, "The Migration of Human Populations," in *The Human Population*, ed. Gerard Piel et al., A Scientific American Book (San Francisco: W. H. Freeman, 1974), p. 65.

10. Page Keeton and Robert E. Keeton, *Cases and Materials on the Law of Torts* (St. Paul, Minn.: West Publishing, 1971), p. 516.

11. Thomas D. Morgan, "The Evolving Concept of Professional Responsibility," in *1977 National Conference on Teaching Professional Responsibility*, ed. Goldberg, pp. 275–316.

12. Auerbach, *Unequal Justice*, p. 263.

13. Carlin, *Lawyers' Ethics*, pp. 161, 170.

*See the bibliography at the back of the book for complete references.

14. Lieberman, *Crisis at the Bar*, p. 207.

15. Ibid.

16. Freidson, *Profession of Medicine*, pp. 139, 158.

17. Abraham Briloff, "Codes of Conduct: Their Sound and Their Fury," in *Ethics, Free Enterprise, and Public Policy*, ed. De George and Pichler, pp. 272–273.

18. Dan H. Pletta, "Ethical Standards for the Engineering Profession: Where Is the Clout?" in *Ethical Problems in Engineering*, ed. Baum and Flores, p. 55.

19. Excerpted from *Problems and Recommendations in Disciplinary Enforcement*, American Bar Association Special Committee on Evaluation of Disciplinary Enforcement, final draft, June, 1970, copyright American Bar Association. Used by permission.

20. Freidson, *Profession of Medicine*, p. 45. (Used by permission.) His comment is meant to apply to all consulting professions. For a comment on expertise as a justification for self-regulation of misconduct, see Auerbach, *Unequal Justice*, p. 302.

21. Freidson, *Profession of Medicine*, p. 163.

22. *French* v. *Fischer*, 50 Tenn. App. 587, 363 S.W.2d 926 (1962).

23. Patterson and Cheatham, *Profession of Law*, p. 89.

24. Lieberman, *Crisis at the Bar*, p. 200; Whitney North Seymour, Jr., *Why Justice Fails* (New York: William Morrow, 1973), p. 17. In Pennsylvania, approximately two-thirds of the complaints are for failure of a lawyer to act competently; Lewis H. Van Dusen, Jr., "The ABA Code of Professional Responsibility," in ABA National Institute Proceedings, "Advisors to Management," p. 16.

25. *Matter of Quinlan*, 70 N.J. 10, 335 A.2d 647 (1976).

26. Carlin, *Lawyers' Ethics*, pp. 73–76.

27. Lawyers recognize an obligation to exercise care that their employees preserve confidentiality; ABA, *Code of Professional Responsibility*, EC 4–2 and DR 4–101(D); ABA, Commission, *Model Rules*, 5.3(a).

28. See also Freidson, *Profession of Medicine*, p. 82.

29. Ibid., pp. 369–370. Used by permission.

30. "A Grievance Committee at Work," pp. 22 ff.

31. "Lawyer Discipline," p. 21.

32. Martin Garbus and Joel Seligman, "Sanctions and Disbarment: They Sit in Judgment," in *Verdicts on Lawyers*, ed. Nader and Green, p. 59.

33. 45 CFR 46, Subpart A Sec. 46.106(b) (1), (4), (5) (revised 1/10/78).

34. *Report of The Professional Organizations Committee*, p. 29.

35. Briloff, "Codes of Conduct" (note 17), p. 277; see Veatch, "Professional Ethics," p. 19, for argument to the same effect for physicians.

36. See Lieberman, *Crisis at the Bar*, pp. 218–222.

37. Freidson, *Profession of Medicine*, p. 158.

38. ABA, Special Committee, *Problems and Recommendations*, pp. 219–220.

39. ABA, *Code of Professional Responsibility*, Canon 1 and DR 1–103(A); ABA, Commission, *Model Rules*, 8.4(a) adopts the Special Committee's suggestion; AMA, *Principles of Medical Ethics*, sec. 2; AMA, *Opinions and Reports*, 6.15; Engineers' Council, "Suggested Guidelines," 1, d.

40. Arlene Kaplan Daniels, "How Free Should Professions Be?" in *Professions and Their Prospects*, ed. Freidson, p. 53.

41. The ABA, Commission, *Model Rules*, 5.1 and 5.2, generally follow these principles.

42. ABA, Special Committee, *Problems and Recommendations*, p. 1.

43. "Grievance Committee at Work," pp. 22, 24.

44. Lieberman, *Crisis at the Bar,* p. 207.

45. Briloff, "Codes of Conduct" (note 17), p. 274.

46. Jeff Sallot, "Closed Hearing for Rights Lawyer, Court Rules," *The Globe and Mail* (Toronto) 13 February 1980, p. 52.

47. See also Briloff, "Codes of Conduct" (note 17), p. 278, and the Report of Association of the Bar of the City of New York cited therein.

48. Carlin, *Lawyers' Ethics,* p. 7; Freidson, *Profession of Medicine,* p. 365.

49. Freidson, *Profession of Medicine,* p. 107.

50. Carlin, *Lawyers' Ethics,* p. 116.

51. Hazard, *Ethics in the Practice of Law,* p. xv.

STUDY QUESTIONS AND PROBLEMS

1. During the early 1960s, Avery Bottoms spent one summer working with a civil rights organization in a southern state. One evening while Bottoms was encouraging blacks at a small church to register to vote, he was arrested for disturbing the peace. Upon conviction, he paid a $75 fine and did not appeal. When appearing before the admissions committee of the state bar after graduating from law school and passing the bar exam, he was asked if he had ever been convicted of a felony or misdemeanor. He frankly told them his story. Should he be denied admission for lack of good moral character? Why or why not? Suppose he had denied the conviction; should he have then been admitted? Why or why not?

2. Charlene Dawson, a recent law school graduate, is visited in her office by a law student, Ephraim Franks. He has just been accused of selling liquor to a minor. He says he knew the person to whom he sold the liquor was too young, but he needed to make some extra money as he was broke. But, Ephraim says, "I told them I thought the person was of age and that he showed me a false driver's license. That is what I will tell everyone but you. If I get convicted, I may not get admitted to the bar." A friend, who was waiting in Charlene's outer office to go to lunch, remarks as they eat that she recognized the fellow who came into the office. He was Eliza Field who had led riots on the campus a few years ago. He had been dating a friend of hers at the time. What, if anything, may Charlene ethically report to the state bar admissions committee? Why? Does she have an obligation to report anything? Why or why not? May or should she report anything to the law school? Why or why not?

3. A nurse, Gloria Henderson, was working in the emergency room of a small hospital when a patient came in with a sprained shoulder. She phoned the patient's private physician who arrived a half-hour later. During the examination, both Gloria and the patient noted alcohol on the physician's breath, and when he left the room the patient remarked that the physician was a little crocked. What should the nurse say? Why? What, if anything, should she subsequently do? Why? If the physician has a high standing at the hospital,

Gloria might get fired if she raises a strong complaint. What then is her ethical duty?

4. A patient arrived at the emergency room, and resident Isaac Jacobs examined him. The patient complained of great weight loss over the past ten weeks, loss of appetite, and a lump in his stomach. His private physician could not be reached. The answering service said he was out of town for the weekend and patients with emergencies should report to the emergency room. Isaac's subsequent discussion with the patient revealed that he had seen and complained to his physician last week about the weight loss and other matters. The physician had checked his blood pressure and listened to his heart and pronounced him fine. (The patient had had a heart attack five years earlier.) The patient died on Tuesday morning from cancer of the lymph glands, a greatly enlarged spleen, and peritonitis (infection of the abdominal lining). Jacobs considered telling the patient's family that they probably had a good case for negligent malpractice and reporting the physician to the hospital board. However, a senior physician advised him not to get involved as he might be subject to a libel suit and the physician might have diagnosed the case and decided it was best not to tell the patient. What should Isaac do? Why?

5. Safeguard, Inc.'s engineers prepared plans and specifications for machinery to be used in manufacturing. Midland Tubing was hired to produce the equipment. Midland's engineers thought Safeguard's design faulty and that the equipment might be dangerous. They reported this to Midland's officials who so informed Safeguard. After a review, Safeguard replied that their engineers thought the design was satisfactory and to go ahead with production. Midland's officials told their engineers to proceed. What should Midland's engineers do? Why?

6. Does the willingness of professionals to report misconduct by others in their profession differ significantly from that of nonprofessionals to report unethical and even illegal conduct by others? Should it? Why or why not?

7. During this semester, how many times in your other courses has there been a discussion of ethical problems raised by or related to the material studied? Should there have been more? Why or why not?

8. Choose the professional organization you know best. If clients have complaints about the service they receive, to whom can they complain? Does the organization have adequate methods to foster ethical conduct by its members? If not, how could some be instituted or current methods improved?

Sources of Study
Problems

Ideas for Study Problems have been freely borrowed from other books that are also valuable sources of many other cases worth considering. The sources used are indicated below; the page in the source where the problem can be found is indicated in parentheses. The chapter and problem numbers refer to this book. These problems are used with permission.

Alger, Philip L., Christensen, N. A., and Olmstead, Sterling P. *Ethical Problems in Engineering.* Edited by Burrington S. Havens and John A. Miller. New York: John Wiley & Sons, 1965. Chapter 2, problem 3 (p. 274); and Chapter 3, problem 4 (p. 35).

American Psychological Association. *Casebook on Ethical Standards of Psychologists.* Washington, D.C.: American Psychological Association, 1967. Chapter 3, problem 6 (p. 38); Chapter 4, problem 9 (p. 11); Chapter 5, problem 3 (p. 29); and Chapter 6, problem 2 (p. 1).

Baum, Robert J., and Flores, Albert, eds. *Ethical Problems in Engineering.* Troy, N.Y.: Center for the Study of the Human Dimensions of Science and Technology, Rensselaer Polytechnic Institute, 1978. Chapter 4, problem 11 (p. 205); Chapter 6, problems 5, 6 (pp. 210, 178); and Chapter 7, problem 5 (p. 186).

Carey, John L. *Professional Ethics of Public Accounting.* New York: American Institute of Accountants, 1946. Chapter 5, problem 7 (p. 64).

Carey, John L., and Doherty, William O. *Ethical Standards of the Accounting Profession.* New York: American Institute of Certified Public Accountants, 1966. Chapter 3, problem 3 (p. 292); Chapter 4, problems, 12, 15 (pp. 235, 236).

Christiansen, Harley D. *Ethics in Counseling: Problem Situations.* Tucson: University of Arizona Press, copyright 1972. Chapter 3, problem 8 (p. 205); and Chapter 4, problem 16 (p. 12).

Garrett, Thomas M., Baumhart, Raymond C., Purcell, Theodore V., and Roets, Perry. *Cases in Business Ethics.* Englewood Cliffs, N.J.: Prentice-Hall, Inc., 1968. Chapter 5, problem 5 (pp. 203–205).

Heine, William C. *Journalism Ethics: A Case Book.* London, Ont.: University of Western Ontario School of Journalism, 1975. Chapter 5, problem 8 (p. 1).

Mantell, Murray I. *Ethics and Professionalism in Engineering.* New York: Macmillan Co., 1964. Chapter 4, problem 6 (p. 118); and Chapter 5, problem 4 (p. 113).

Mathews, Robert E. *Problems Illustrative of the Responsibilities of Members of the Legal Profession.* 2d ed. New York: Council on Legal Education for Professional Responsibility, 1968. Chapter 4, problem 10 (p. 116); Chapter 5, problem 6 (p. 124); and Chapter 7, problem 1 (p. 257).

Morgan, Thomas D., and Rotunda, Ronald D. *Problems and Materials on Professional Responsibility.* Mineola, N.Y.: Foundation Press, 1976. Chapter 3, problem 1 (p. 69); Chapter 4, problem 14 (p. 48); Chapter 5, problem 2 (p. 17); Chapter 6, problems 4, 9 (pp. 270, 15); and Chapter 7, problem 2 (p. 141).

Redlich, Norman. *Professional Responsibility: A Problem Approach.* Boston: Little, Brown and Co., 1976. Chapter 4, problem 2 (p. 35); and Chapter 6, problem 7 (p. 65).

Veatch, Robert M. *Case Studies in Medical Ethics.* Cambridge: Harvard University Press, 1977. Chapter 4, problem 7 (p. 151); Chapter 5, problem 1 (p. 129); Chapter 6, problem 1 (p. 299); and Chapter 7, problems 3, 4 (pp. 115, 113).

Select Bibliography

Alger, Philip L., Christensen, N. A., and Olmstead, Sterling P. *Ethical Problems in Engineering.* Edited by Burrington S. Havens and John A. Miller. New York: John Wiley & Sons, 1965.

American Bar Association. *Code of Professional Responsibility and Code of Judicial Conduct.* Chicago: American Bar Association, 1979.

———. Commission on Evaluation of Professional Standards. *Model Rules of Professional Conduct.* Proposed Final Draft. Chicago: American Bar Association, May 30, 1981.

———. National Institute Proceedings. "Advisors to Management: Responsibilities and Liabilities of Lawyers and Accountants." *The Business Lawyer* (30 March 1975; Special Issue): 1–227.

———. Special Committee on Evaluation of Disciplinary Enforcement. *Problems and Recommendations in Disciplinary Enforcement.* Preliminary Draft. January 15, 1970. Chicago: American Bar Association, 1970.

American College of Trial Lawyers. *Code of Trial Conduct.* Los Angeles: American College of Trial Lawyers, 1972.

American Institute of Certified Public Accountants. "Rules of Conduct." In *Ethics, Free Enterprise, and Public Policy: Original Essays on Moral Issues in Business,* edited by Richard T. De George and Joseph A. Pichler. New York: Oxford University Press, 1978, pp. 280-287.

American Medical Association. *Opinions and Reports of the Judicial Council.* Chicago: American Medical Association, 1977.

———. *Principles of Medical Ethics.* Chicago: American Medical Association, 1980.

———. *Principles of Medical Ethics* (1957). In *Opinions and Reports of the Judicial Council.* Chicago: American Medical Association, 1977.

Auerbach, Jerold S. *Unequal Justice: Lawyers and Social Change in Modern America.* New York: Oxford University Press, 1976.

Bates v. *State Bar of Arizona,* 433 U.S. 350 (1977).

Baum, Robert J., and Flores, Albert, eds. *Ethical Problems in Engineering.* Troy, N.Y.: Center for the Study of the Human Dimensions of Science and Technology, Rensselaer Polytechnic Institute, 1978.

Bayles, Michael D. "National Health Insurance and Noncovered Services." *Journal of Health Politics, Policy and Law* 2 (1977): 335–348.

———. *Principles of Legislation: The Uses of Political Authority.* Detroit: Wayne State University Press, 1978.

———. "A Problem of Clean Hands: Refusal to Provide Professional Services." *Social Theory and Practice* 5 (1979): 165–181.

Bloom, Murray Teigh, ed. *Lawyers, Clients, & Ethics.* New York: Council on Legal Education for Professional Responsibility, 1974.

Bok, Sissela. *Lying: Moral Choice in Public and Private Life.* New York: Pantheon Books, 1978.

Branson, Roy. "The Secularization of American Medicine." *Hastings Center Studies* 1, no. 2 (1973): 17–28.

Briloff, Abraham J. *More Debits Than Credits: The Burnt Investor's Guide to Financial Statements.* New York: Harper & Row, 1976.

Buchanan, Allen. "Medical Paternalism." *Philosophy & Public Affairs* 7 (1978): 370–390.

"Business and Professional Ethics." *National Forum* 58 (Summer 1978).

Callahan, Daniel. "Recombinant DNA: Science and the Public." *Hastings Center Report* 7 (April 1977): 20–22.

Carlin, Jerome E. *Lawyers' Ethics: A Survey of the New York City Bar.* New York: Russell Sage Foundation, 1966.

Cheek, James H. "Professional Responsibility and Self-Regulation of the Securities Lawyer." *Washington and Lee Law Review* 32 (1975): 597–636.

Comment. *"Tarasoff* and the Psychotherapist's Duty to Warn." *San Diego Law Review* 12 (1975): 932–951.

Davis, John W., Hoffmaster, Barry, and Shorten, Sarah, eds. *Contemporary Issues in Biomedical Ethics.* Clifton, N.J.: Humana Press, 1978.

De George, Richard T., and Pichler, Joseph A., eds. *Ethics, Free Enterprise, and Public Policy: Original Essays on Moral Issues in Business.* New York: Oxford University Press, 1978.

Deneke, Arno H. "The Dilemma of the Virtuous Lawyer or When Do You Have to Blow the Whistle on Your Client." *Arizona State Law Journal,* 1979, pp. 245–252.

Drinker, Henry S. *Legal Ethics.* New York: Columbia University Press, 1953.

Engineers' Council for Professional Development. "Codes of Ethics of Engineers." In *Ethical Problems in Engineering,* edited by Robert J. Baum and Albert Flores. Troy, N.Y.: Center for the Study of the Human Dimensions of Science and Technology, Rensselaer Polytechnic Institute, 1978, p. 36.

———. "Suggested Guidelines for Use with the Fundamental Canons of Ethics." In *Ethical Problems in Engineering,* edited by Robert J. Baum and Albert Flores. Troy, N.Y.: Center for the Study of the Human Dimensions of Science and Technology, Rensselaer Polytechnic Institute, 1978, pp. 37–40.

Englehardt, H. Tristram, Jr. "Rights and Responsibilities of Patients and Physicians." In *Medical Treatment of the Dying: Moral Issues,* edited by Michael D. Bayles and Dallas M. High. Cambridge, Mass.: G. K. Hall & Co. and Schenkman Publishing Co., 1978.

Freedman, Benjamin. "A Meta-Ethics for Professional Morality." *Ethics* 89 (1978):1–19.

Freedman, Monroe H. "A Civil Libertarian Looks at Securities Regulations." *Ohio State Law Journal* 35 (1974): 280–289.

———. *Lawyers' Ethics in an Adversary System.* Indianapolis: Bobbs-Merrill Co., 1975.

Freidson, Eliot. *Profession of Medicine: A Study of the Sociology of Applied Knowledge.* New York: Harper & Row, 1970.

————, ed. *The Professions and Their Prospects.* Beverly Hills: Sage Publications, 1973.

Fried, Charles. *Right and Wrong.* Cambridge: Harvard University Press, 1978.

Gaylin, Willard. "What's an FBI Poster Doing in a Nice Journal Like That?" *Hastings Center Report* 2 (April 1972): 1–3.

Gert, Bernard, and Culver, Charles M. "Paternalistic Behavior." *Philosophy & Public Affairs* 6 (1976): 45–57.

Goldberg, Stuart C., ed. *1977 National Conference on Teaching Professional Responsibility: Pre-Conference Materials.* Detroit: University of Detroit School of Law, 1977.

Goldfarb v. *Virginia State Bar,* 421 U.S. 733 (1975).

Goldman, Alan H. *The Moral Foundations of Professional Ethics.* Totowa, N.J.: Rowman and Littlefield, 1980.

Gorovitz, Samuel, et al., eds. *Moral Problems in Medicine.* Englewood Cliffs, N.J.: Prentice-Hall, 1976.

Grace, Roger M. "Invading the Privacy of the Attorney–Client Relationship." *Case and Comment* 81 (July-August 1976): 46–49.

"A Grievance Committee at Work: The Michigan Story." *Juris Doctor* 3 (October 1973): 22 ff.

Hazard, Geoffrey C., Jr. *Ethics in the Practice of Law.* New Haven and London: Yale University Press, 1978.

Hegland, Kenney. "Beyond Enthusiasm and Commitment." *Arizona Law Review* 13 (1971): 805–817.

In re Primus, 436 U.S. 412 (1978).

Kardestuncer, Hayrettin, ed. *Social Consequences of Engineering.* San Francisco: Boyd & Fraser Publishing, 1979.

Kaufman, Andrew I., ed. *Problems in Professional Responsibility.* Boston: Little, Brown and Co., 1976.

Konigsberg v. *State Bar of California,* 353 U.S. 252 (1957).

Larson, Magali Sarfletti. *The Rise of Professionalism.* Berkeley: University of California Press, 1977.

"Lawyer Discipline: The Public Is Banging at the Door." *Juris Doctor* 3 (October 1973): 21.

Layton, Edwin T., Jr. *The Revolt of the Engineers: Social Responsibility and the American Engineering Profession.* Cleveland: Press of Case Western Reserve University, 1971.

Lieberman, Jethro K. *Crisis at the Bar: Lawyers' Unethical Ethics and What To Do About It.* New York: W. W. Norton & Co., 1978.

Llewellyn, Karl N. "The Bar Specializes—With What Results?" *Annals of the American Academy of Political and Social Science* 167 (May 1933): 177–192.

————. "The Bar's Troubles and Poultices—and Cures?" In *Jurisprudence: Realism in Theory and Practice.* Chicago: University of Chicago Press, 1962, pp. 243–281.

Luban, David. "Professional Ethics: A New Code for Lawyers?" *Hastings Center Report* 10 (June 1980): 11–15.

Lynn, Kenneth S., ed. *The Professions in America.* Boston: Beacon Press, 1965.

Masters, Roger D. "Is Contract an Adequate Basis for Medical Ethics?" *Hastings Center Report* 5 (December 1975): 24–28.

May, William F. "Code, Covenant, Contract, or Philanthropy?" *Hastings Center Report* 5 (December 1975): 29–38.

Moore, Wilbert E. *The Professions: Roles and Rules.* New York: Russell Sage Foundation, 1970.

Nader, Ralph, and Green, Mark, eds. *Verdicts on Lawyers.* New York: Thomas Y. Crowell Co., 1976.

National Society of Professional Engineers. "Codes of Ethics for Engineers." In *Ethical Problems in Engineering,* edited by Robert J. Baum and Albert Flores. Troy, N.Y.: Center for the Study of the Human Dimensions of Science and Technology, Rensselaer Polytechnic Institute, 1978, pp. 42–43.

National Society of Professional Engineers v. *United States,* 435 U.S. 679 (1978).

Newton, Lisa. "A Framework for Responsible Medicine." *Journal of Medicine and Philosophy* 4 (1979): 57–69.

Note. "Legal Services—Past and Present." *Cornell Law Quarterly* 59 (1974): 960–988.

Novak, Dennis H., et al. "Changes in Physicians' Attitudes Toward Telling the Cancer Patient." *Journal of the American Medical Association* 241 (1979): 897–900.

Ohralik v. *Ohio State Bar Association,* 436 U.S. 447 (1978).

Oken, Donald. "What to Tell Cancer Patients: A Study of Medical Attitudes." *Journal of the American Medical Association* 175 (1961): 1120–1128.

Orkin, Mark M. *Legal Ethics: A Study of Professional Conduct.* Toronto: Cartwright & Sons, 1957.

Parsons, Talcott. "Professions." In *International Encyclopedia of the Social Sciences,* edited by Daniel L. Sills. 2d ed. New York: The Macmillan Co. and the Free Press, 1968.

Patterson, L. Ray, and Cheatham, Elliott E. *The Profession of Law.* Mineola, N.Y.: Foundation Press, 1971.

Pirsig, Maynard E., ed. *Cases and Materials on Professional Responsibility.* 2d ed. St. Paul, Minn.: West Publishing Co., 1965.

Pound, Roscoe. "What Is a Profession? The Rise of the Legal Profession in Antiquity." *Notre Dame Lawyer* 19 (1944): 203–228.

Regents of the University of California v. *Bakke,* 98 S.Ct. 3140 (1978).

The Report of the Professional Organizations Committee. Toronto: Ministry of the Attorney General, 1980.

Robison, Wade L., and Pritchard, Michael S., eds. *Medical Responsibility: Paternalism, Informed Consent, and Euthanasia.* Clifton, N.J.: Humana Press, 1979.

Rosenthal, Douglas E. *Lawyer and Client: Who's in Charge?* New York: Russell Sage Foundation, 1974.

Schware v. *Board of Bar Examiners,* 353 U.S. 232 (1957).

Sharswood, George. *An Essay on Professional Ethics.* 6th ed. Philadelphia: George T. Bird Co., 1844; reprint 1930.

Simon, William H. "The Ideology of Advocacy: Procedural Justice and Professional Ethics." *Wisconsin Law Review,* 1978, pp. 29–144.

Swain, Bruce M. *Reporter's Ethics.* Ames: Iowa State University Press, 1978.

United States. National Commission for the Protection of Human Subjects of Biomedical and Behavioral Research. *The Belmont Report: Ethical Principles and Guidelines for the Protection of Human Subjects of Research.* Washington, D.C.: U.S. Government Printing Office, 1978. See other reports and appendixes.

Veatch, Robert M. "Medical Ethics: Professional or Universal?" *Harvard Theological Review* 65 (1972): 531–559.

———. "Models for Ethical Medicine in a Revolutionary Age." *Hastings Center Report* 2 (June 1972): 5–7.

———. "Professional Ethics: New Principles for Physicians." *Hastings Center Report* 10 (June 1980): 16–19.

———. "Professional Medical Ethics: The Grounding of Its Principles." *Journal of Medicine and Philosophy* 4 (1979): 1–19.

———, and Branson, Roy, eds. *Ethics and Health Policy.* Cambridge, Mass.: Ballinger, 1976.

Virginia State Board of Pharmacy v. *Virginia Citizens Consumer Council,* 425 U.S. 748 (1976).

Index